STAR WARS®
·❧· LEGACY ·❧·

LEGACY

(Forty years after the Battle of Yavin and beyond)

As this era began, Luke Skywalker had unified the Jedi Order into a cohesive group of powerful Jedi Knights. It was a time of relative peace, yet darkness approached on the horizon. Now, Skywalker's descendants face new and resurgent threats to the galaxy, and to the balance of the Force.

The events in this story begin approximately 137 years after the Battle of Yavin.

STAR WARS® LEGACY

VOLUME NINE
MONSTER

STORY
John Ostrander and Jan Duursema

SCRIPT
John Ostrander

PENCILS
**Jan Duursema and
Dave Ross**

INKS
Dan Parsons

COLORS
**Brad Anderson and
Jesus Aburto**

LETTERING
Michael Heisler

COVER ART
Chris Scalf

DARK HORSE BOOKS®

PUBLISHER
Mike Richardson

EDITOR
Randy Stradley

COLLECTION DESIGNER
Scott Cook

ASSISTANT EDITOR
Freddye Lins

Special thanks to Jann Moorhead, David Anderman, Troy Alders,
Leland Chee, Sue Rostoni, and Carol Roeder at Lucas Licensing.

STAR WARS: LEGACY VOLUME NINE—MONSTER

Star Wars © 2010 Lucasfilm Ltd. & ™. All rights reserved. Used under authorization. Text and illustrations for Star Wars are © 2010 Lucasfilm Ltd. Dark Horse Books® and the Dark Horse logo are registered trademarks of Dark Horse Comics, Inc. All rights reserved. No portion of this publication may be reproduced or transmitted, in any form or by any means, without the express written permission of Dark Horse Comics, Inc. Names, characters, places, and incidents featured in this publication either are the product of the author's imagination or are used fictitiously. Any resemblance to actual persons (living or dead), events, institutions, or locales, without satiric intent, is coincidental.

This volume collects issues #42–#46 of the
Dark Horse comic-book series *Star Wars: Legacy*.

Published by
Dark Horse Books
A division of Dark Horse Comics, Inc.
10956 SE Main Street
Milwaukie, OR 97222

darkhorse.com
starwars.com

To find a comics shop in your area, call the Comic Shop Locator Service toll-free at 1-888-266-4226

Library of Congress Cataloging-in-Publication Data

Ostrander, John.
Star Wars, legacy. volume nine : monster / story, John Ostrander and Jan Duursema ; script, John Ostrander ; pencils, Jan Duursema, Dave Ross ; inks, Dan Parsons ; colors, Brad Anderson, Jesus Aburto ; letters, Michael Heisler ; front & back cover art, Chris Scalf. -- 1st ed.
p. cm.
"This volume collects issues #42-#46 of the Dark Horse comic-book series Star Wars: Legacy."
ISBN 978-1-59582-485-1
1. Science fiction comic books, strips, etc. I. Duursema, Jan. II. Ross, Dave. III. Title. IV. Title: Monster.
PN6728.S73O8853 2010
741.5'973--dc22
                                    2010004009

First edition: July 2010
ISBN 978-1-59582-485-1

1 3 5 7 9 10 8 6 4 2
Printed at Midas Printing International, Ltd., Huizhou, China

MIKE RICHARDSON president and publisher NEIL HANKERSON executive vice president TOM WEDDLE chief financial officer RANDY STRADLEY vice president of publishing MICHAEL MARTENS vice president of business development ANITA NELSON vice president of marketing, sales, and licensing DAVID SCROGGY vice president of product development DALE LAFOUNTAIN vice president of information technology DARLENE VOGEL director of purchasing KEN LIZZI general counsel DAVEY ESTRADA editorial director SCOTT ALLIE senior managing editor CHRIS WARNER senior books editor DIANA SCHUTZ executive editor CARY GRAZZINI director of design and production LIA RIBACCHI art director CARA NIECE director of scheduling

The rumored death of Darth Krayt and his actions as Emperor prior to his losing encounter with Cade Skywalker have set into motion many events across the galaxy.

As the Sith struggle to accept a placeholder for their leader, dissension grows among the Moffs and other supporting members of the Empire. A partnership has been born between Admiral Gar Stazi of the Galactic Alliance and the forces of deposed Emperor Roan Fel, and now the Jedi are ready to explore an association against the Sith.

And, though he does not wish to be involved in the struggle for the fate of the galaxy, Cade may find that it will be easier to accept his legacy than to fight against it . . .

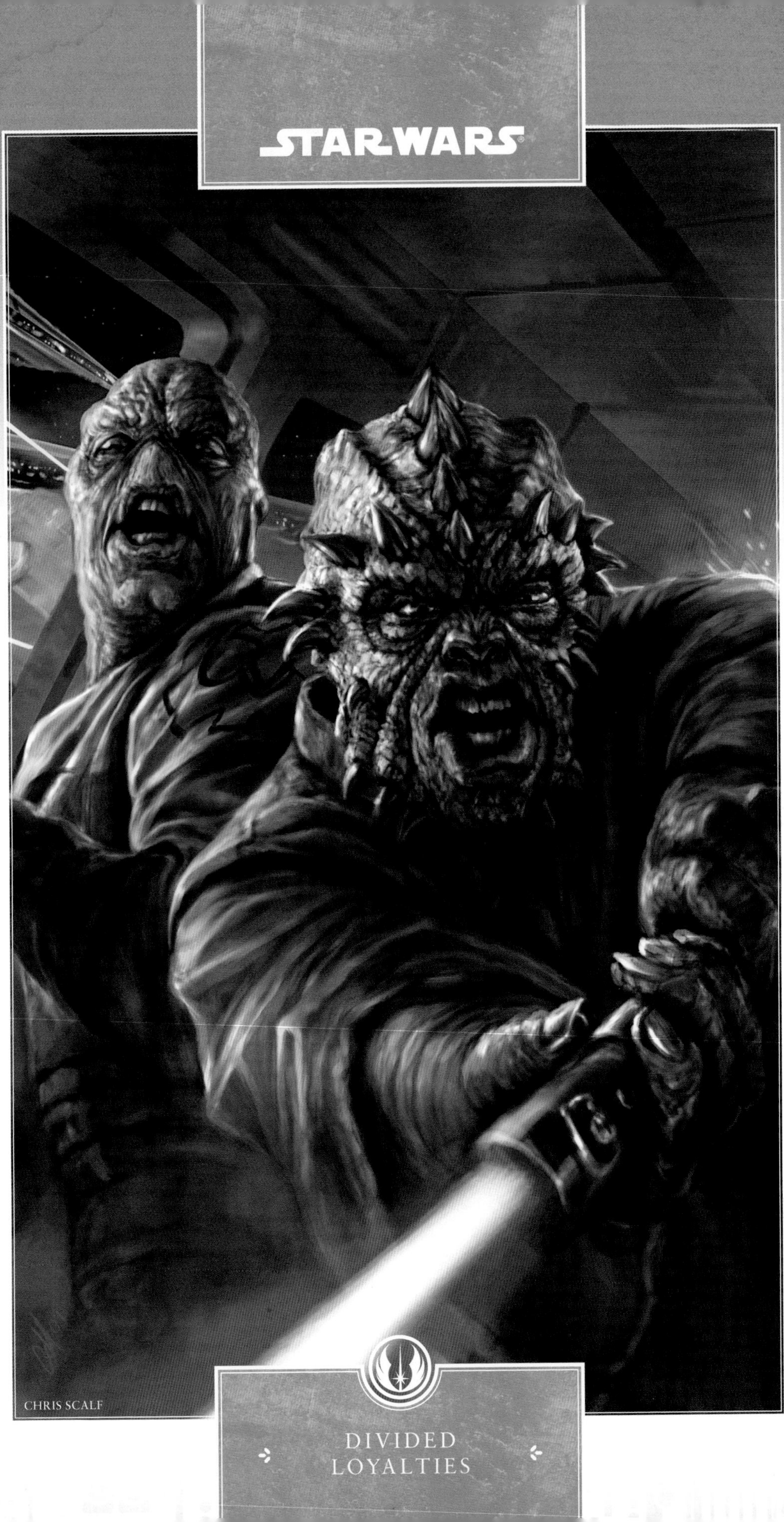
STAR WARS
CHRIS SCALF

DIVIDED
LOYALTIES

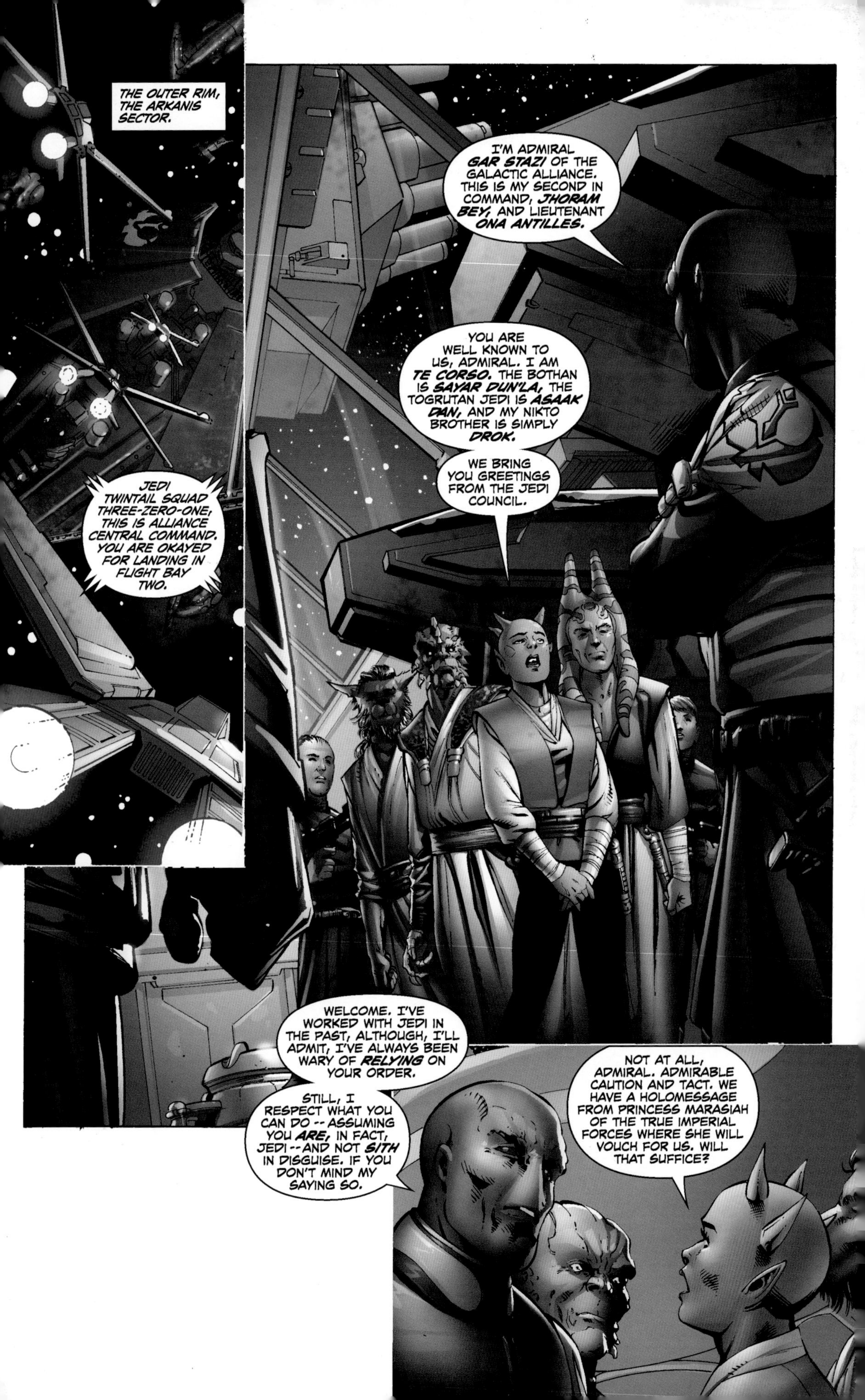
THE OUTER RIM, THE ARKANIS SECTOR.
JEDI TWINTAIL SQUAD THREE-ZERO-ONE, THIS IS ALLIANCE CENTRAL COMMAND. YOU ARE OKAYED FOR LANDING IN FLIGHT BAY TWO.
I'M ADMIRAL GAR STAZI OF THE GALACTIC ALLIANCE. THIS IS MY SECOND IN COMMAND, JHORAM BEY, AND LIEUTENANT ONA ANTILLES.
YOU ARE WELL KNOWN TO US, ADMIRAL. I AM TE CORSO. THE BOTHAN IS SAYAR DUN'LA, THE TOGRUTAN JEDI IS ASAAK DAN, AND MY NIKTO BROTHER IS SIMPLY DROK.
WE BRING YOU GREETINGS FROM THE JEDI COUNCIL.
WELCOME. I'VE WORKED WITH JEDI IN THE PAST, ALTHOUGH, I'LL ADMIT, I'VE ALWAYS BEEN WARY OF RELYING ON YOUR ORDER.
STILL, I RESPECT WHAT YOU CAN DO -- ASSUMING YOU ARE, IN FACT, JEDI -- AND NOT SITH IN DISGUISE. IF YOU DON'T MIND MY SAYING SO.
NOT AT ALL, ADMIRAL. ADMIRABLE CAUTION AND TACT. WE HAVE A HOLOMESSAGE FROM PRINCESS MARASIAH OF THE TRUE IMPERIAL FORCES WHERE SHE WILL VOUCH FOR US. WILL THAT SUFFICE?

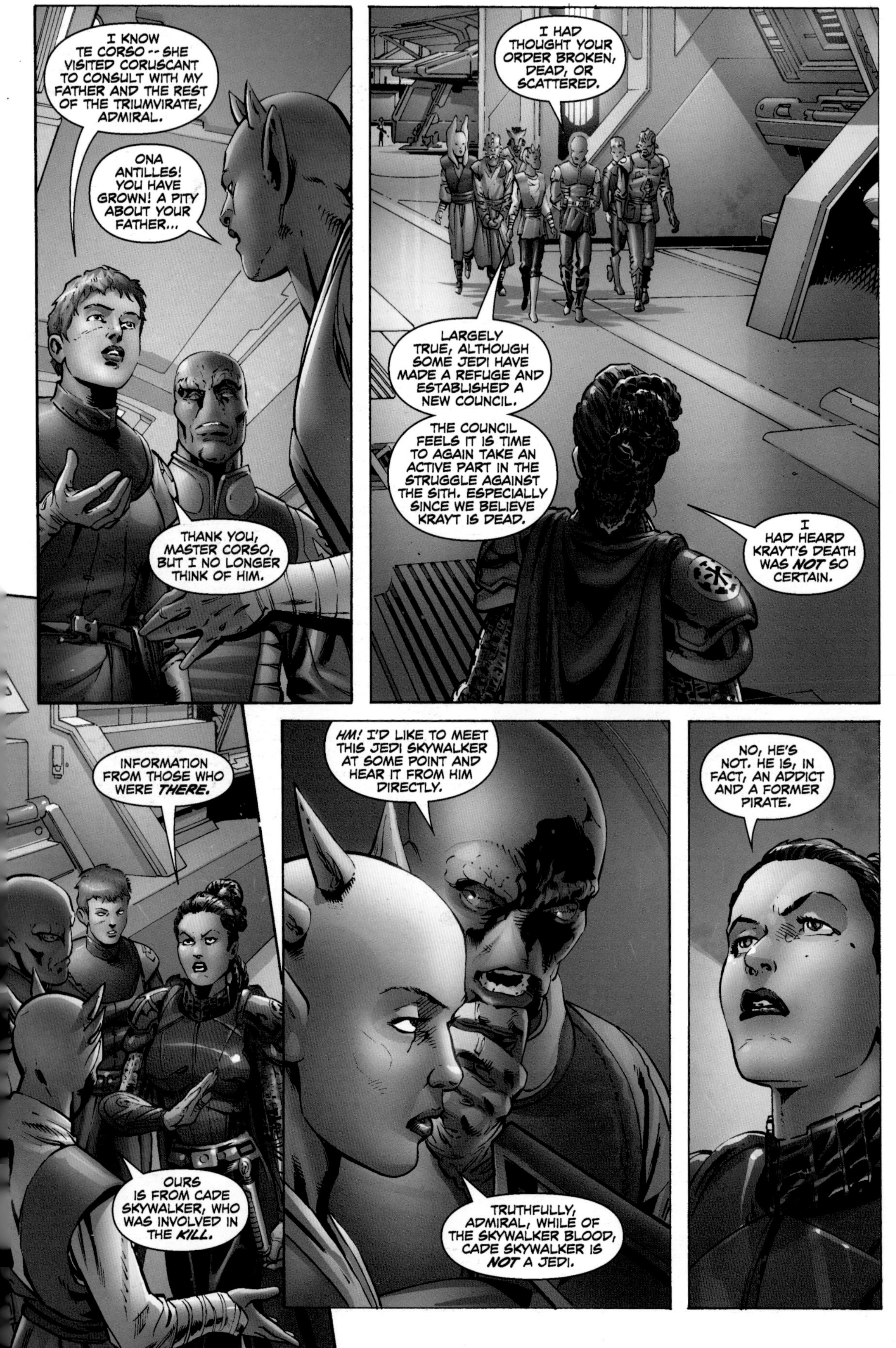

I KNOW TE CORSO -- SHE VISITED CORUSCANT TO CONSULT WITH MY FATHER AND THE REST OF THE TRIUMVIRATE, ADMIRAL.
ONA ANTILLES! YOU HAVE GROWN! A PITY ABOUT YOUR FATHER...
THANK YOU, MASTER CORSO, BUT I NO LONGER THINK OF HIM.
I HAD THOUGHT YOUR ORDER BROKEN, DEAD, OR SCATTERED.
LARGELY TRUE, ALTHOUGH SOME JEDI HAVE MADE A REFUGE AND ESTABLISHED A NEW COUNCIL.
THE COUNCIL FEELS IT IS TIME TO AGAIN TAKE AN ACTIVE PART IN THE STRUGGLE AGAINST THE SITH. ESPECIALLY SINCE WE BELIEVE KRAYT IS DEAD.
I HAD HEARD KRAYT'S DEATH WAS NOT SO CERTAIN.
INFORMATION FROM THOSE WHO WERE THERE.
OURS IS FROM CADE SKYWALKER, WHO WAS INVOLVED IN THE KILL.
HM! I'D LIKE TO MEET THIS JEDI SKYWALKER AT SOME POINT AND HEAR IT FROM HIM DIRECTLY.
TRUTHFULLY, ADMIRAL, WHILE OF THE SKYWALKER BLOOD, CADE SKYWALKER IS NOT A JEDI.
NO, HE'S NOT. HE IS, IN FACT, AN ADDICT AND A FORMER PIRATE.

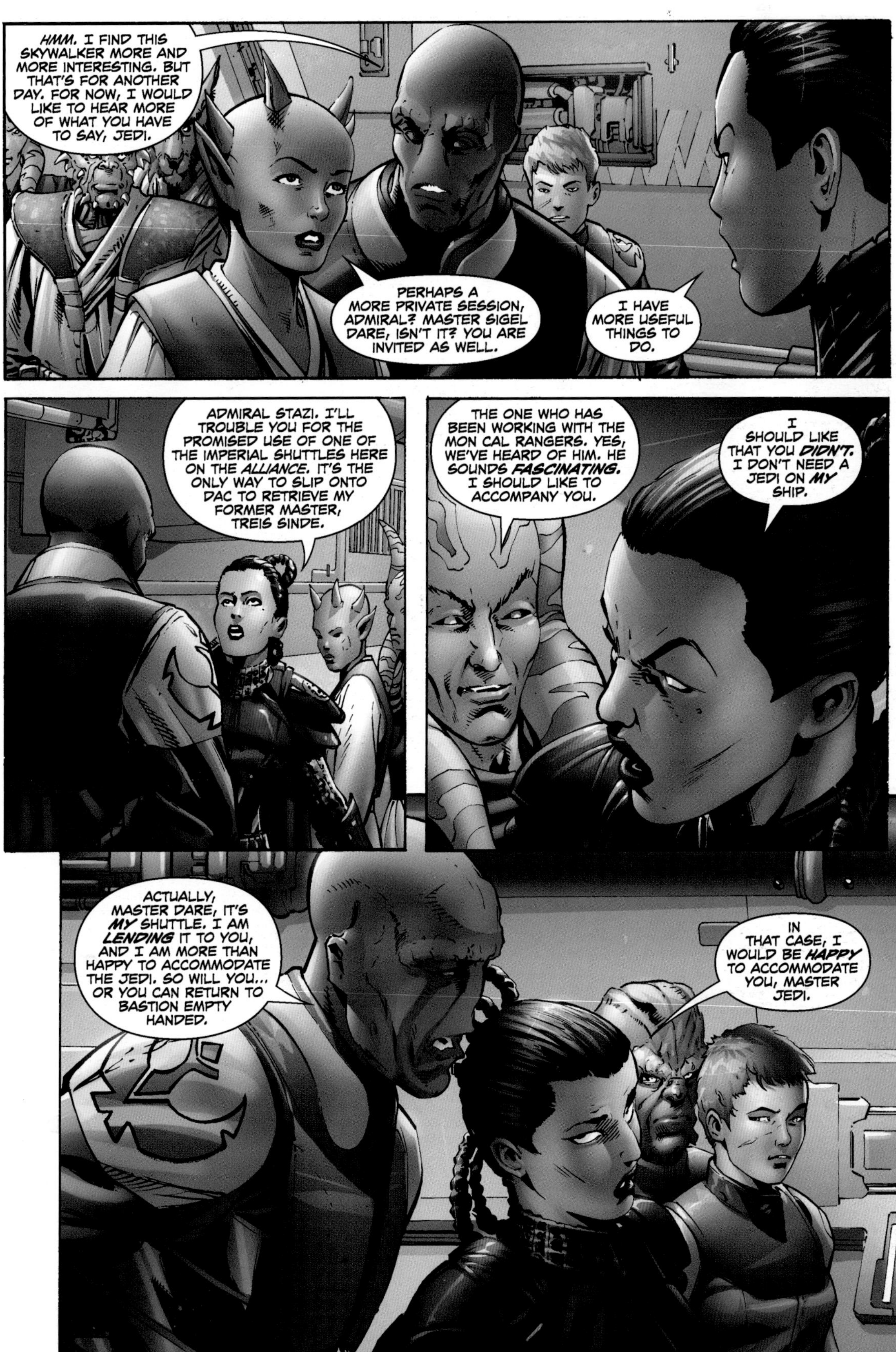
HMM. I FIND THIS SKYWALKER MORE AND MORE INTERESTING. BUT THAT'S FOR ANOTHER DAY. FOR NOW, I WOULD LIKE TO HEAR MORE OF WHAT YOU HAVE TO SAY, JEDI.
PERHAPS A MORE PRIVATE SESSION, ADMIRAL? MASTER SIGEL DARE, ISN'T IT? YOU ARE INVITED AS WELL.
I HAVE MORE USEFUL THINGS TO DO.
ADMIRAL STAZI. I'LL TROUBLE YOU FOR THE PROMISED USE OF ONE OF THE IMPERIAL SHUTTLES HERE ON THE ALLIANCE. IT'S THE ONLY WAY TO SLIP ONTO DAC TO RETRIEVE MY FORMER MASTER, TREIS SINDE.
THE ONE WHO HAS BEEN WORKING WITH THE MON CAL RANGERS. YES, WE'VE HEARD OF HIM. HE SOUNDS FASCINATING. I SHOULD LIKE TO ACCOMPANY YOU.
I SHOULD LIKE THAT YOU DIDN'T. I DON'T NEED A JEDI ON MY SHIP.
ACTUALLY, MASTER DARE, IT'S MY SHUTTLE. I AM LENDING IT TO YOU, AND I AM MORE THAN HAPPY TO ACCOMMODATE THE JEDI. SO WILL YOU... OR YOU CAN RETURN TO BASTION EMPTY HANDED.
IN THAT CASE, I WOULD BE HAPPY TO ACCOMMODATE YOU, MASTER JEDI.

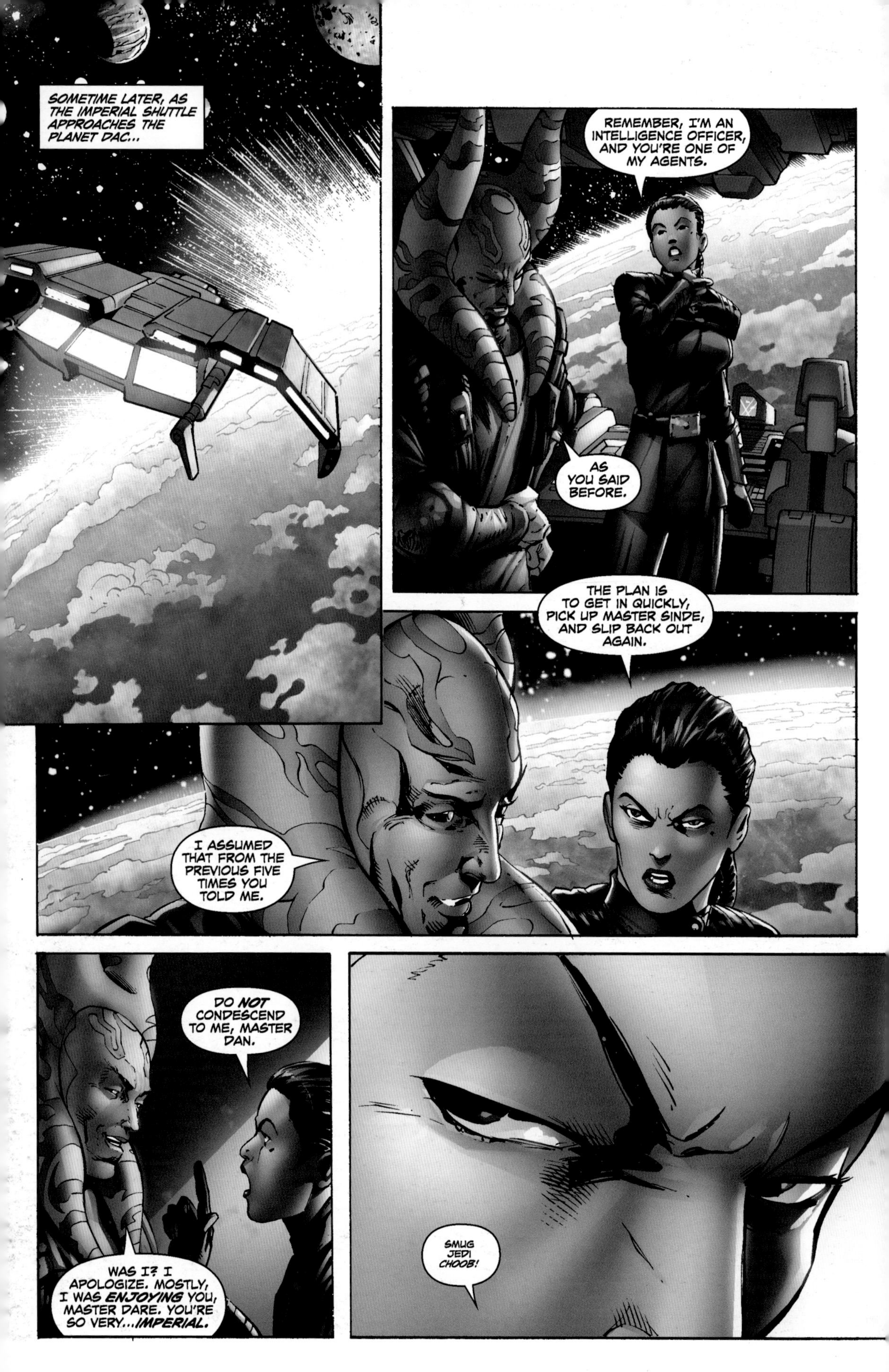
SOMETIME LATER, AS THE IMPERIAL SHUTTLE APPROACHES THE PLANET DAC...
REMEMBER, I'M AN INTELLIGENCE OFFICER, AND YOU'RE ONE OF MY AGENTS.
AS YOU SAID BEFORE.
THE PLAN IS TO GET IN QUICKLY, PICK UP MASTER SINDE, AND SLIP BACK OUT AGAIN.
I ASSUMED THAT FROM THE PREVIOUS FIVE TIMES YOU TOLD ME.
DO *NOT* CONDESCEND TO ME, MASTER DAN.
WAS I? I APOLOGIZE. MOSTLY, I WAS *ENJOYING* YOU, MASTER DARE. YOU'RE SO VERY...*IMPERIAL.*
SMUG JEDI *CHOOB!*

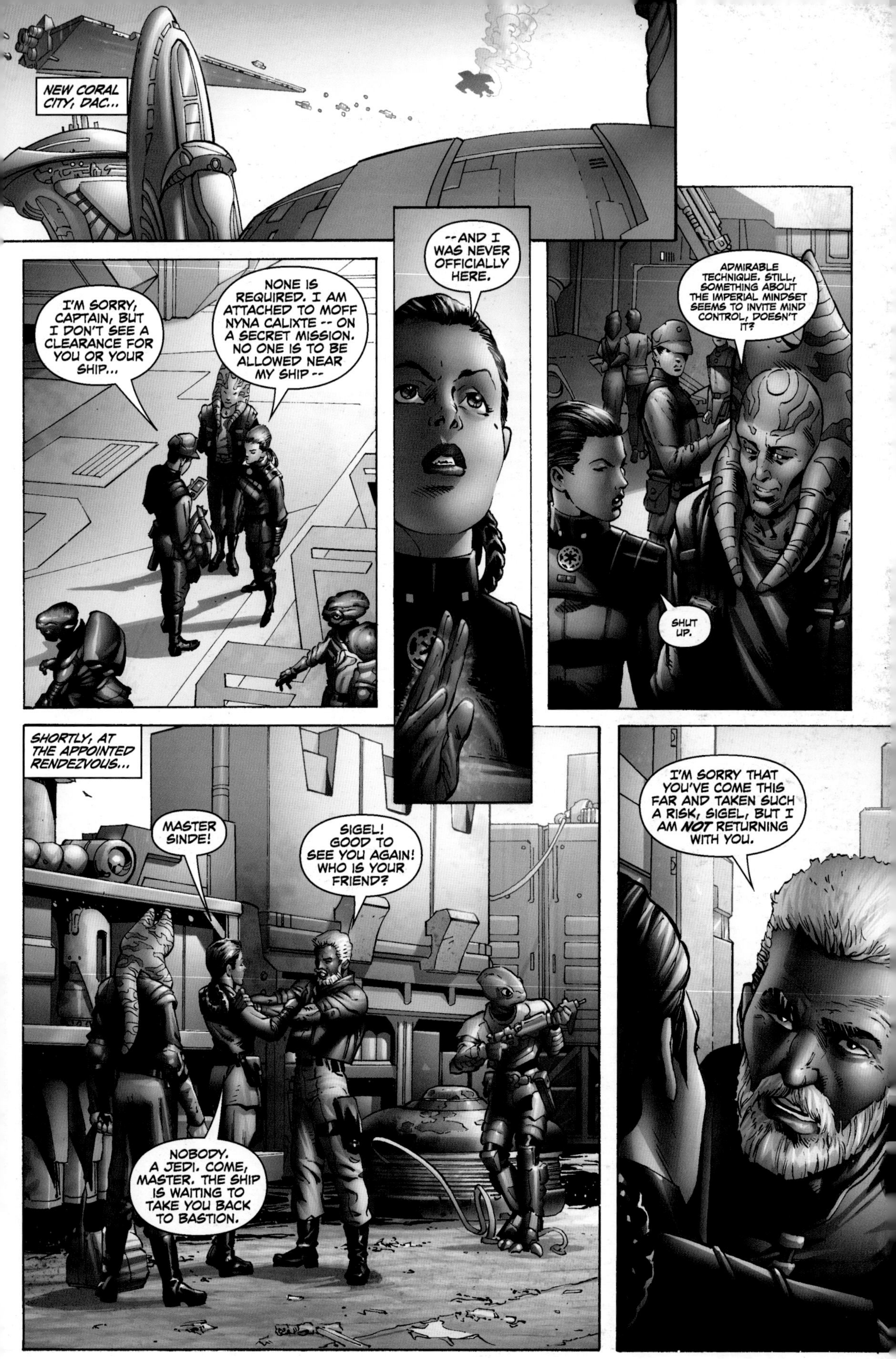
NEW CORAL CITY, DAC...
I'M SORRY, CAPTAIN, BUT I DON'T SEE A CLEARANCE FOR YOU OR YOUR SHIP...
NONE IS REQUIRED. I AM ATTACHED TO MOFF NYNA CALIXTE -- ON A SECRET MISSION. NO ONE IS TO BE ALLOWED NEAR MY SHIP --
--AND I WAS NEVER OFFICIALLY HERE.
ADMIRABLE TECHNIQUE. STILL, SOMETHING ABOUT THE IMPERIAL MINDSET SEEMS TO INVITE MIND CONTROL, DOESN'T IT?
SHUT UP.
SHORTLY, AT THE APPOINTED RENDEZVOUS...
MASTER SINDE!
SIGEL! GOOD TO SEE YOU AGAIN! WHO IS YOUR FRIEND?
NOBODY. A JEDI. COME, MASTER. THE SHIP IS WAITING TO TAKE YOU BACK TO BASTION.
I'M SORRY THAT YOU'VE COME THIS FAR AND TAKEN SUCH A RISK, SIGEL, BUT I AM NOT RETURNING WITH YOU.

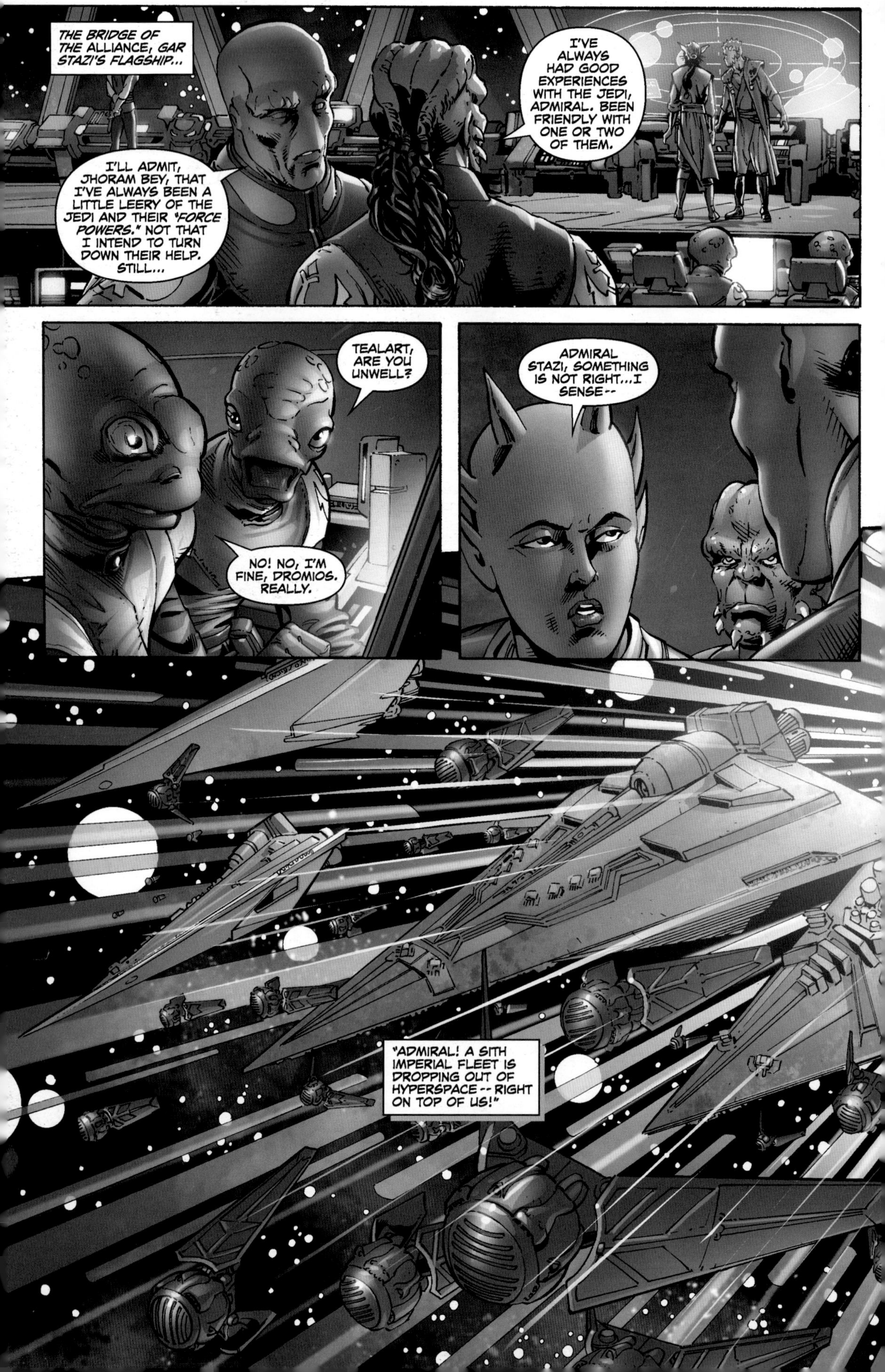
THE BRIDGE OF THE ALLIANCE, GAR STAZI'S FLAGSHIP...
I'LL ADMIT, JHORAM BEY, THAT I'VE ALWAYS BEEN A LITTLE LEERY OF THE JEDI AND THEIR "FORCE POWERS." NOT THAT I INTEND TO TURN DOWN THEIR HELP. STILL...
I'VE ALWAYS HAD GOOD EXPERIENCES WITH THE JEDI, ADMIRAL. BEEN FRIENDLY WITH ONE OR TWO OF THEM.
TEALART, ARE YOU UNWELL?
NO! NO, I'M FINE, DROMIOS. REALLY.
ADMIRAL STAZI, SOMETHING IS NOT RIGHT...I SENSE--
"ADMIRAL! A SITH IMPERIAL FLEET IS DROPPING OUT OF HYPERSPACE -- RIGHT ON TOP OF US!"

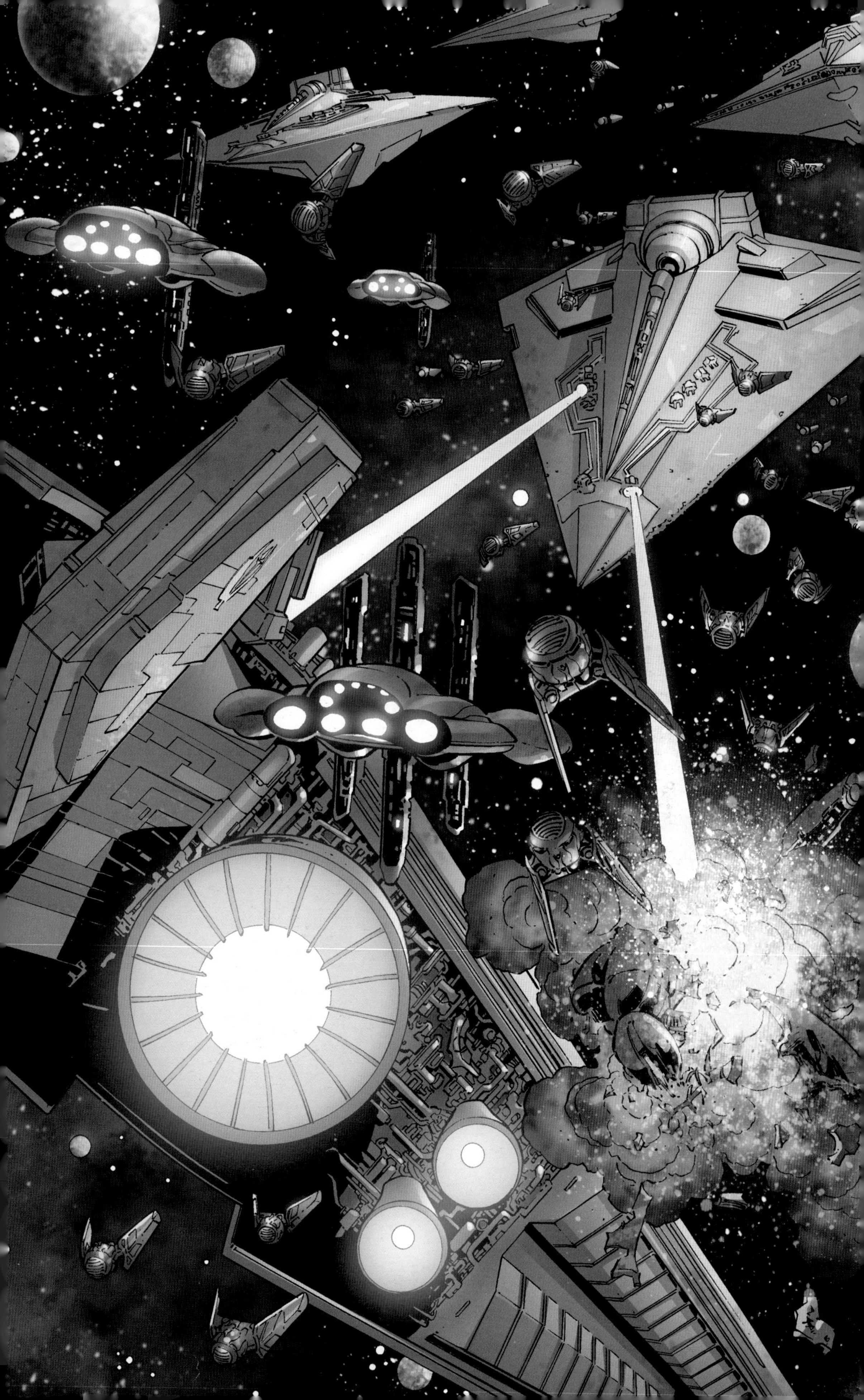

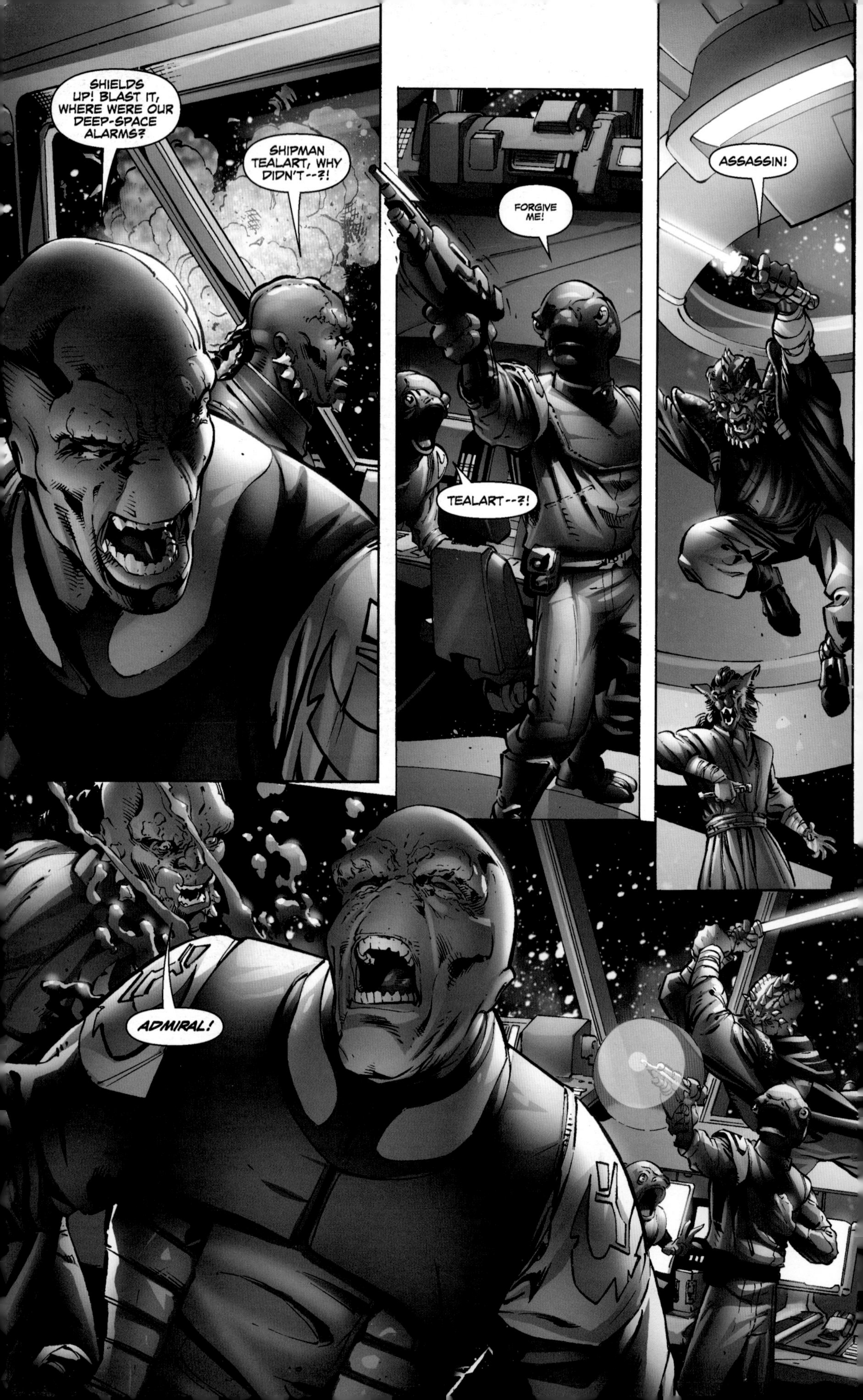
SHIELDS UP! BLAST IT, WHERE WERE OUR DEEP-SPACE ALARMS?
SHIPMAN TEALART, WHY DIDN'T--?!
FORGIVE ME!
TEALART--?!
ASSASSIN!
ADMIRAL!

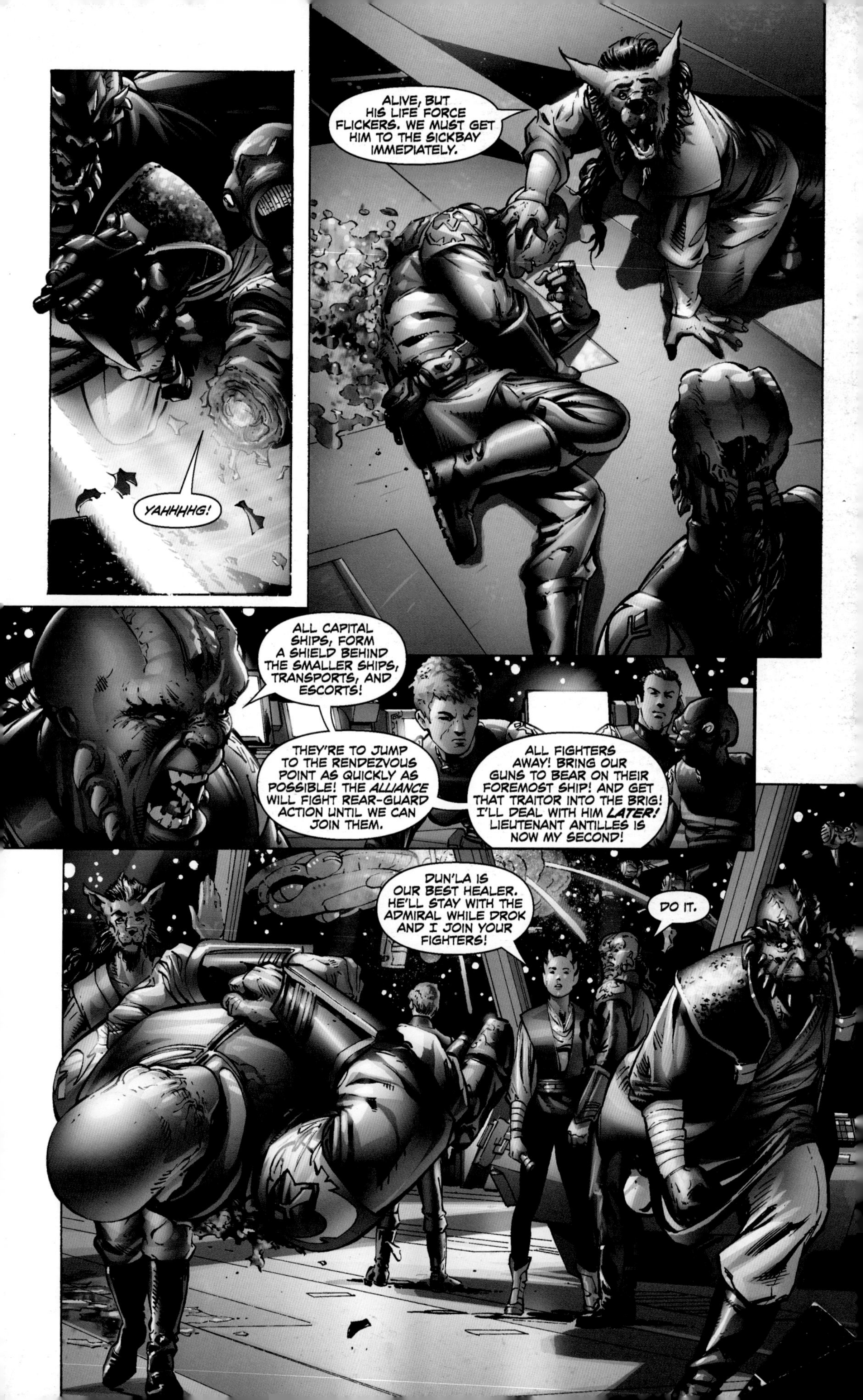
YAHHHHG!
ALIVE, BUT HIS LIFE FORCE FLICKERS. WE MUST GET HIM TO THE SICKBAY IMMEDIATELY.
ALL CAPITAL SHIPS, FORM A SHIELD BEHIND THE SMALLER SHIPS, TRANSPORTS, AND ESCORTS!
THEY'RE TO JUMP TO THE RENDEZVOUS POINT AS QUICKLY AS POSSIBLE! THE ALLIANCE WILL FIGHT REAR-GUARD ACTION UNTIL WE CAN JOIN THEM.
ALL FIGHTERS AWAY! BRING OUR GUNS TO BEAR ON THEIR FOREMOST SHIP! AND GET THAT TRAITOR INTO THE BRIG! I'LL DEAL WITH HIM LATER! LIEUTENANT ANTILLES IS NOW MY SECOND!
DUN'LA IS OUR BEST HEALER. HE'LL STAY WITH THE ADMIRAL WHILE DROK AND I JOIN YOUR FIGHTERS!
DO IT.

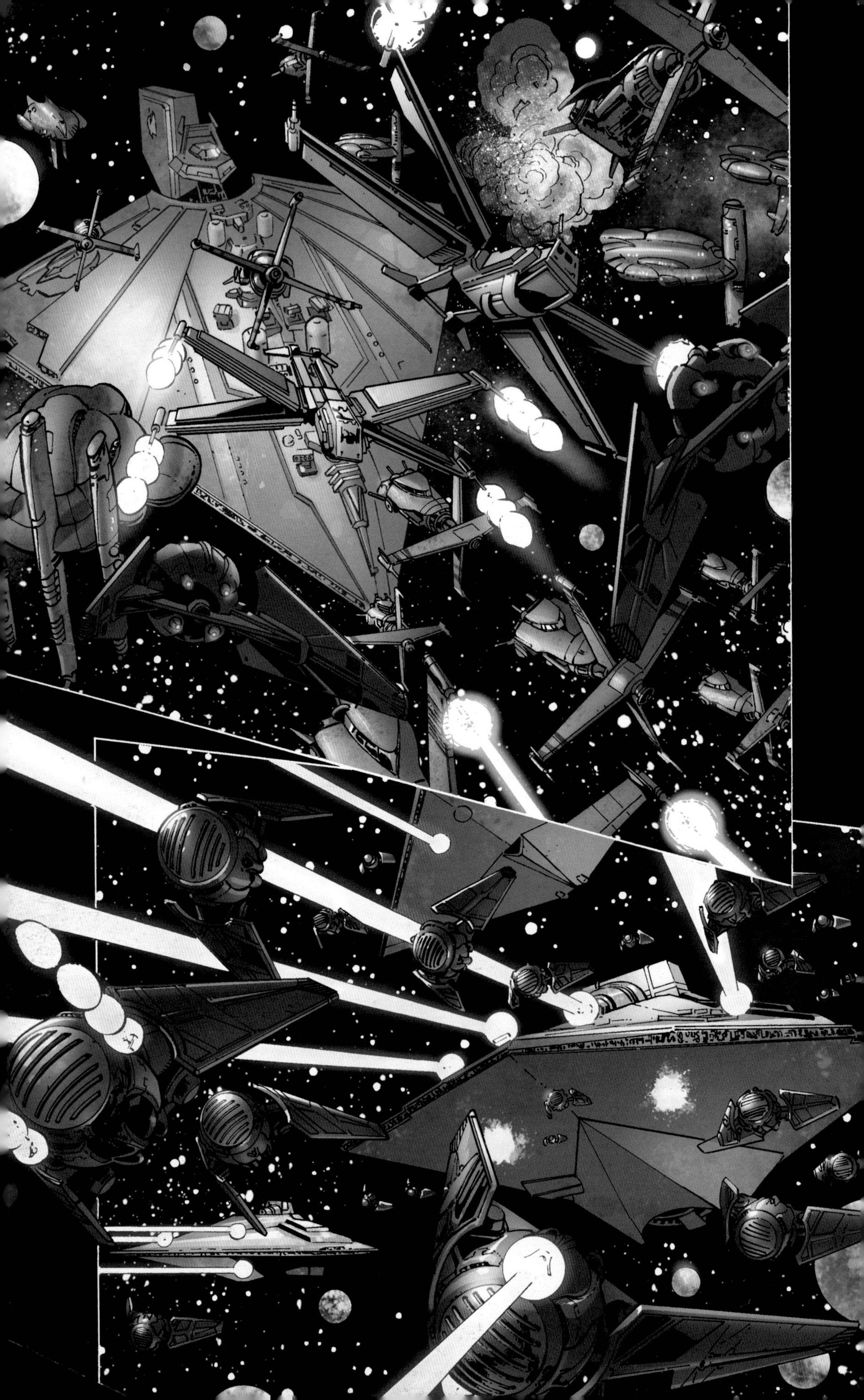

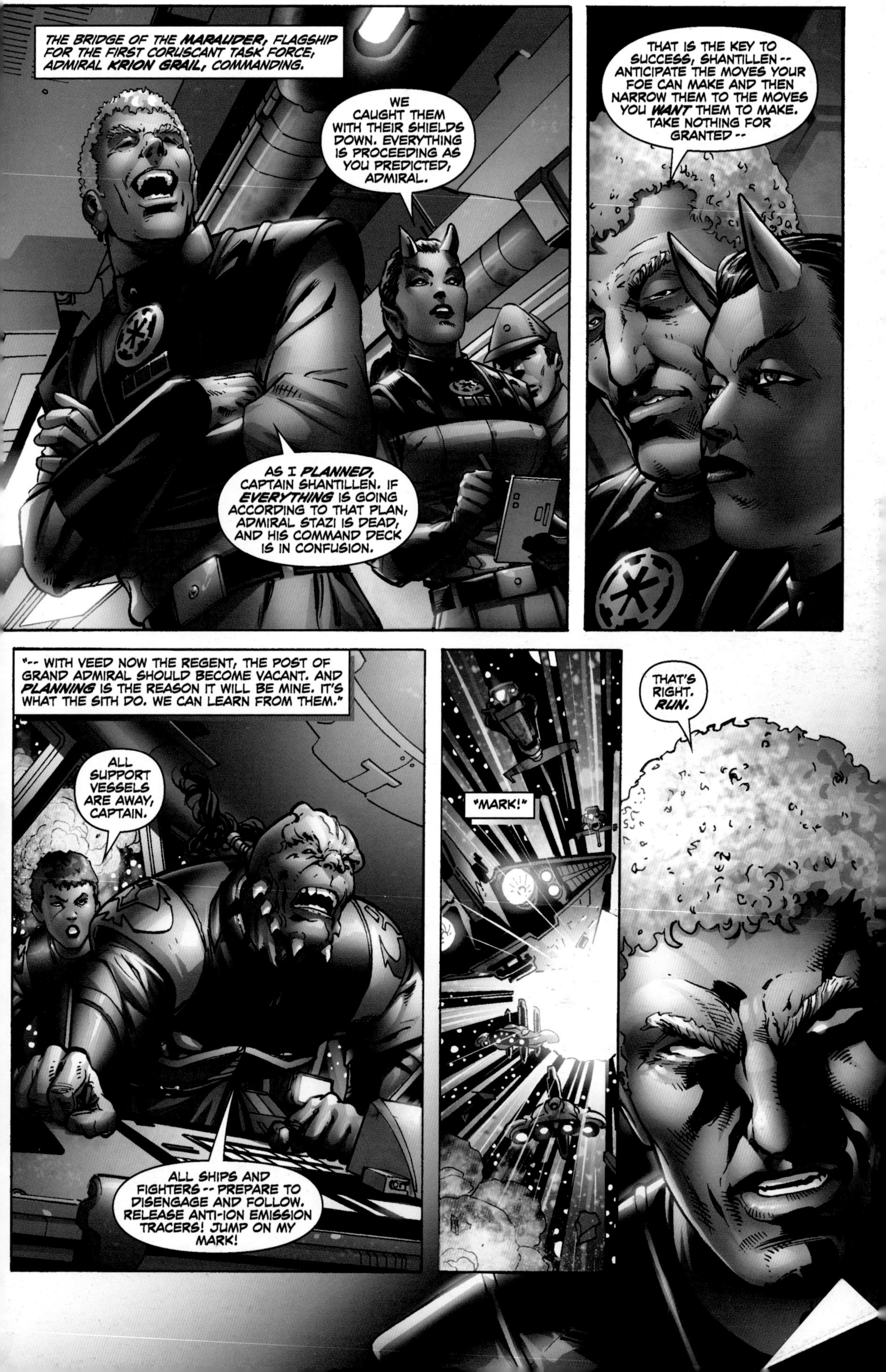
THE BRIDGE OF THE MARAUDER, FLAGSHIP FOR THE FIRST CORUSCANT TASK FORCE, ADMIRAL KRION GRAIL, COMMANDING.
WE CAUGHT THEM WITH THEIR SHIELDS DOWN. EVERYTHING IS PROCEEDING AS YOU PREDICTED, ADMIRAL.
AS I PLANNED, CAPTAIN SHANTILLEN. IF EVERYTHING IS GOING ACCORDING TO THAT PLAN, ADMIRAL STAZI IS DEAD, AND HIS COMMAND DECK IS IN CONFUSION.
THAT IS THE KEY TO SUCCESS, SHANTILLEN -- ANTICIPATE THE MOVES YOUR FOE CAN MAKE AND THEN NARROW THEM TO THE MOVES YOU WANT THEM TO MAKE. TAKE NOTHING FOR GRANTED --
"-- WITH VEED NOW THE REGENT, THE POST OF GRAND ADMIRAL SHOULD BECOME VACANT. AND PLANNING IS THE REASON IT WILL BE MINE. IT'S WHAT THE SITH DO. WE CAN LEARN FROM THEM."
ALL SUPPORT VESSELS ARE AWAY, CAPTAIN.
ALL SHIPS AND FIGHTERS -- PREPARE TO DISENGAGE AND FOLLOW. RELEASE ANTI-ION EMISSION TRACERS! JUMP ON MY MARK!
"MARK!"
THAT'S RIGHT. RUN.

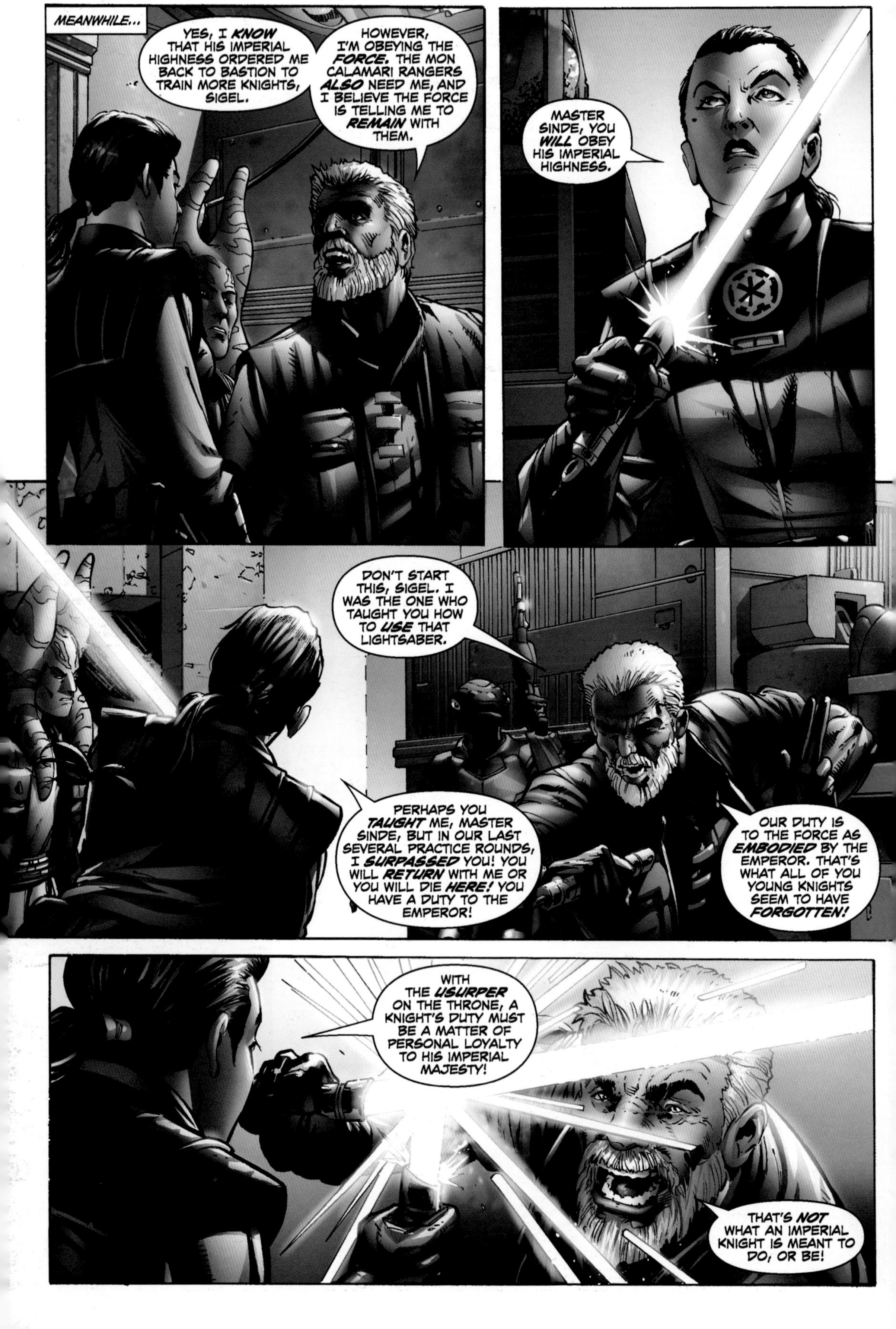
MEANWHILE...
YES, I KNOW THAT HIS IMPERIAL HIGHNESS ORDERED ME BACK TO BASTION TO TRAIN MORE KNIGHTS, SIGEL.
HOWEVER, I'M OBEYING THE FORCE. THE MON CALAMARI RANGERS ALSO NEED ME, AND I BELIEVE THE FORCE IS TELLING ME TO REMAIN WITH THEM.
MASTER SINDE, YOU WILL OBEY HIS IMPERIAL HIGHNESS.
DON'T START THIS, SIGEL. I WAS THE ONE WHO TAUGHT YOU HOW TO USE THAT LIGHTSABER.
PERHAPS YOU TAUGHT ME, MASTER SINDE, BUT IN OUR LAST SEVERAL PRACTICE ROUNDS, I SURPASSED YOU! YOU WILL RETURN WITH ME OR YOU WILL DIE HERE! YOU HAVE A DUTY TO THE EMPEROR!
OUR DUTY IS TO THE FORCE AS EMBODIED BY THE EMPEROR. THAT'S WHAT ALL OF YOU YOUNG KNIGHTS SEEM TO HAVE FORGOTTEN!
WITH THE USURPER ON THE THRONE, A KNIGHT'S DUTY MUST BE A MATTER OF PERSONAL LOYALTY TO HIS IMPERIAL MAJESTY!
THAT'S NOT WHAT AN IMPERIAL KNIGHT IS MEANT TO DO, OR BE!

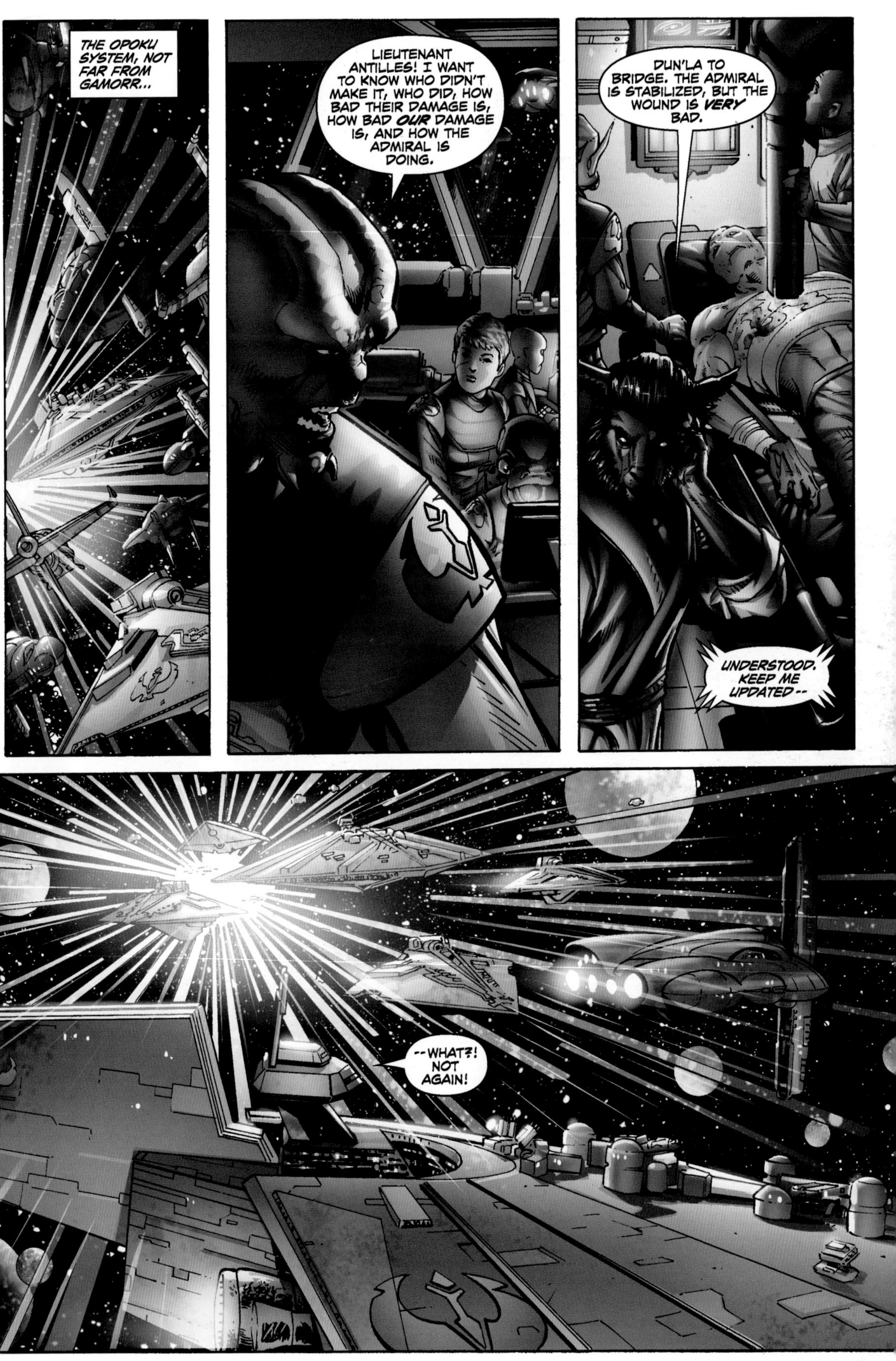
THE OPOKU SYSTEM, NOT FAR FROM GAMORR...
LIEUTENANT ANTILLES! I WANT TO KNOW WHO DIDN'T MAKE IT, WHO DID, HOW BAD THEIR DAMAGE IS, HOW BAD OUR DAMAGE IS, AND HOW THE ADMIRAL IS DOING.
DUN'LA TO BRIDGE. THE ADMIRAL IS STABILIZED, BUT THE WOUND IS VERY BAD.
UNDERSTOOD. KEEP ME UPDATED--
--WHAT?! NOT AGAIN!

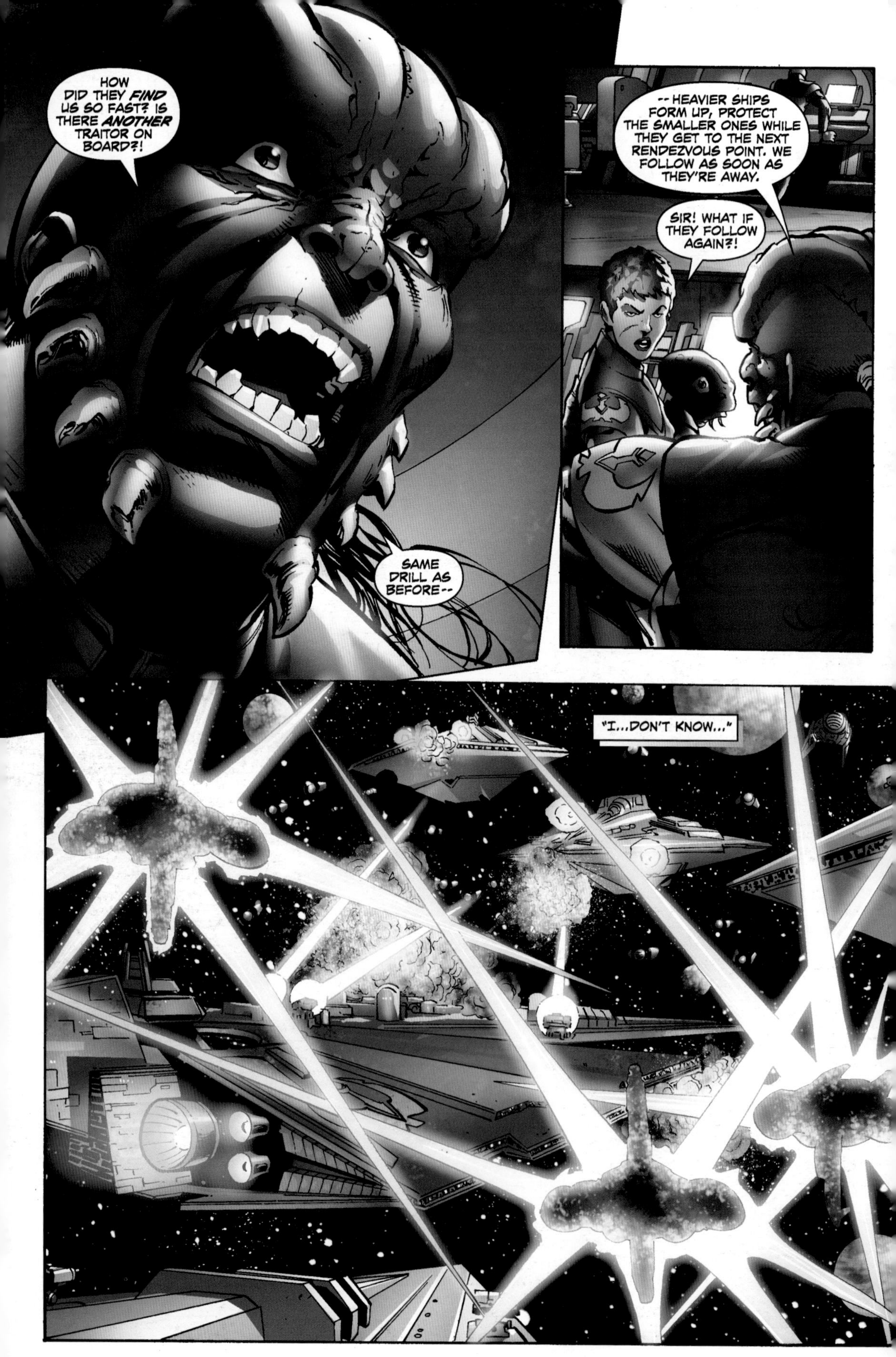
HOW DID THEY FIND US SO FAST? IS THERE ANOTHER TRAITOR ON BOARD?!
SAME DRILL AS BEFORE--
--HEAVIER SHIPS FORM UP, PROTECT THE SMALLER ONES WHILE THEY GET TO THE NEXT RENDEZVOUS POINT. WE FOLLOW AS SOON AS THEY'RE AWAY.
SIR! WHAT IF THEY FOLLOW AGAIN?!
"I...DON'T KNOW..."

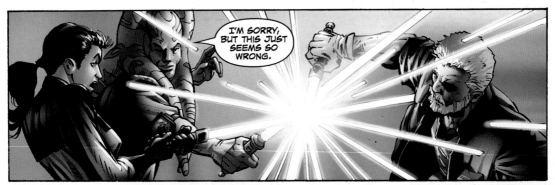

I'M SORRY, BUT THIS JUST SEEMS SO WRONG.

YOU DARE?!

AH! BETTER! NOW YOU'RE NO LONGER FIGHTING EACH OTHER!

MAY I SUGGEST AN *ALTERNATIVE* TO YOUR CURRENT SOLUTION?

NO!

I WAS MERELY BEING POLITE.

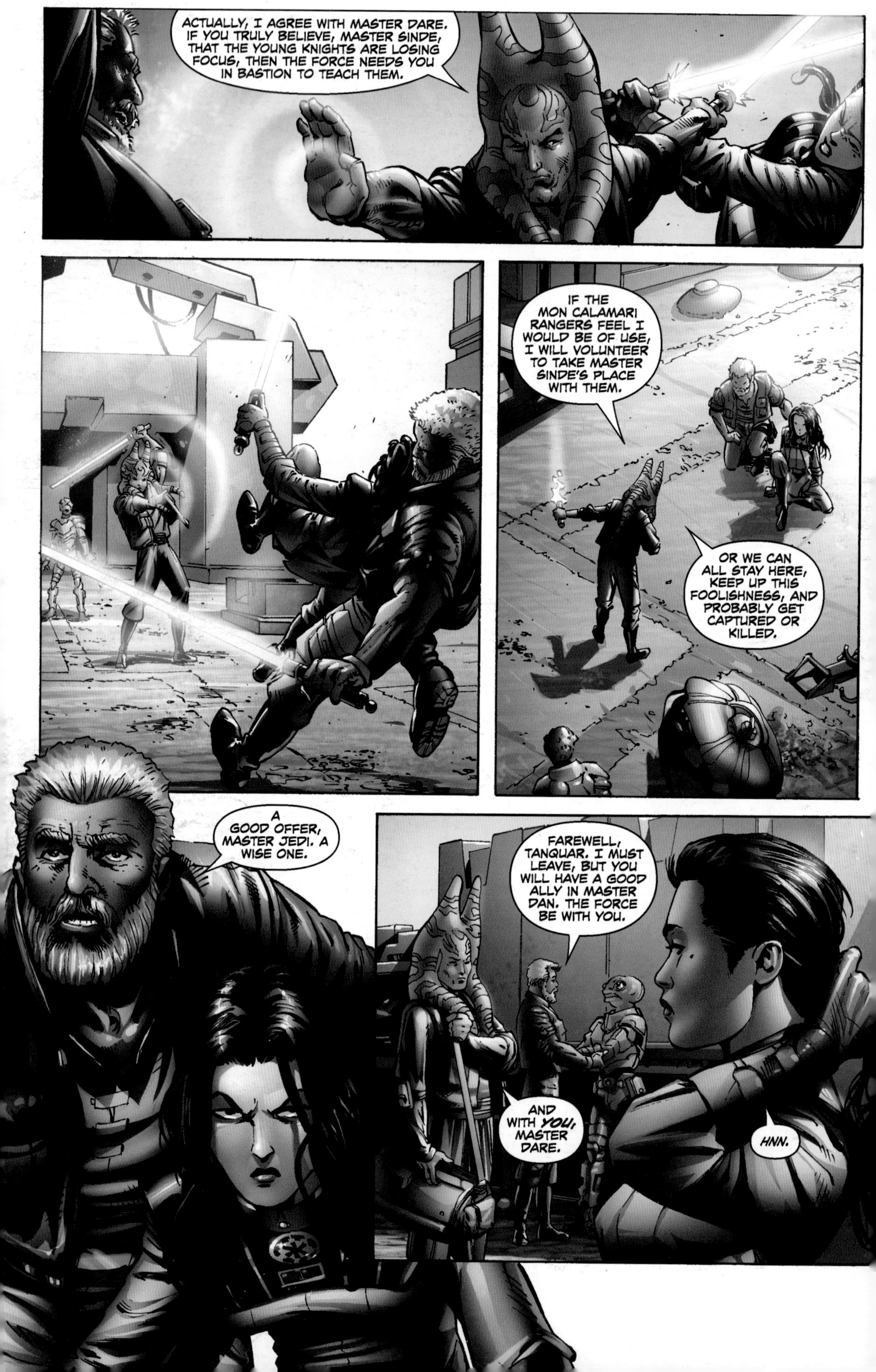
ACTUALLY, I AGREE WITH MASTER DARE. IF YOU TRULY BELIEVE, MASTER SINDE, THAT THE YOUNG KNIGHTS ARE LOSING FOCUS, THEN THE FORCE NEEDS YOU IN BASTION TO TEACH THEM.
IF THE MON CALAMARI RANGERS FEEL I WOULD BE OF USE, I WILL VOLUNTEER TO TAKE MASTER SINDE'S PLACE WITH THEM.
OR WE CAN ALL STAY HERE, KEEP UP THIS FOOLISHNESS, AND PROBABLY GET CAPTURED OR KILLED.
A GOOD OFFER, MASTER JEDI. A WISE ONE.
FAREWELL, TANQUAR. I MUST LEAVE, BUT YOU WILL HAVE A GOOD ALLY IN MASTER DAN. THE FORCE BE WITH YOU.
AND WITH *YOU*, MASTER DARE.
HNN.

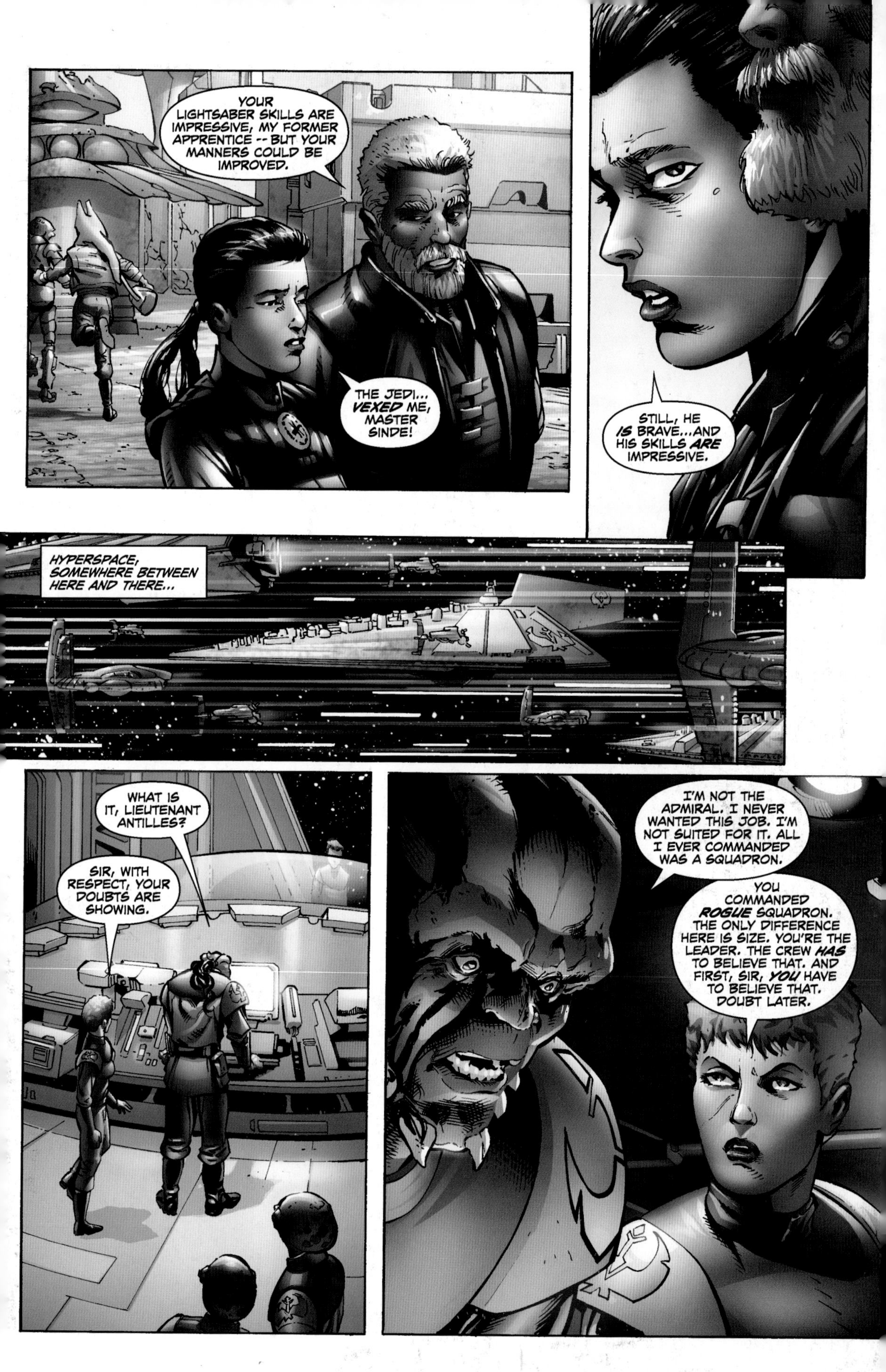
YOUR LIGHTSABER SKILLS ARE IMPRESSIVE, MY FORMER APPRENTICE -- BUT YOUR MANNERS COULD BE IMPROVED.
THE JEDI... VEXED ME, MASTER SINDE!
STILL, HE IS BRAVE...AND HIS SKILLS ARE IMPRESSIVE.
HYPERSPACE, SOMEWHERE BETWEEN HERE AND THERE...
WHAT IS IT, LIEUTENANT ANTILLES?
SIR, WITH RESPECT, YOUR DOUBTS ARE SHOWING.
I'M NOT THE ADMIRAL. I NEVER WANTED THIS JOB. I'M NOT SUITED FOR IT. ALL I EVER COMMANDED WAS A SQUADRON.
YOU COMMANDED ROGUE SQUADRON. THE ONLY DIFFERENCE HERE IS SIZE. YOU'RE THE LEADER. THE CREW HAS TO BELIEVE THAT. AND FIRST, SIR, YOU HAVE TO BELIEVE THAT. DOUBT LATER.

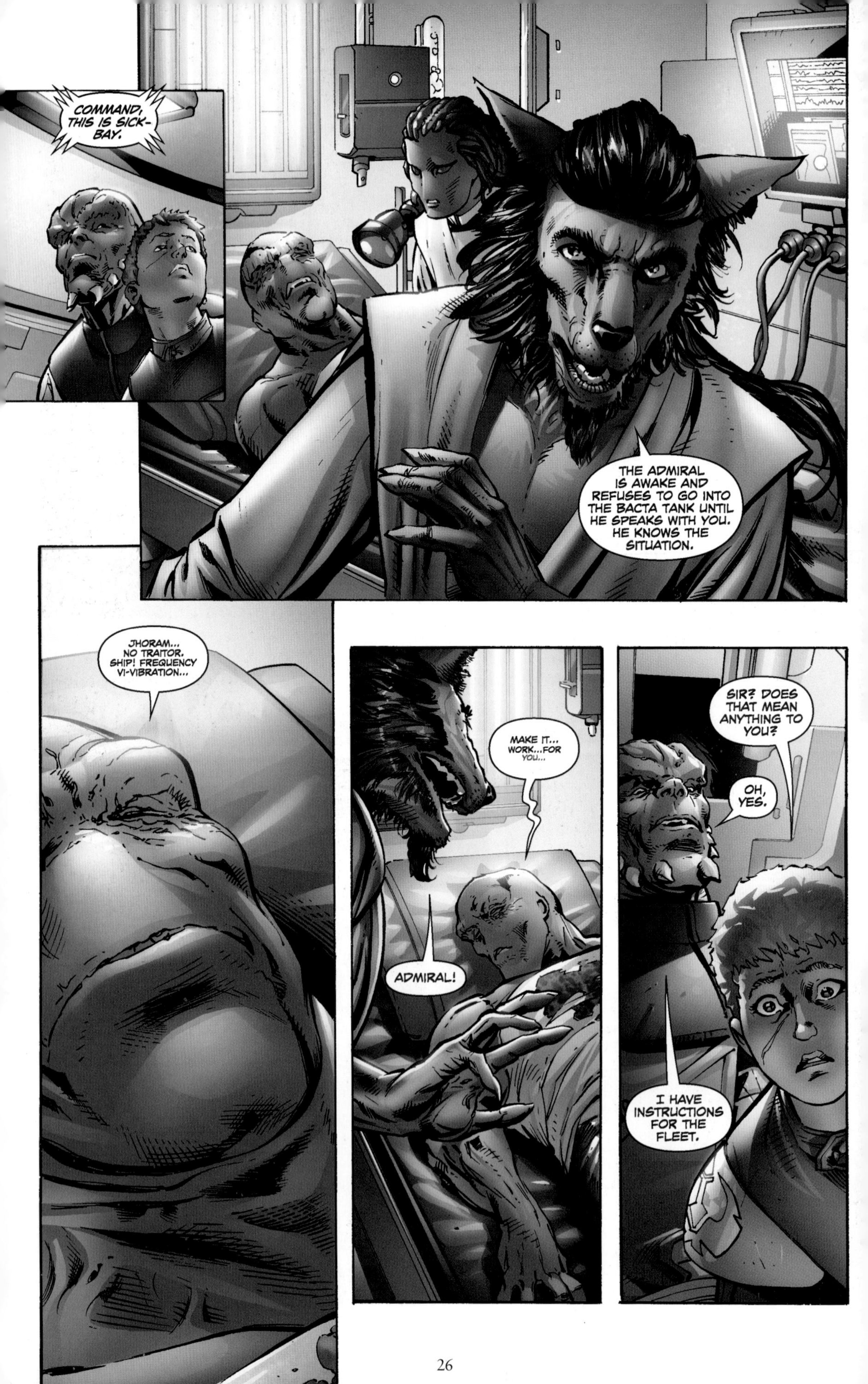
COMMAND, THIS IS SICK-BAY.
THE ADMIRAL IS AWAKE AND REFUSES TO GO INTO THE BACTA TANK UNTIL HE SPEAKS WITH YOU. HE KNOWS THE SITUATION.
JHORAM... NO TRAITOR. SHIP! FREQUENCY VI-VIBRATION...
MAKE IT... WORK...FOR YOU...
ADMIRAL!
SIR? DOES THAT MEAN ANYTHING TO YOU?
OH, YES.
I HAVE INSTRUCTIONS FOR THE FLEET.

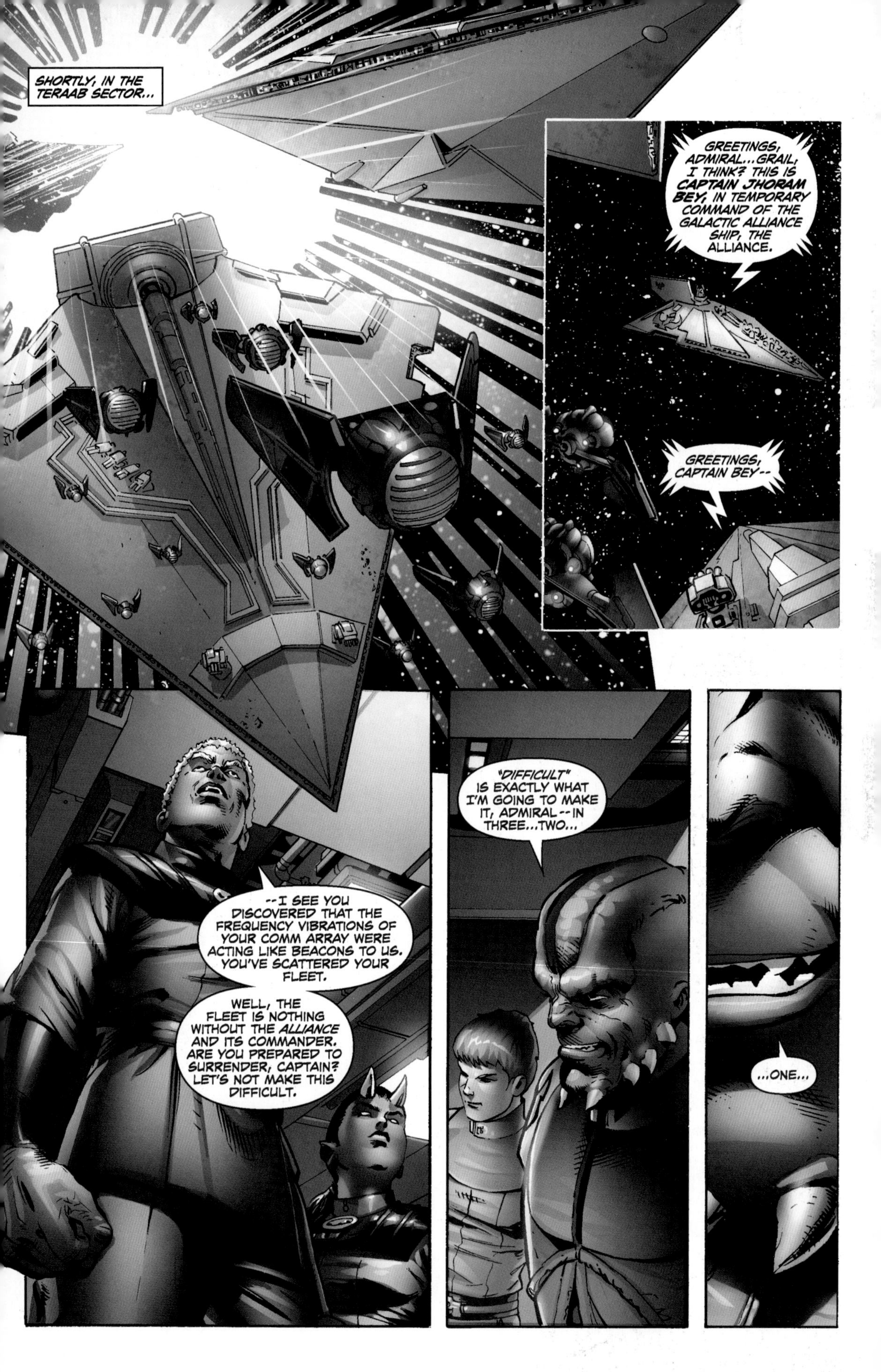
SHORTLY, IN THE TERAAB SECTOR...
GREETINGS, ADMIRAL...GRAIL, I THINK? THIS IS CAPTAIN JHORAM BEY, IN TEMPORARY COMMAND OF THE GALACTIC ALLIANCE SHIP, THE ALLIANCE.
GREETINGS, CAPTAIN BEY--
--I SEE YOU DISCOVERED THAT THE FREQUENCY VIBRATIONS OF YOUR COMM ARRAY WERE ACTING LIKE BEACONS TO US. YOU'VE SCATTERED YOUR FLEET.
WELL, THE FLEET IS NOTHING WITHOUT THE ALLIANCE AND ITS COMMANDER. ARE YOU PREPARED TO SURRENDER, CAPTAIN? LET'S NOT MAKE THIS DIFFICULT.
"DIFFICULT" IS EXACTLY WHAT I'M GOING TO MAKE IT, ADMIRAL--IN THREE...TWO...
...ONE...

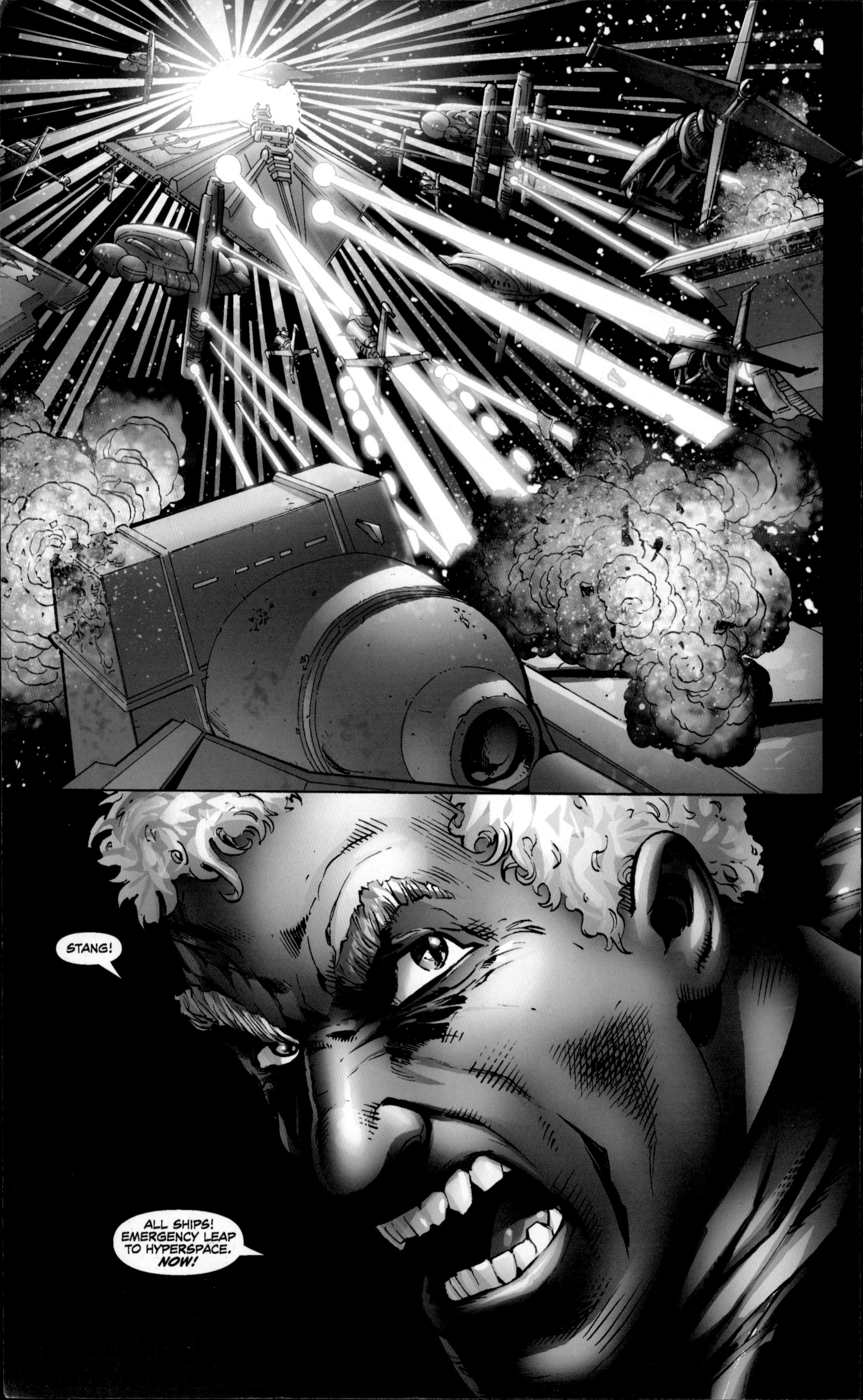
STANG!
ALL SHIPS! EMERGENCY LEAP TO HYPERSPACE. *NOW!*

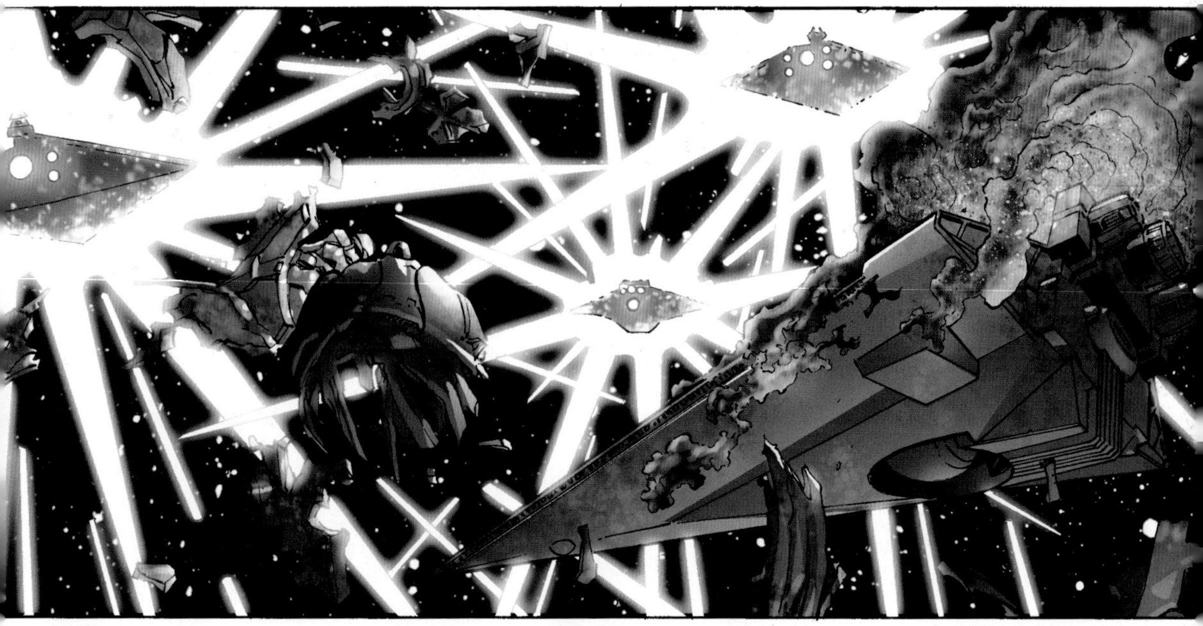

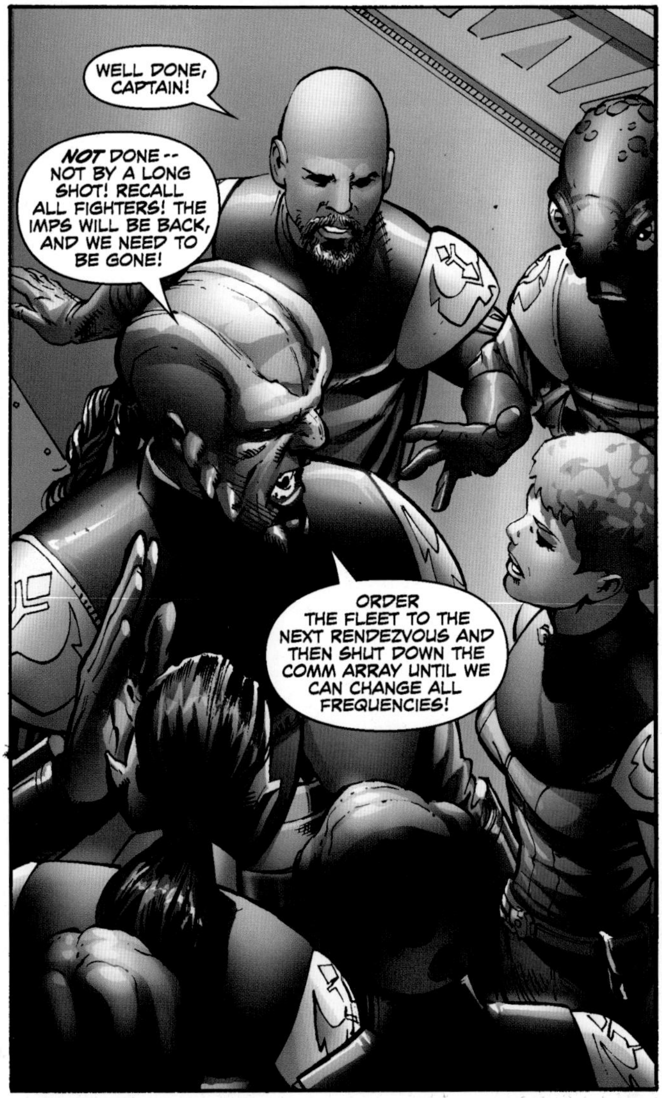
WELL DONE, CAPTAIN!
NOT DONE -- NOT BY A LONG SHOT! RECALL ALL FIGHTERS! THE IMPS WILL BE BACK, AND WE NEED TO BE GONE!
ORDER THE FLEET TO THE NEXT RENDEZVOUS AND THEN SHUT DOWN THE COMM ARRAY UNTIL WE CAN CHANGE ALL FREQUENCIES!

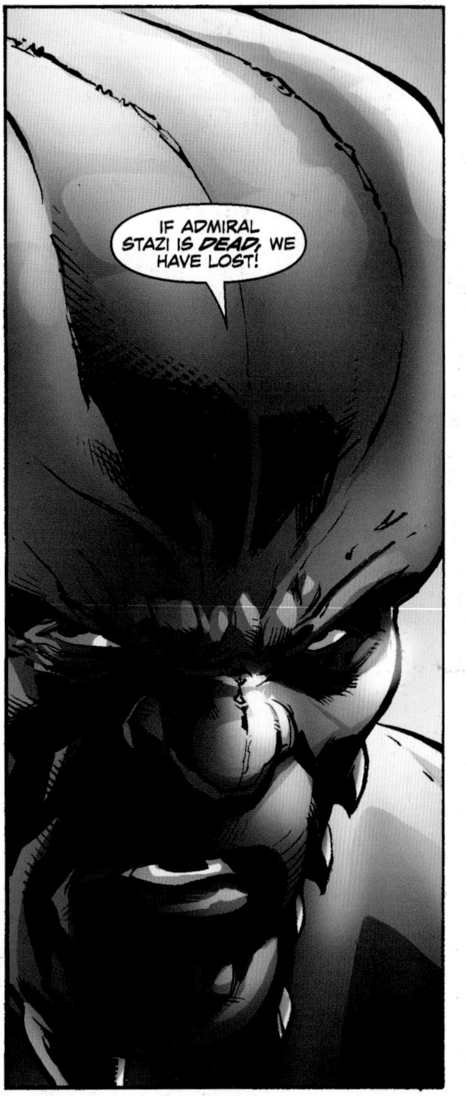
IF ADMIRAL STAZI IS DEAD, WE HAVE LOST!

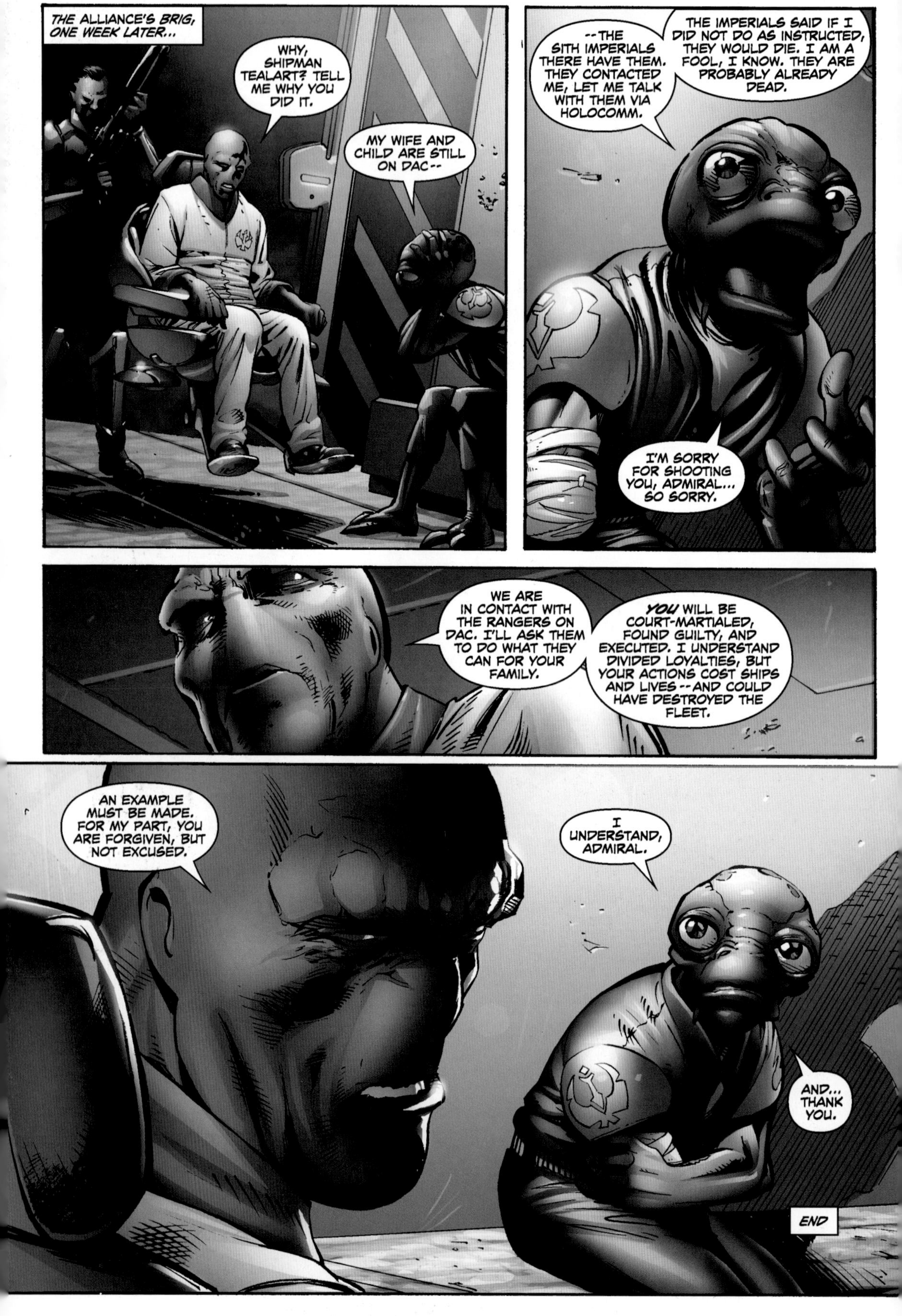
THE ALLIANCE'S BRIG, ONE WEEK LATER...
WHY, SHIPMAN TEALART? TELL ME WHY YOU DID IT.
MY WIFE AND CHILD ARE STILL ON DAC--
--THE SITH IMPERIALS THERE HAVE THEM. THEY CONTACTED ME, LET ME TALK WITH THEM VIA HOLOCOMM.
THE IMPERIALS SAID IF I DID NOT DO AS INSTRUCTED, THEY WOULD DIE. I AM A FOOL, I KNOW. THEY ARE PROBABLY ALREADY DEAD.
I'M SORRY FOR SHOOTING YOU, ADMIRAL... SO SORRY.
WE ARE IN CONTACT WITH THE RANGERS ON DAC. I'LL ASK THEM TO DO WHAT THEY CAN FOR YOUR FAMILY.
YOU WILL BE COURT-MARTIALED, FOUND GUILTY, AND EXECUTED. I UNDERSTAND DIVIDED LOYALTIES, BUT YOUR ACTIONS COST SHIPS AND LIVES--AND COULD HAVE DESTROYED THE FLEET.
AN EXAMPLE MUST BE MADE. FOR MY PART, YOU ARE FORGIVEN, BUT NOT EXCUSED.
I UNDERSTAND, ADMIRAL.
AND... THANK YOU.
END

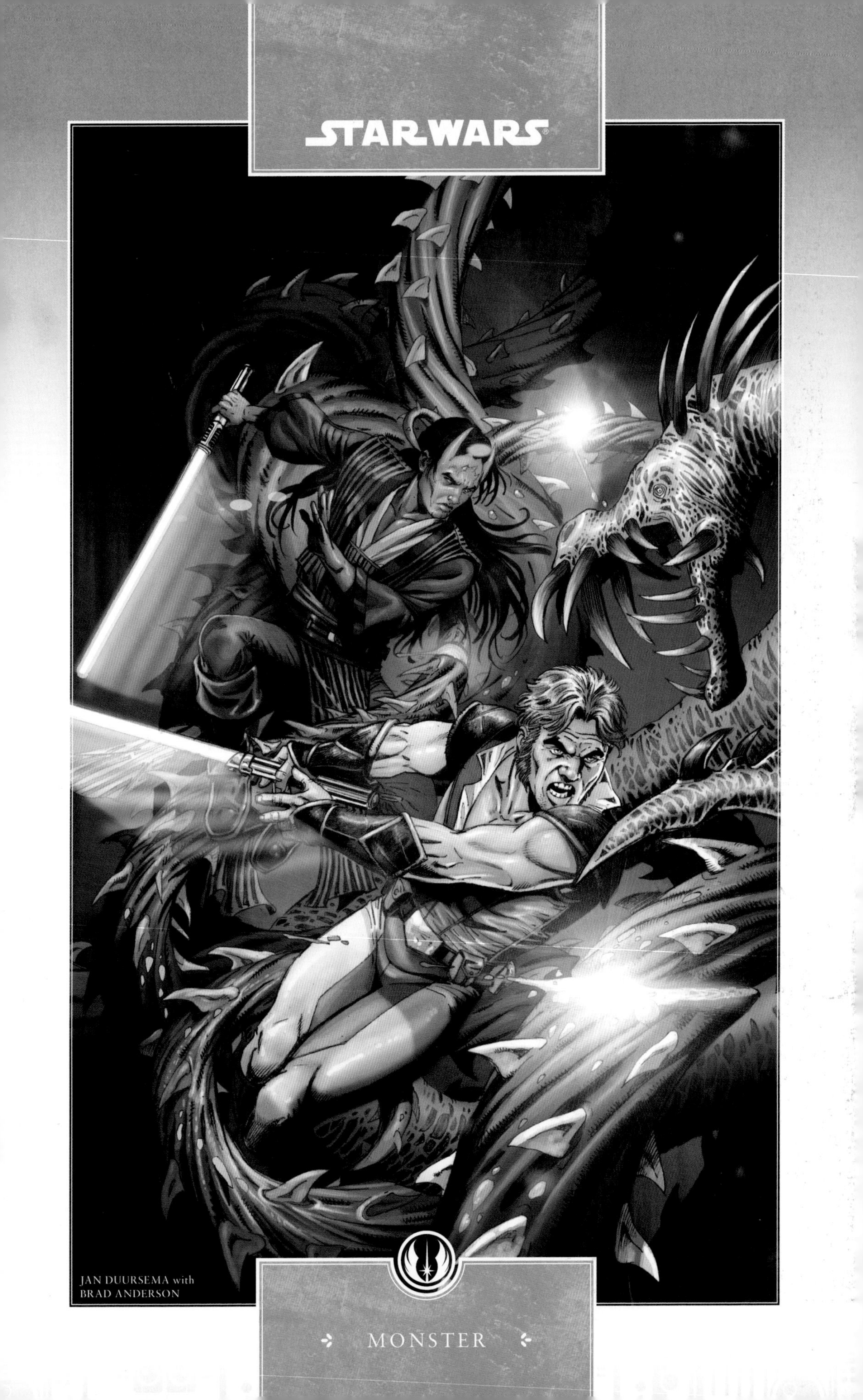
STAR WARS
JAN DUURSEMA with
BRAD ANDERSON
MONSTER

MEMORY FALLS BACK TO BEFORE THE FALL OF OSSUS. A YEAR BEFORE THE SITH-IMPERIAL WAR.

CHROM-VRONES, LEGACY OF THE YUUZHAN VONG OCCUPATION, STILL POCK THE PLANET WAYLAND. SCARS OF WAR.

GROWN FROM YORIK CORAL, THE ENORMOUS WORMS DIGEST ROCK, SPEWING PLASMA OVER ONCE-LUSH TERRAIN. TERRIBLE, EFFECTIVE WEAPONS OF WAR.

NEARLY ALL THE SENTIENTS WHO SURVIVED THE YUUZHAN VONG WAR ON WAYLAND HAD ABANDONED THE DYING WORLD, BUT SOME MYNEYRSHI WOULD NOT LEAVE THE PLANET THAT HAD SPAWNED THEIR SPECIES.

THEY LIVED WITHOUT HOPE.

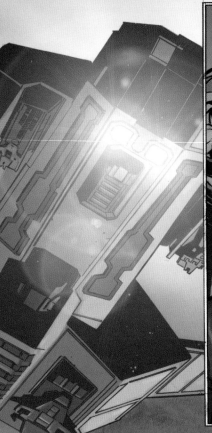

WE CAME TO GIVE IT BACK TO THEM.

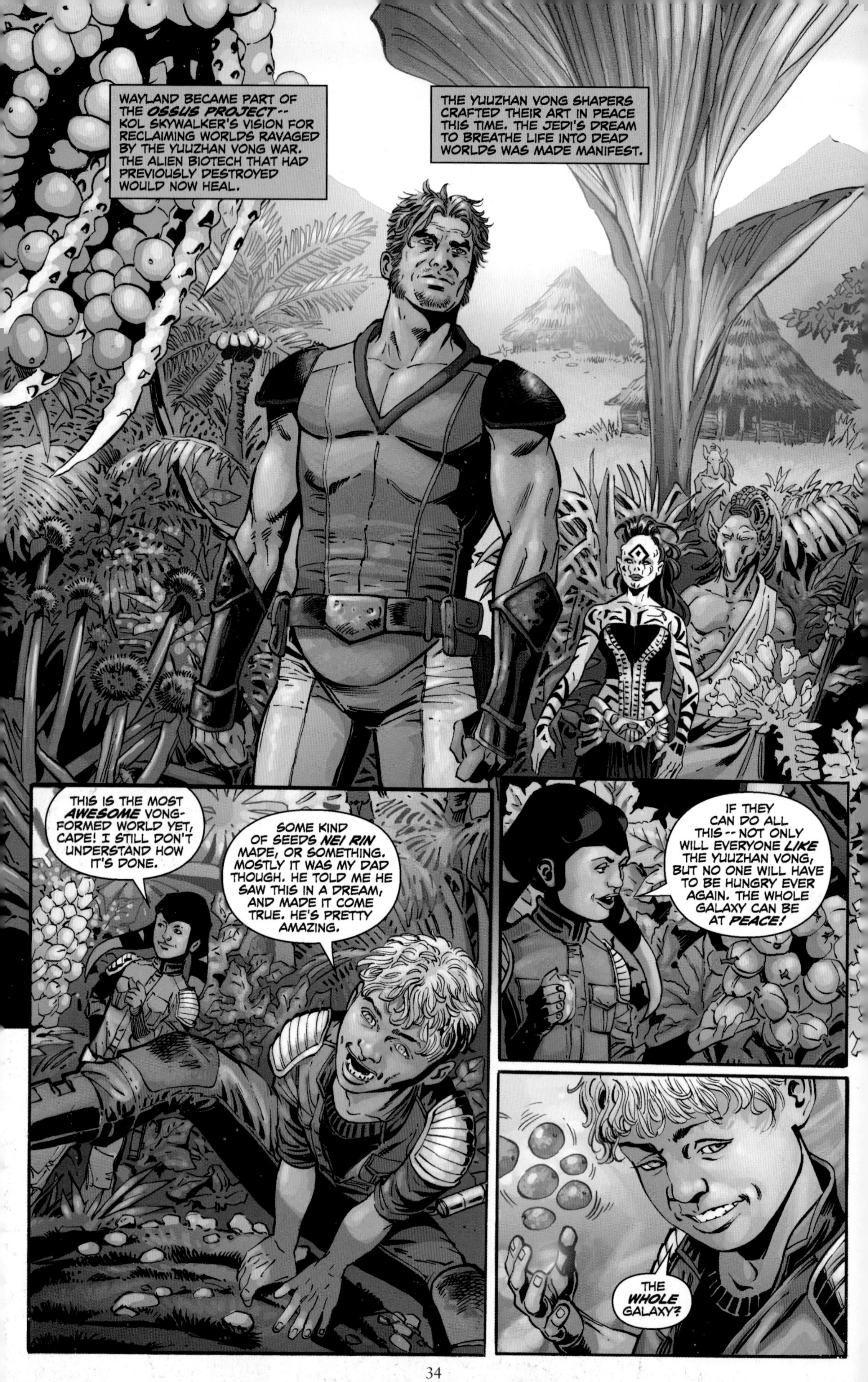
WAYLAND BECAME PART OF THE OSSUS PROJECT -- KOL SKYWALKER'S VISION FOR RECLAIMING WORLDS RAVAGED BY THE YUUZHAN VONG WAR. THE ALIEN BIOTECH THAT HAD PREVIOUSLY DESTROYED WOULD NOW HEAL.
THE YUUZHAN VONG SHAPERS CRAFTED THEIR ART IN PEACE THIS TIME. THE JEDI'S DREAM TO BREATHE LIFE INTO DEAD WORLDS WAS MADE MANIFEST.
THIS IS THE MOST AWESOME VONG-FORMED WORLD YET, CADE! I STILL DON'T UNDERSTAND HOW IT'S DONE.
SOME KIND OF SEEDS NEI RIN MADE, OR SOMETHING. MOSTLY IT WAS MY DAD THOUGH. HE TOLD ME HE SAW THIS IN A DREAM, AND MADE IT COME TRUE. HE'S PRETTY AMAZING.
IF THEY CAN DO ALL THIS -- NOT ONLY WILL EVERYONE LIKE THE YUUZHAN VONG, BUT NO ONE WILL HAVE TO BE HUNGRY EVER AGAIN. THE WHOLE GALAXY CAN BE AT PEACE!
THE WHOLE GALAXY?

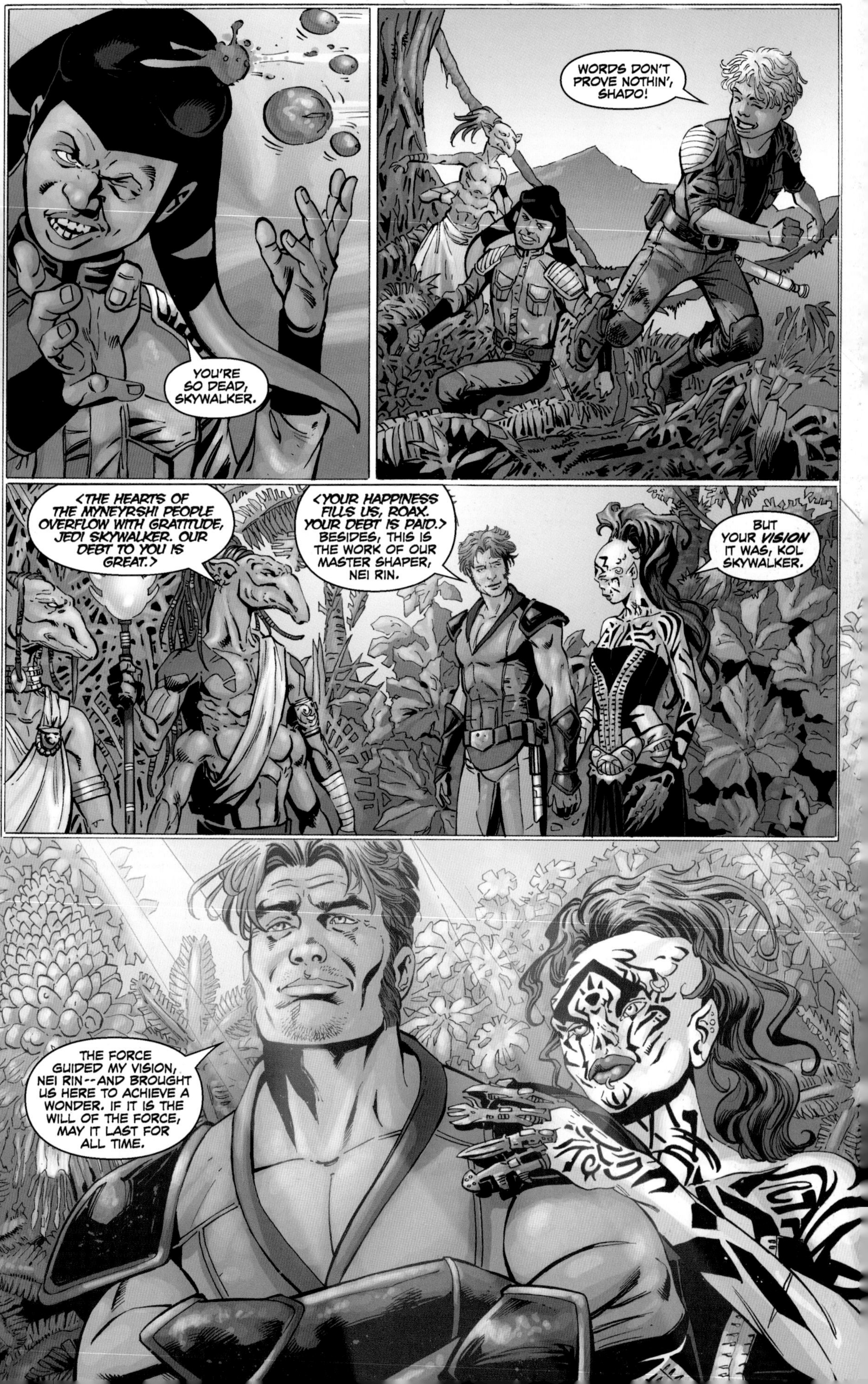

YOU'RE SO DEAD, SKYWALKER.
WORDS DON'T PROVE NOTHIN', SHADO!
<THE HEARTS OF THE MYNEYRSHI PEOPLE OVERFLOW WITH GRATITUDE, JEDI SKYWALKER. OUR DEBT TO YOU IS GREAT.>
<YOUR HAPPINESS FILLS US, ROAX. YOUR DEBT IS PAID.> BESIDES, THIS IS THE WORK OF OUR MASTER SHAPER, NEI RIN.
BUT YOUR VISION IT WAS, KOL SKYWALKER.
THE FORCE GUIDED MY VISION, NEI RIN--AND BROUGHT US HERE TO ACHIEVE A WONDER. IF IT IS THE WILL OF THE FORCE, MAY IT LAST FOR ALL TIME.

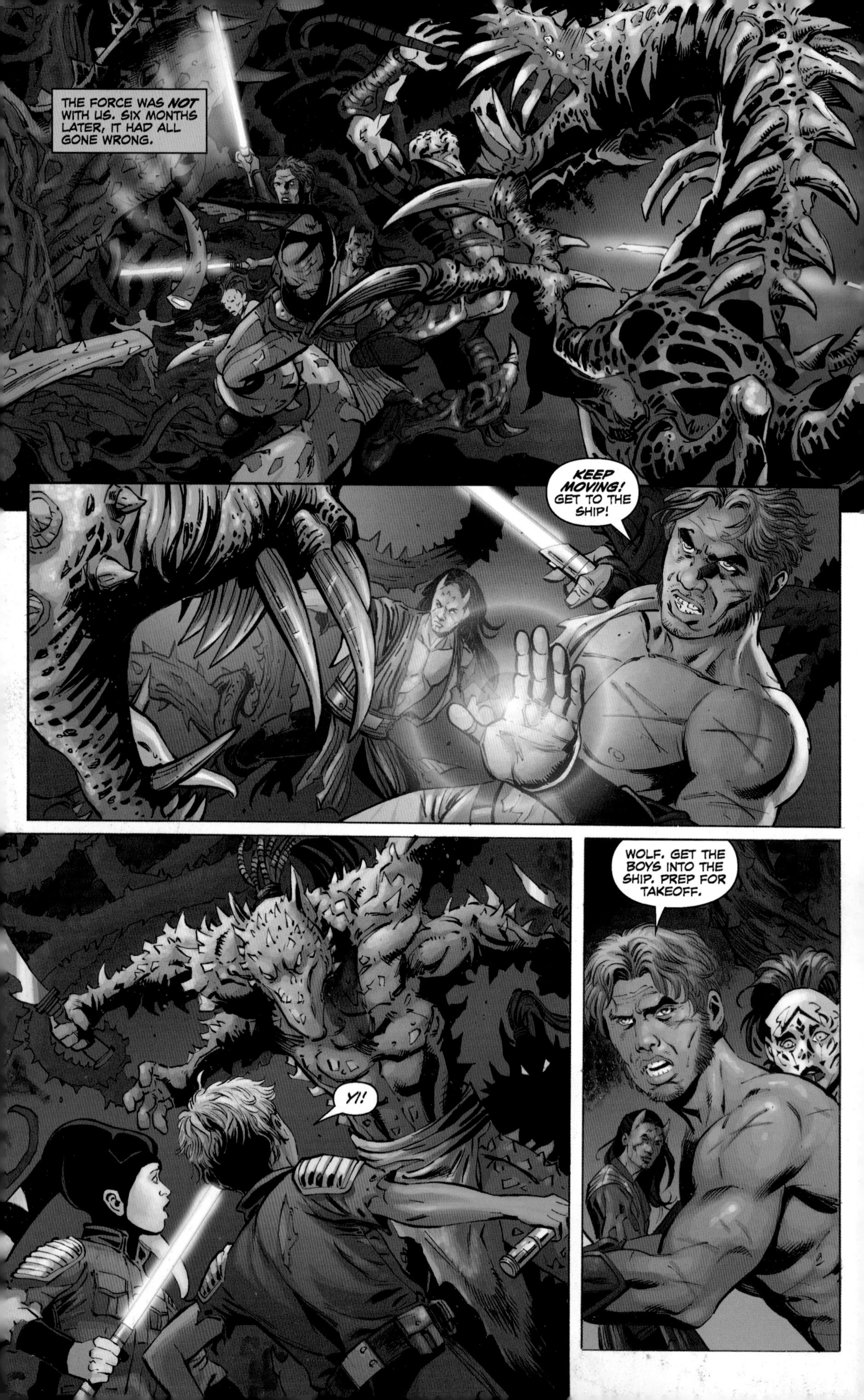
THE FORCE WAS NOT WITH US. SIX MONTHS LATER, IT HAD ALL GONE WRONG.
KEEP MOVING! GET TO THE SHIP!
YI!
WOLF. GET THE BOYS INTO THE SHIP. PREP FOR TAKEOFF.

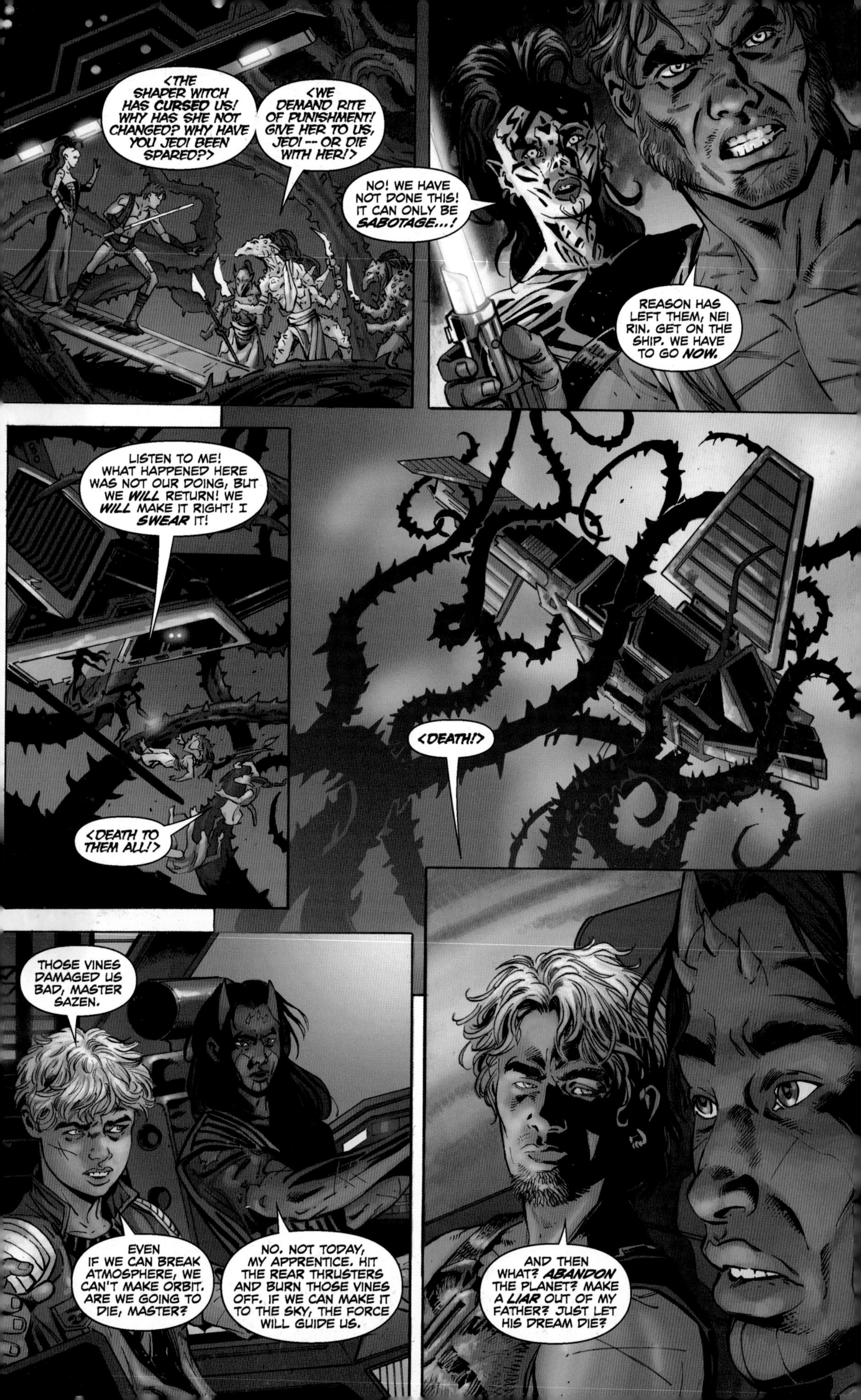
<THE SHAPER WITCH HAS CURSED US! WHY HAS SHE NOT CHANGED? WHY HAVE YOU JEDI BEEN SPARED?>
<WE DEMAND RITE OF PUNISHMENT! GIVE HER TO US, JEDI -- OR DIE WITH HER!>
NO! WE HAVE NOT DONE THIS! IT CAN ONLY BE SABOTAGE...!
REASON HAS LEFT THEM, NEI RIN. GET ON THE SHIP. WE HAVE TO GO NOW.
LISTEN TO ME! WHAT HAPPENED HERE WAS NOT OUR DOING, BUT WE WILL RETURN! WE WILL MAKE IT RIGHT! I SWEAR IT!
<DEATH TO THEM ALL!>
<DEATH!>
THOSE VINES DAMAGED US BAD, MASTER SAZEN.
EVEN IF WE CAN BREAK ATMOSPHERE, WE CAN'T MAKE ORBIT. ARE WE GOING TO DIE, MASTER?
NO. NOT TODAY, MY APPRENTICE. HIT THE REAR THRUSTERS AND BURN THOSE VINES OFF. IF WE CAN MAKE IT TO THE SKY, THE FORCE WILL GUIDE US.
AND THEN WHAT? ABANDON THE PLANET? MAKE A LIAR OUT OF MY FATHER? JUST LET HIS DREAM DIE?

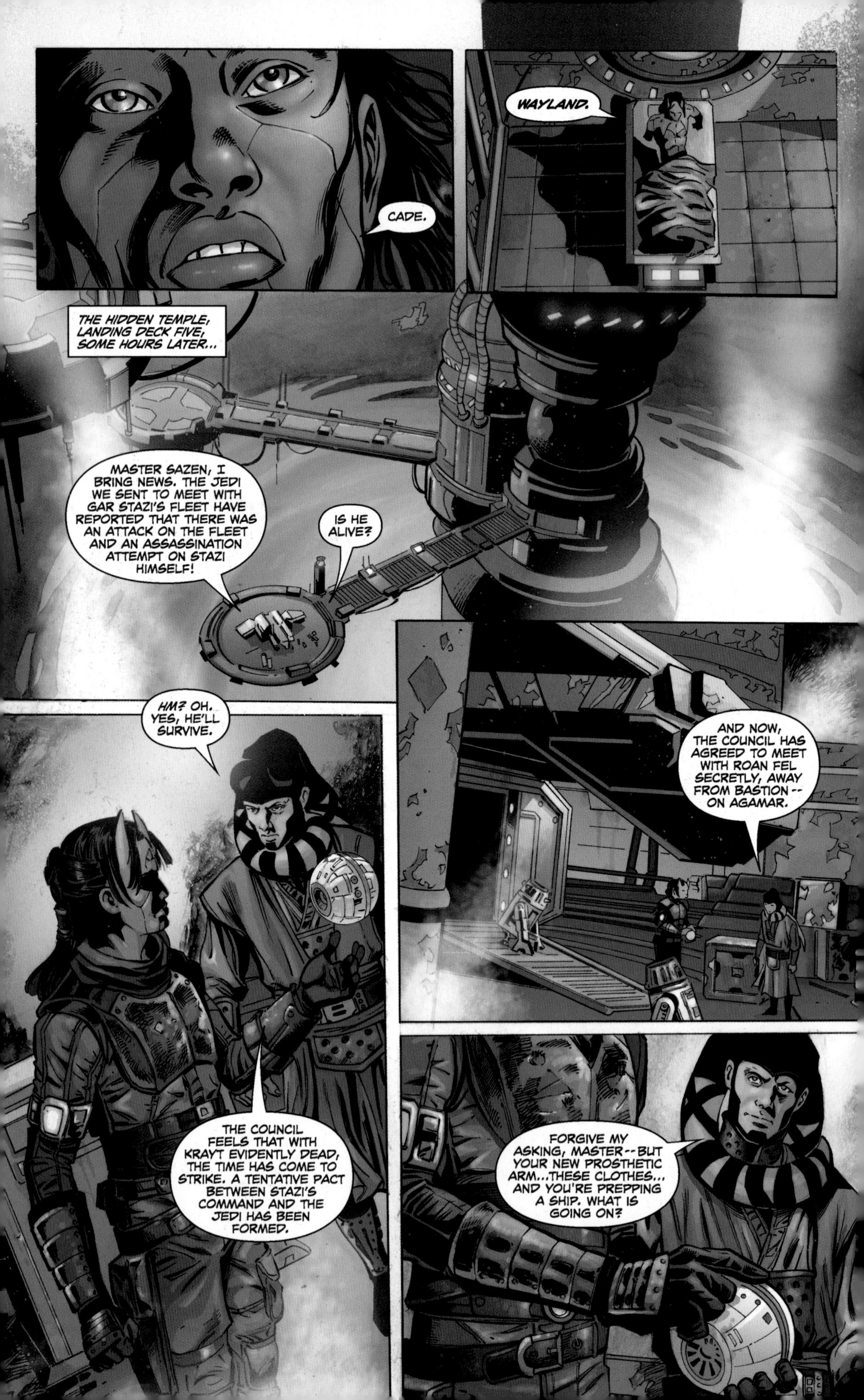
CADE.
WAYLAND.
THE HIDDEN TEMPLE, LANDING DECK FIVE, SOME HOURS LATER...
MASTER SAZEN, I BRING NEWS. THE JEDI WE SENT TO MEET WITH GAR STAZI'S FLEET HAVE REPORTED THAT THERE WAS AN ATTACK ON THE FLEET AND AN ASSASSINATION ATTEMPT ON STAZI HIMSELF!
IS HE ALIVE?
HM? OH. YES, HE'LL SURVIVE.
THE COUNCIL FEELS THAT WITH KRAYT EVIDENTLY DEAD, THE TIME HAS COME TO STRIKE. A TENTATIVE PACT BETWEEN STAZI'S COMMAND AND THE JEDI HAS BEEN FORMED.
AND NOW, THE COUNCIL HAS AGREED TO MEET WITH ROAN FEL SECRETLY, AWAY FROM BASTION -- ON AGAMAR.
FORGIVE MY ASKING, MASTER -- BUT YOUR NEW PROSTHETIC ARM... THESE CLOTHES... AND YOU'RE PREPPING A SHIP. WHAT IS GOING ON?

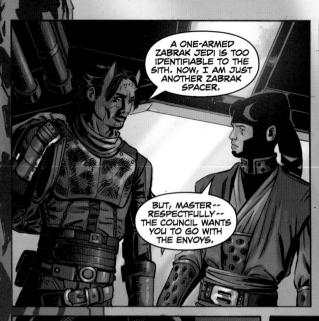

A ONE-ARMED ZABRAK JEDI IS TOO IDENTIFIABLE TO THE SITH. NOW, I AM JUST ANOTHER ZABRAK SPACER.

BUT, MASTER-- RESPECTFULLY-- THE COUNCIL WANTS YOU TO GO WITH THE ENVOYS.

I REGRET THAT I CANNOT. I'VE HAD A VISION.

MASTER, I RESPECT YOUR VISIONS -- ALL THE JEDI DO, BUT...

SHADO...IT IS WHAT IT IS. I DO NOT QUESTION THE WILL OF THE FORCE. NOR SHOULD YOU--FORMER APPRENTICE.

IT'S ABOUT CADE.

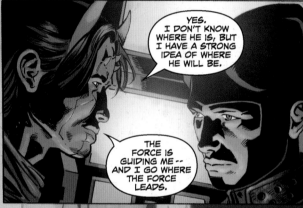

YES. I DON'T KNOW WHERE HE IS, BUT I HAVE A STRONG IDEA OF WHERE HE WILL BE.

THE FORCE IS GUIDING ME -- AND I GO WHERE THE FORCE LEADS.

THEN -- THE FORCE BE WITH YOU, WOLF.

THANK YOU, MY FRIEND.

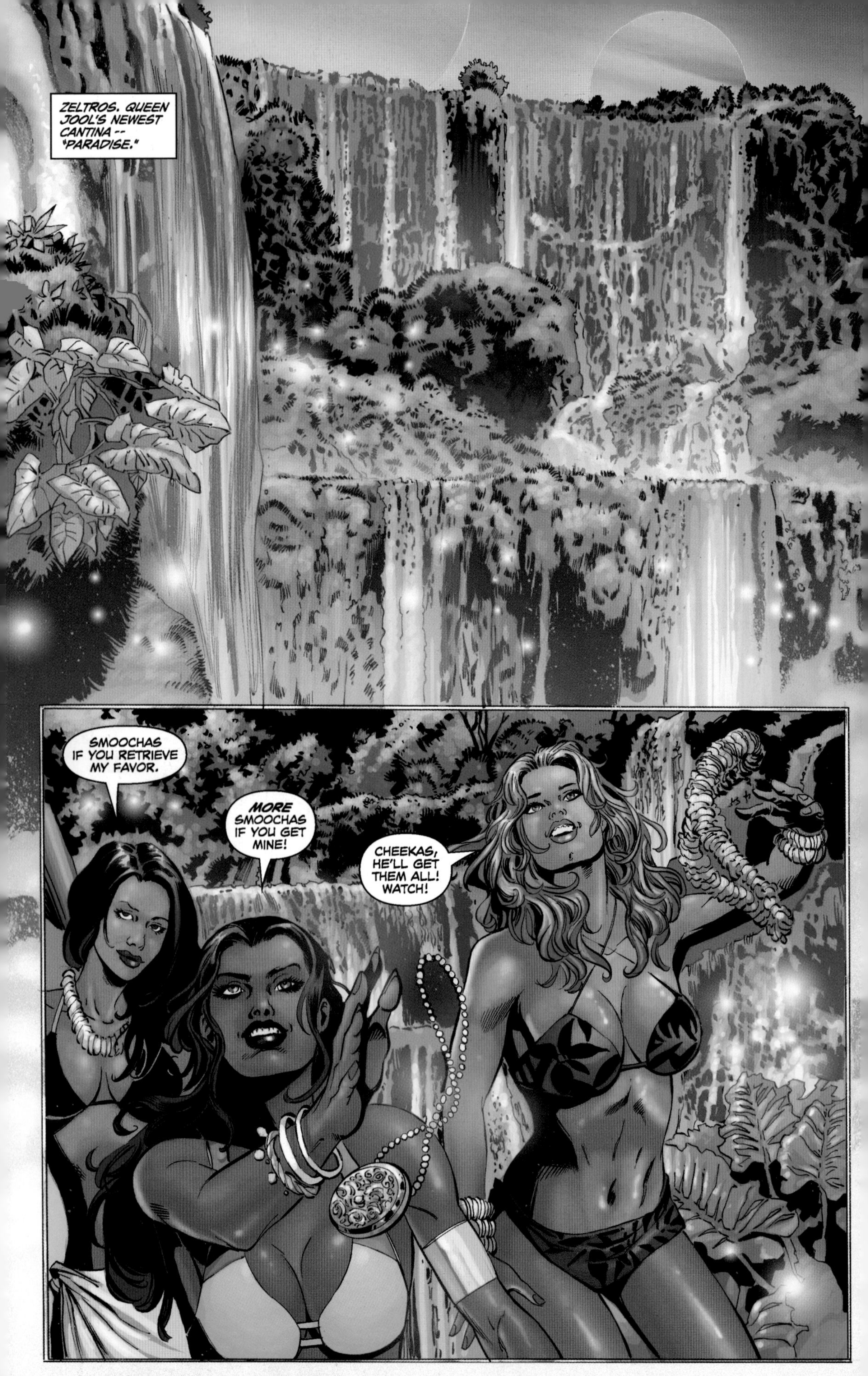
ZELTROS. QUEEN JOOL'S NEWEST CANTINA -- "PARADISE."
SMOOCHAS IF YOU RETRIEVE MY FAVOR.
MORE SMOOCHAS IF YOU GET MINE!
CHEEKAS, HE'LL GET THEM ALL! WATCH!

NO WORRIES, SYN. ZELTRONS DO THIS ALL THE TIME.

SANE ZELTRONS?

LIVE, SANE ZELTRONS?

YEEEAHHH!

WE'RE GONNA DIE!

NOT TODAY.

HUH -- FEELS LIKE... I'M FLYING?!

FORCE IS WITH US, PATEESA!

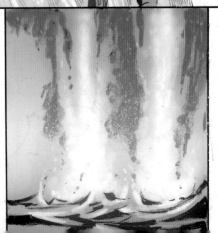

41

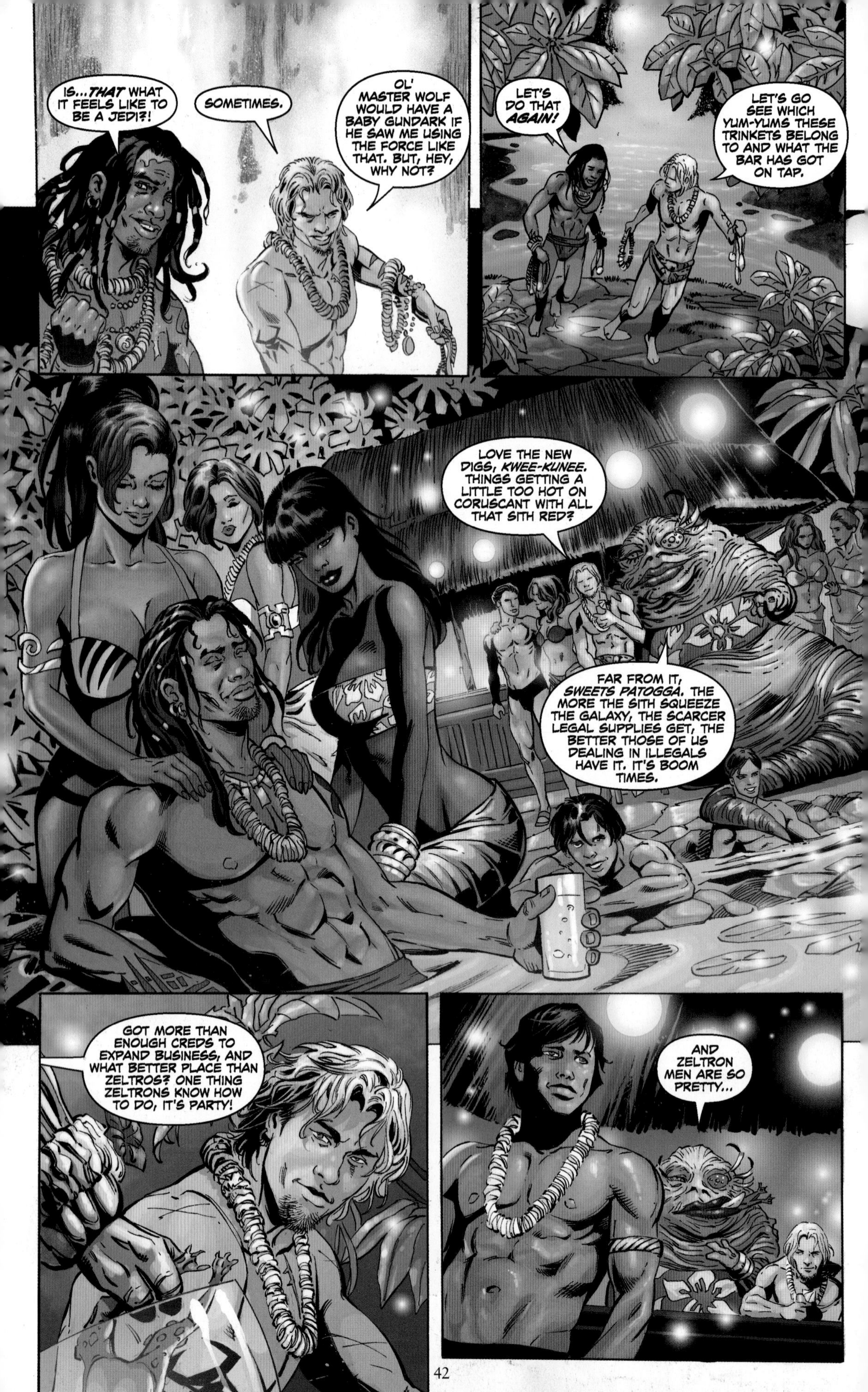
IS...THAT WHAT IT FEELS LIKE TO BE A JEDI?!
SOMETIMES.
OL' MASTER WOLF WOULD HAVE A BABY GUNDARK IF HE SAW ME USING THE FORCE LIKE THAT. BUT, HEY, WHY NOT?
LET'S DO THAT AGAIN!
LET'S GO SEE WHICH YUM-YUMS THESE TRINKETS BELONG TO AND WHAT THE BAR HAS GOT ON TAP.
LOVE THE NEW DIGS, KWEE-KUNEE. THINGS GETTING A LITTLE TOO HOT ON CORUSCANT WITH ALL THAT SITH RED?
FAR FROM IT, SWEETS PATOGGA. THE MORE THE SITH SQUEEZE THE GALAXY, THE SCARCER LEGAL SUPPLIES GET, THE BETTER THOSE OF US DEALING IN ILLEGALS HAVE IT. IT'S BOOM TIMES.
GOT MORE THAN ENOUGH CREDS TO EXPAND BUSINESS, AND WHAT BETTER PLACE THAN ZELTROS? ONE THING ZELTRONS KNOW HOW TO DO, IT'S PARTY!
AND ZELTRON MEN ARE SO PRETTY...

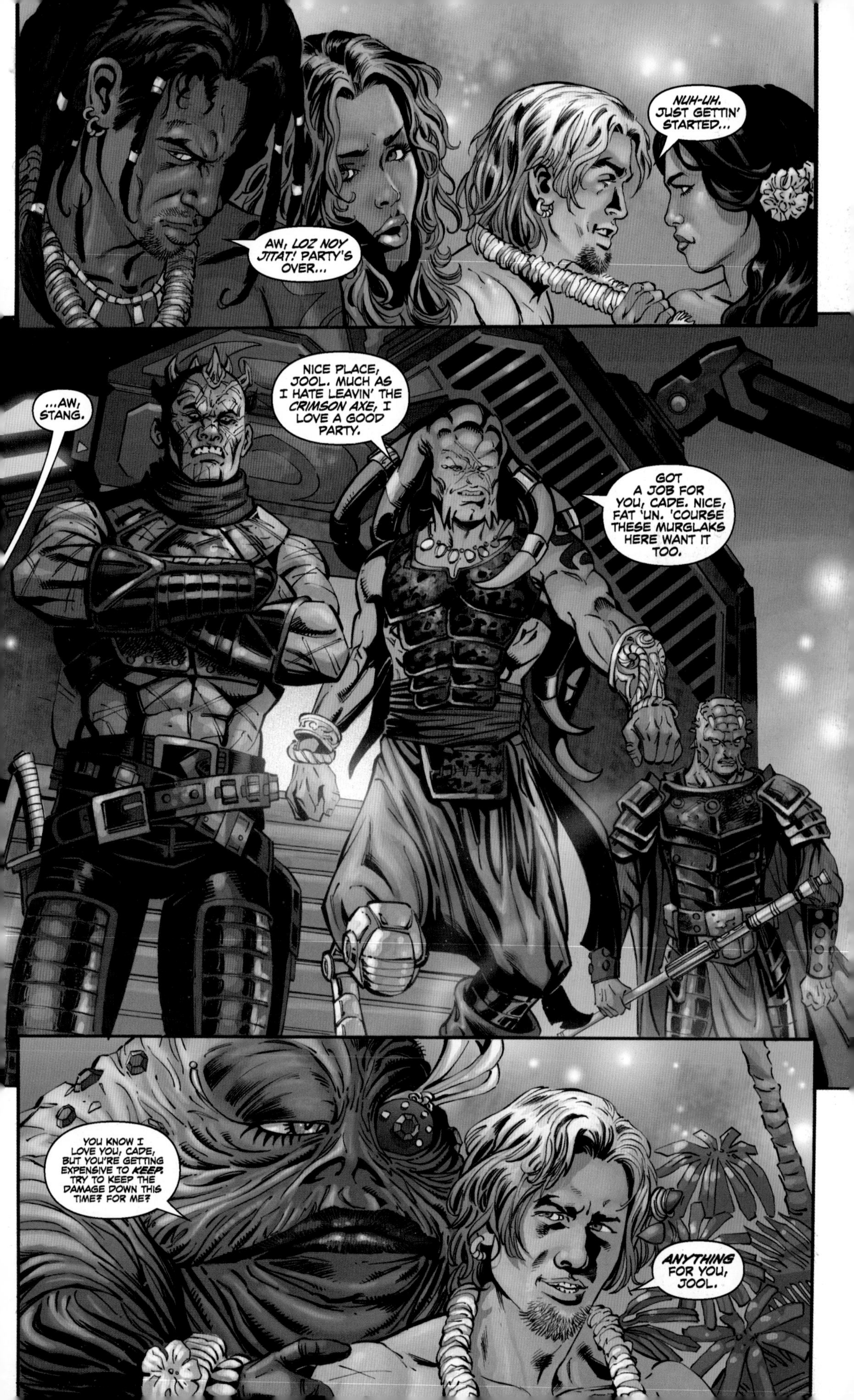
AW, LOZ NOY JITAT! PARTY'S OVER...
NUH-UH. JUST GETTIN' STARTED...
...AW, STANG.
NICE PLACE, JOOL. MUCH AS I HATE LEAVIN' THE CRIMSON AXE, I LOVE A GOOD PARTY.
GOT A JOB FOR YOU, CADE. NICE, FAT 'UN. 'COURSE THESE MURGLAKS HERE WANT IT TOO.
YOU KNOW I LOVE YOU, CADE, BUT YOU'RE GETTING EXPENSIVE TO KEEP. TRY TO KEEP THE DAMAGE DOWN THIS TIME? FOR ME?
ANYTHING FOR YOU, JOOL.

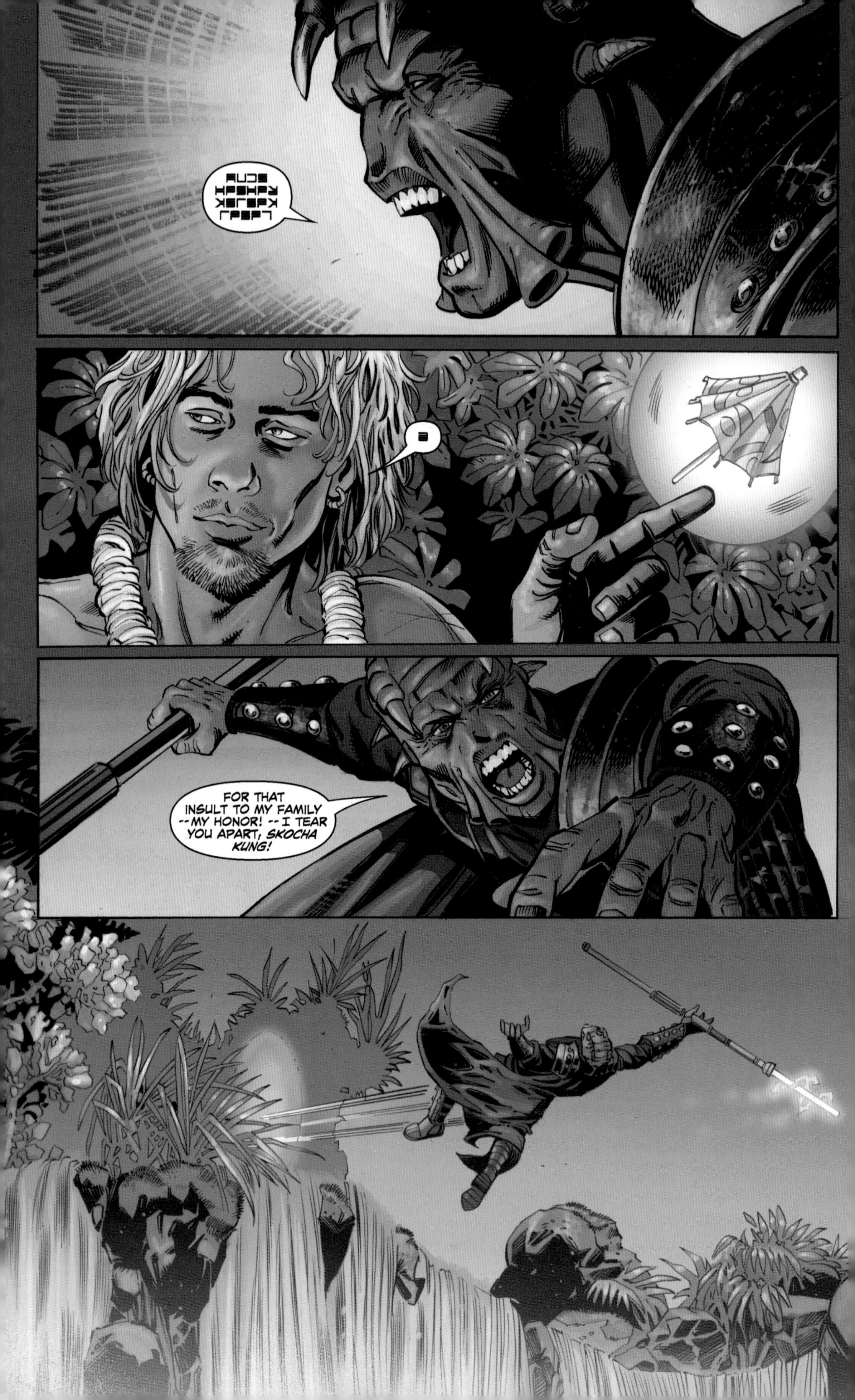
FOR THAT INSULT TO MY FAMILY --MY HONOR! --I TEAR YOU APART, *SKOCHA KUNG!*

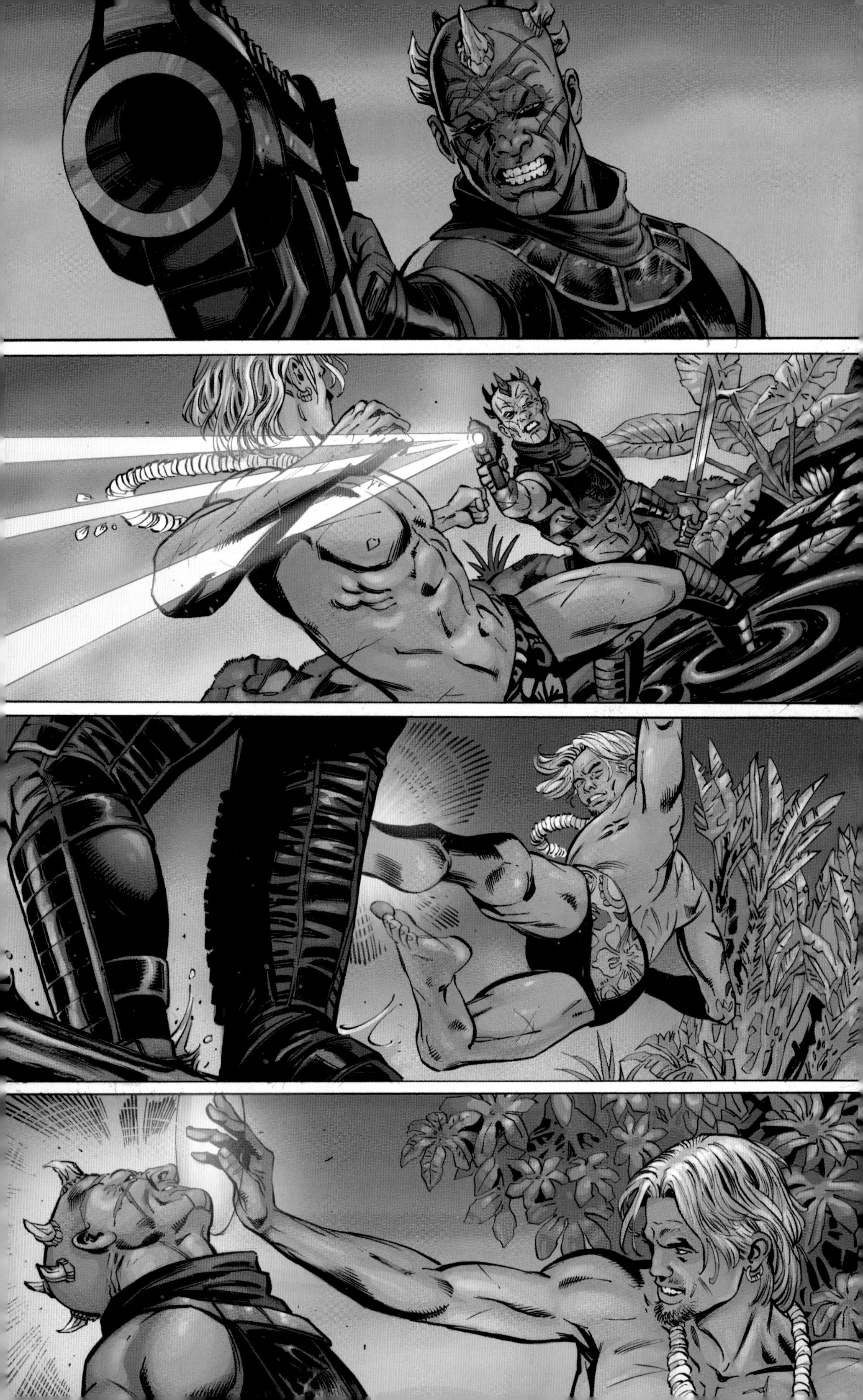

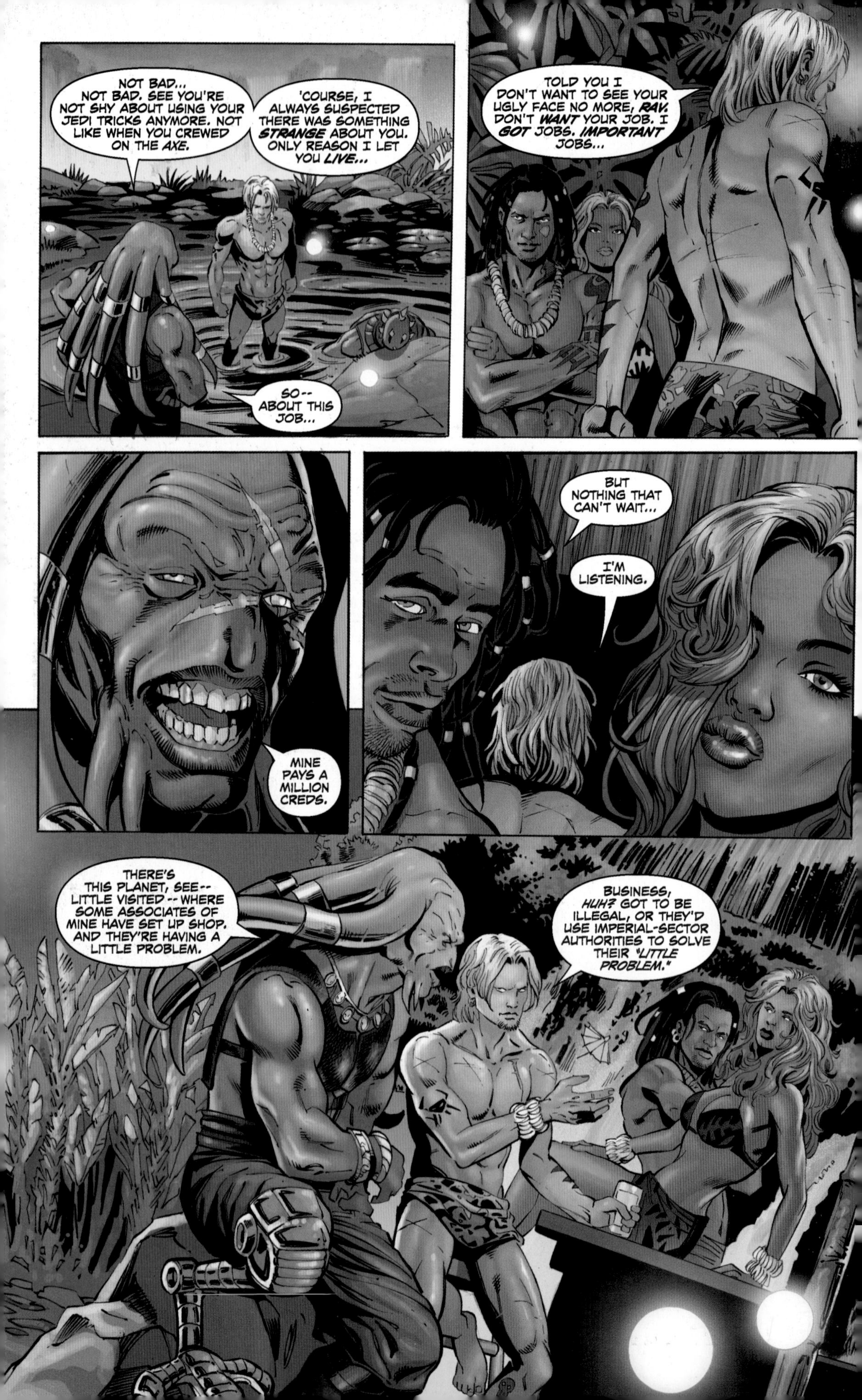
NOT BAD... NOT BAD. SEE YOU'RE NOT SHY ABOUT USING YOUR JEDI TRICKS ANYMORE. NOT LIKE WHEN YOU CREWED ON THE AXE.
'COURSE, I ALWAYS SUSPECTED THERE WAS SOMETHING STRANGE ABOUT YOU. ONLY REASON I LET YOU LIVE...
SO-- ABOUT THIS JOB...
TOLD YOU I DON'T WANT TO SEE YOUR UGLY FACE NO MORE, RAV. DON'T WANT YOUR JOB. I GOT JOBS. IMPORTANT JOBS...
BUT NOTHING THAT CAN'T WAIT...
MINE PAYS A MILLION CREDS.
I'M LISTENING.
THERE'S THIS PLANET, SEE-- LITTLE VISITED -- WHERE SOME ASSOCIATES OF MINE HAVE SET UP SHOP. AND THEY'RE HAVING A LITTLE PROBLEM.
BUSINESS, HUH? GOT TO BE ILLEGAL, OR THEY'D USE IMPERIAL-SECTOR AUTHORITIES TO SOLVE THEIR "LITTLE PROBLEM."

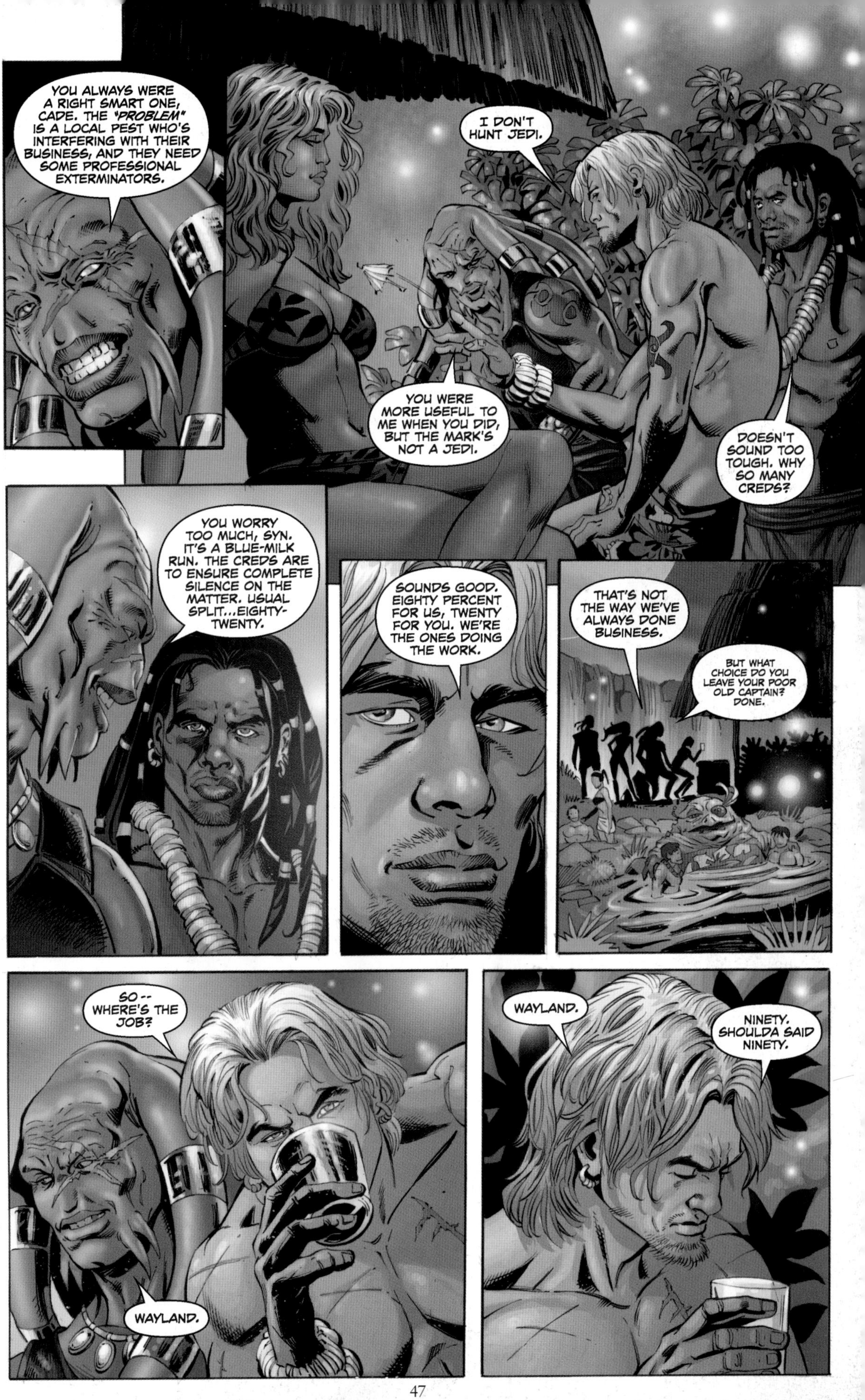
YOU ALWAYS WERE A RIGHT SMART ONE, CADE. THE "PROBLEM" IS A LOCAL PEST WHO'S INTERFERING WITH THEIR BUSINESS, AND THEY NEED SOME PROFESSIONAL EXTERMINATORS.
I DON'T HUNT JEDI.
YOU WERE MORE USEFUL TO ME WHEN YOU DID, BUT THE MARK'S NOT A JEDI.
DOESN'T SOUND TOO TOUGH. WHY SO MANY CREDS?
YOU WORRY TOO MUCH, SYN. IT'S A BLUE-MILK RUN. THE CREDS ARE TO ENSURE COMPLETE SILENCE ON THE MATTER. USUAL SPLIT...EIGHTY-TWENTY.
SOUNDS GOOD. EIGHTY PERCENT FOR US, TWENTY FOR YOU. WE'RE THE ONES DOING THE WORK.
THAT'S NOT THE WAY WE'VE ALWAYS DONE BUSINESS.
BUT WHAT CHOICE DO YOU LEAVE YOUR POOR OLD CAPTAIN? DONE.
SO -- WHERE'S THE JOB?
WAYLAND.
WAYLAND.
NINETY. SHOULDA SAID NINETY.

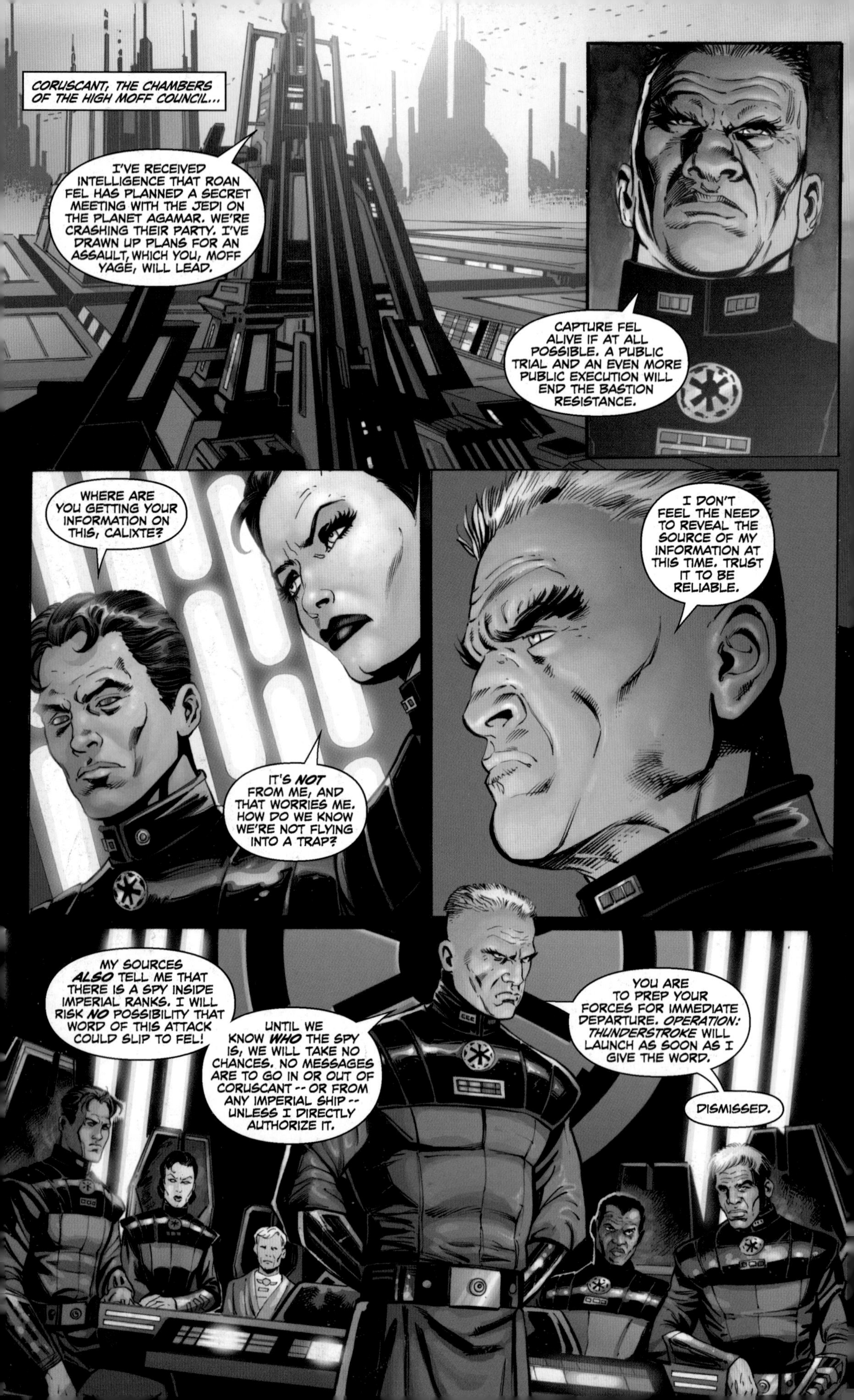
CORUSCANT, THE CHAMBERS OF THE HIGH MOFF COUNCIL...
I'VE RECEIVED INTELLIGENCE THAT ROAN FEL HAS PLANNED A SECRET MEETING WITH THE JEDI ON THE PLANET AGAMAR. WE'RE CRASHING THEIR PARTY. I'VE DRAWN UP PLANS FOR AN ASSAULT, WHICH YOU, MOFF YAGE, WILL LEAD.
CAPTURE FEL ALIVE IF AT ALL POSSIBLE. A PUBLIC TRIAL AND AN EVEN MORE PUBLIC EXECUTION WILL END THE BASTION RESISTANCE.
WHERE ARE YOU GETTING YOUR INFORMATION ON THIS, CALIXTE?
IT'S ***NOT*** FROM ME, AND THAT WORRIES ME. HOW DO WE KNOW WE'RE NOT FLYING INTO A TRAP?
I DON'T FEEL THE NEED TO REVEAL THE SOURCE OF MY INFORMATION AT THIS TIME. TRUST IT TO BE RELIABLE.
MY SOURCES ***ALSO*** TELL ME THAT THERE IS A SPY INSIDE IMPERIAL RANKS. I WILL RISK ***NO*** POSSIBILITY THAT WORD OF THIS ATTACK COULD SLIP TO FEL!
UNTIL WE KNOW ***WHO*** THE SPY IS, WE WILL TAKE NO CHANCES. NO MESSAGES ARE TO GO IN OR OUT OF CORUSCANT -- OR FROM ANY IMPERIAL SHIP -- UNLESS I DIRECTLY AUTHORIZE IT.
YOU ARE TO PREP YOUR FORCES FOR IMMEDIATE DEPARTURE. *OPERATION: THUNDERSTROKE* WILL LAUNCH AS SOON AS I GIVE THE WORD.
DISMISSED.

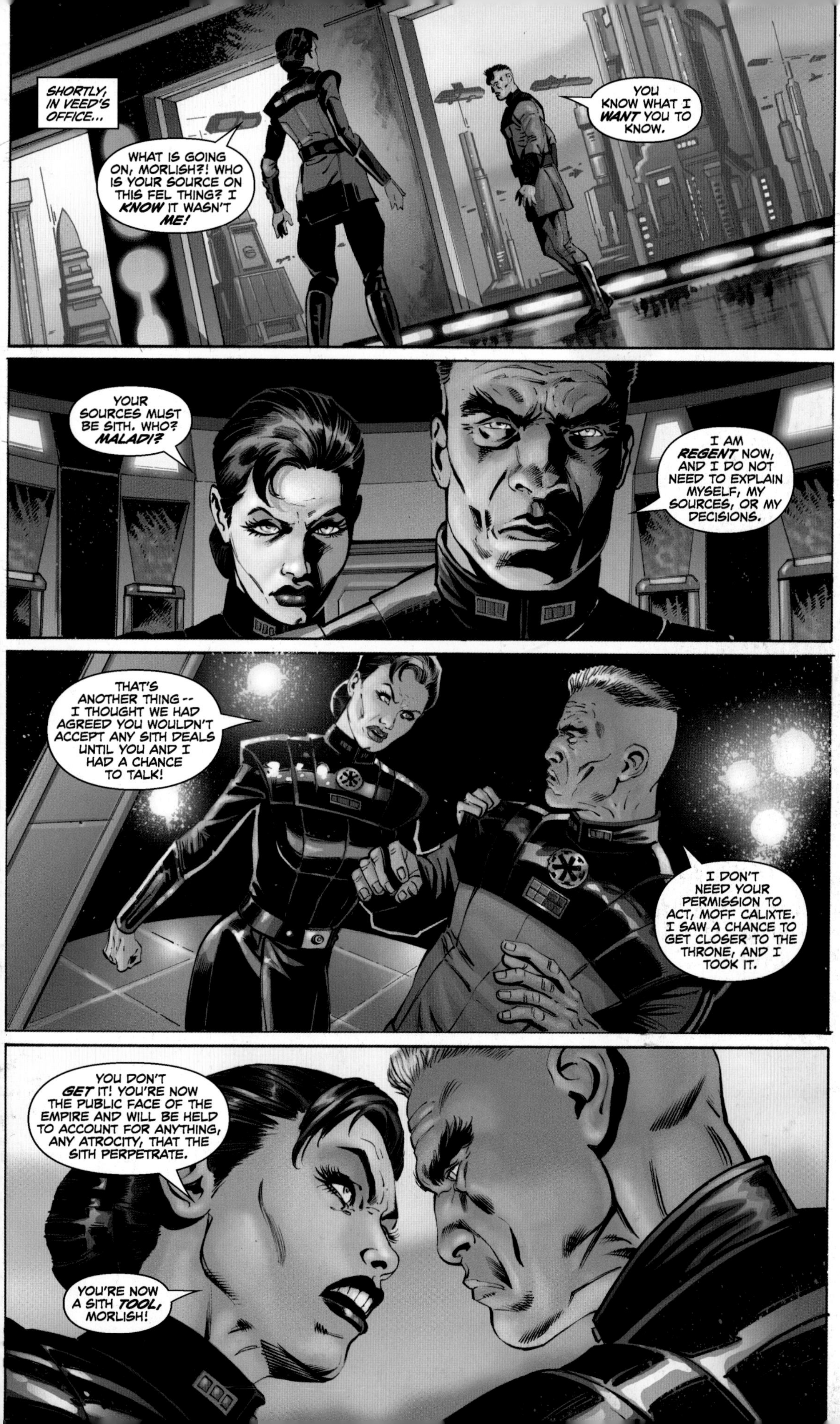
SHORTLY, IN VEED'S OFFICE...
WHAT IS GOING ON, MORLISH?! WHO IS YOUR SOURCE ON THIS FEL THING? I KNOW IT WASN'T ME!
YOU KNOW WHAT I WANT YOU TO KNOW.
YOUR SOURCES MUST BE SITH. WHO? MALADI?
I AM REGENT NOW, AND I DO NOT NEED TO EXPLAIN MYSELF, MY SOURCES, OR MY DECISIONS.
THAT'S ANOTHER THING -- I THOUGHT WE HAD AGREED YOU WOULDN'T ACCEPT ANY SITH DEALS UNTIL YOU AND I HAD A CHANCE TO TALK!
I DON'T NEED YOUR PERMISSION TO ACT, MOFF CALIXTE. I SAW A CHANCE TO GET CLOSER TO THE THRONE, AND I TOOK IT.
YOU DON'T GET IT! YOU'RE NOW THE PUBLIC FACE OF THE EMPIRE AND WILL BE HELD TO ACCOUNT FOR ANYTHING, ANY ATROCITY, THAT THE SITH PERPETRATE.
YOU'RE NOW A SITH TOOL, MORLISH!

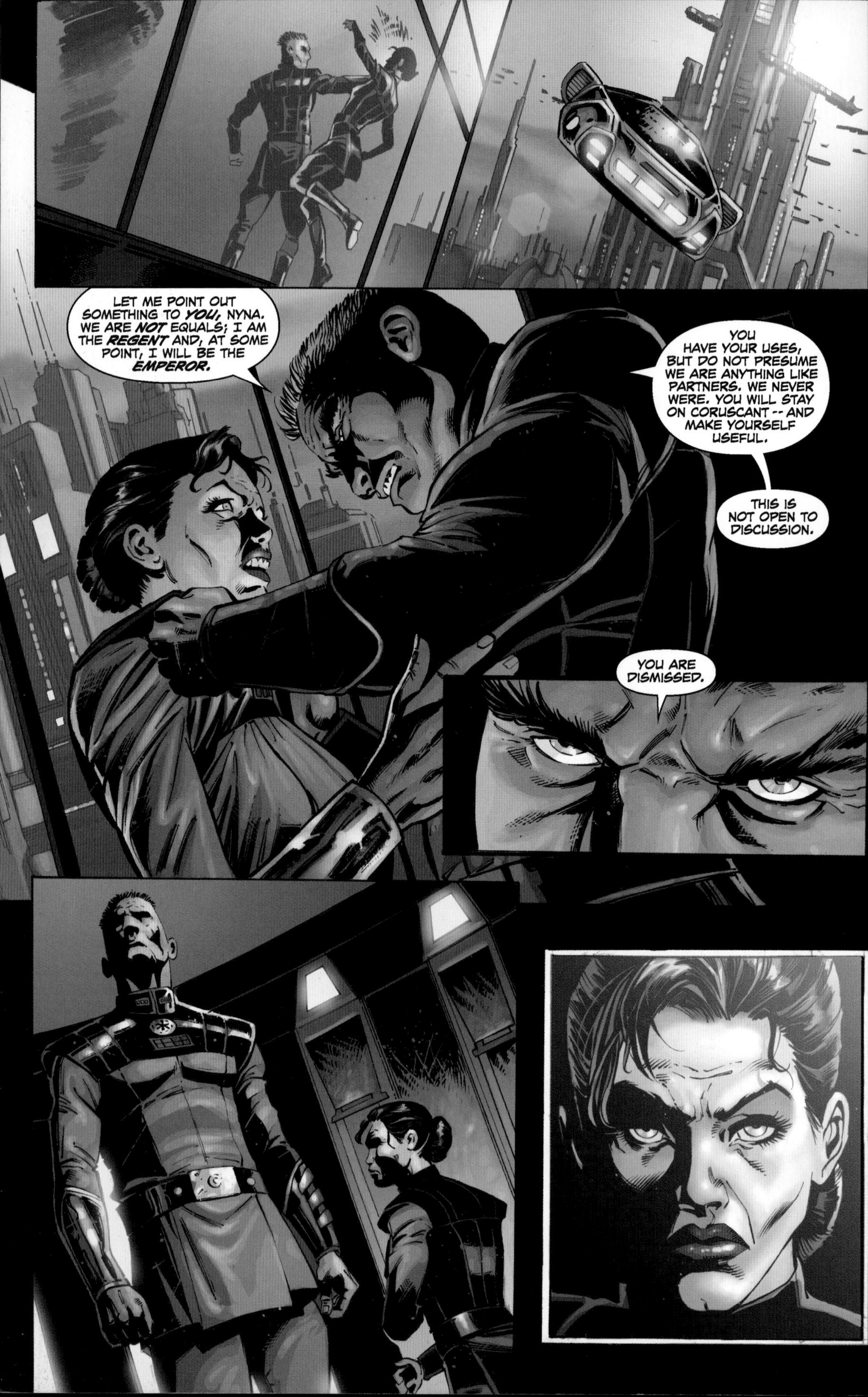
LET ME POINT OUT SOMETHING TO YOU, NYNA. WE ARE NOT EQUALS; I AM THE REGENT AND, AT SOME POINT, I WILL BE THE EMPEROR.
YOU HAVE YOUR USES, BUT DO NOT PRESUME WE ARE ANYTHING LIKE PARTNERS. WE NEVER WERE. YOU WILL STAY ON CORUSCANT -- AND MAKE YOURSELF USEFUL.
THIS IS NOT OPEN TO DISCUSSION.
YOU ARE DISMISSED.

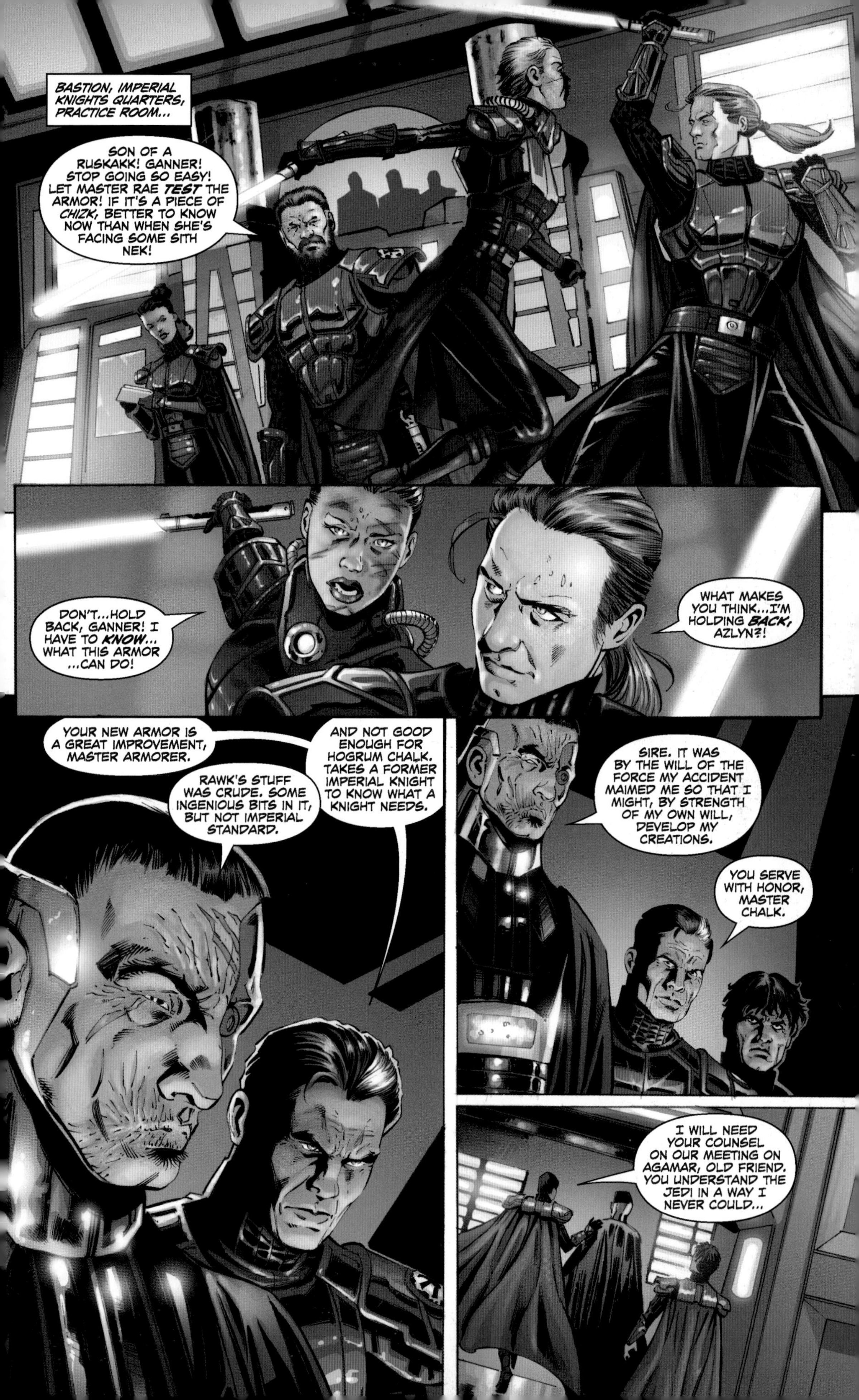
BASTION, IMPERIAL KNIGHTS QUARTERS, PRACTICE ROOM...
SON OF A RUSKAKK! GANNER! STOP GOING SO EASY! LET MASTER RAE TEST THE ARMOR! IF IT'S A PIECE OF CHIZK, BETTER TO KNOW NOW THAN WHEN SHE'S FACING SOME SITH NEK!
DON'T...HOLD BACK, GANNER! I HAVE TO KNOW... WHAT THIS ARMOR ...CAN DO!
WHAT MAKES YOU THINK...I'M HOLDING BACK, AZLYN?!
YOUR NEW ARMOR IS A GREAT IMPROVEMENT, MASTER ARMORER.
RAWK'S STUFF WAS CRUDE. SOME INGENIOUS BITS IN IT, BUT NOT IMPERIAL STANDARD.
AND NOT GOOD ENOUGH FOR HOGRUM CHALK. TAKES A FORMER IMPERIAL KNIGHT TO KNOW WHAT A KNIGHT NEEDS.
SIRE. IT WAS BY THE WILL OF THE FORCE MY ACCIDENT MAIMED ME SO THAT I MIGHT, BY STRENGTH OF MY OWN WILL, DEVELOP MY CREATIONS.
YOU SERVE WITH HONOR, MASTER CHALK.
I WILL NEED YOUR COUNSEL ON OUR MEETING ON AGAMAR, OLD FRIEND. YOU UNDERSTAND THE JEDI IN A WAY I NEVER COULD...

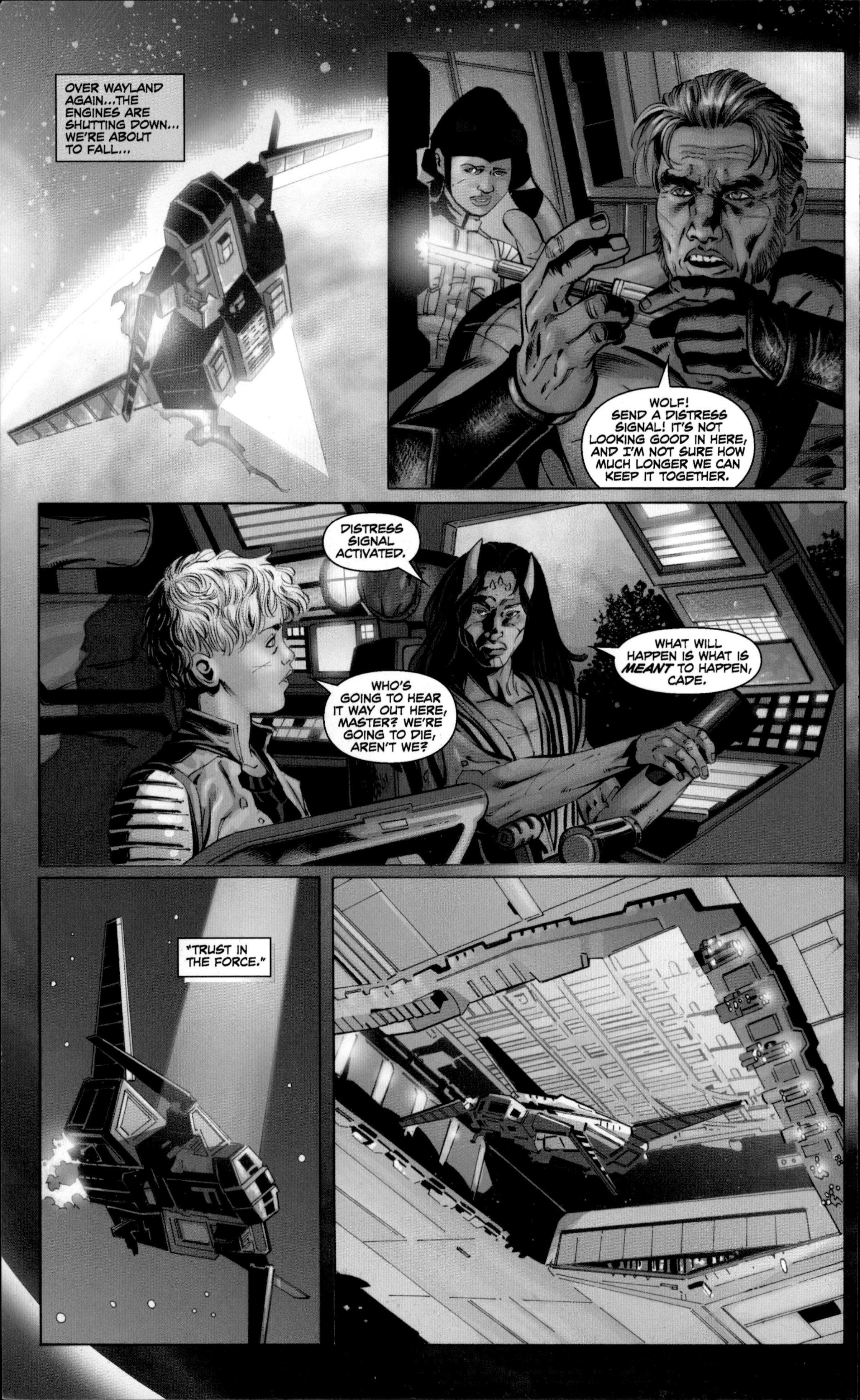
OVER WAYLAND AGAIN...THE ENGINES ARE SHUTTING DOWN... WE'RE ABOUT TO FALL...
WOLF! SEND A DISTRESS SIGNAL! IT'S NOT LOOKING GOOD IN HERE, AND I'M NOT SURE HOW MUCH LONGER WE CAN KEEP IT TOGETHER.
DISTRESS SIGNAL ACTIVATED.
WHO'S GOING TO HEAR IT WAY OUT HERE, MASTER? WE'RE GOING TO DIE, AREN'T WE?
WHAT WILL HAPPEN IS WHAT IS *MEANT* TO HAPPEN, CADE.
"TRUST IN THE FORCE."

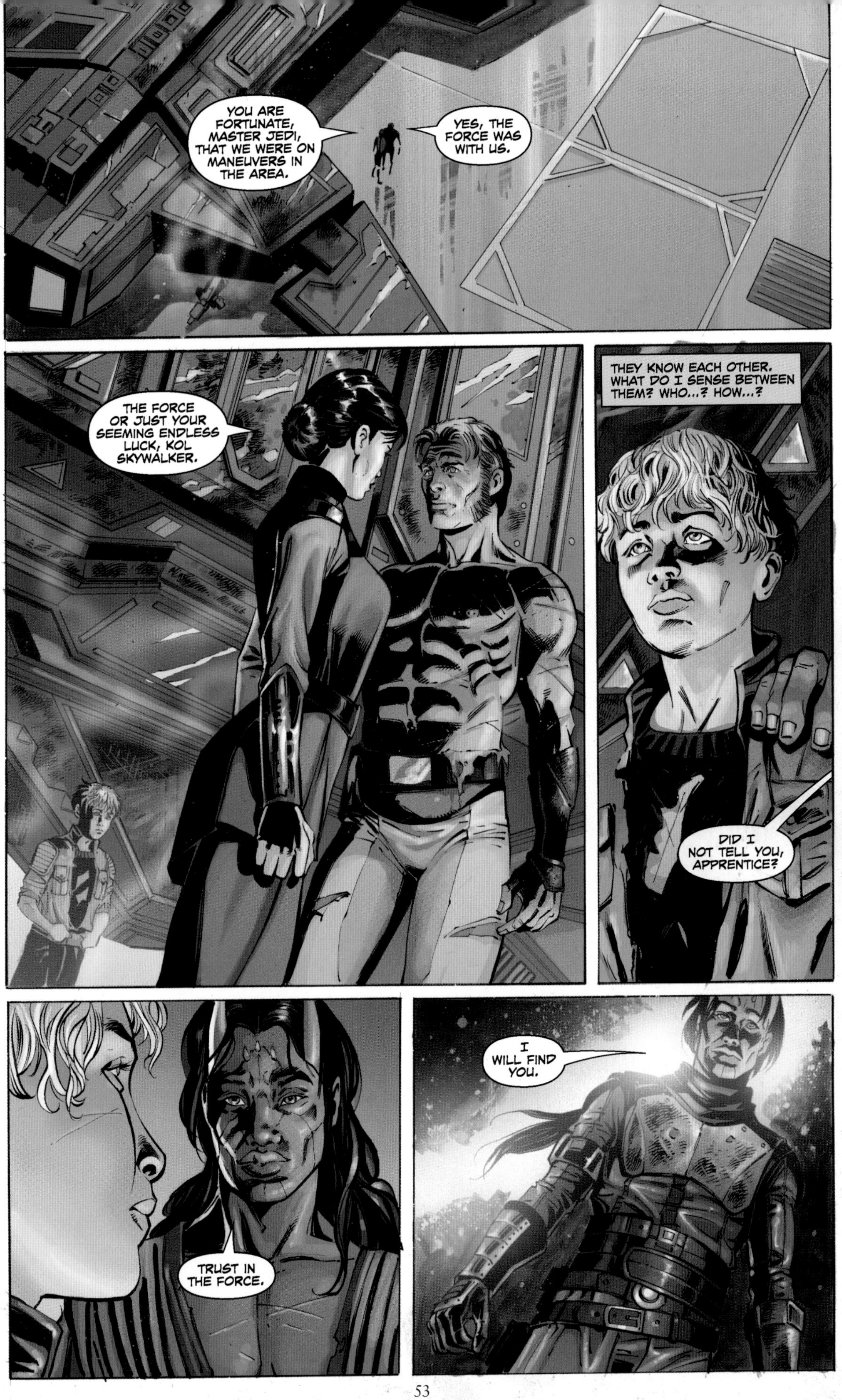
YOU ARE FORTUNATE, MASTER JEDI, THAT WE WERE ON MANEUVERS IN THE AREA.
YES, THE FORCE WAS WITH US.
THE FORCE OR JUST YOUR SEEMING ENDLESS LUCK, KOL SKYWALKER.
THEY KNOW EACH OTHER. WHAT DO I SENSE BETWEEN THEM? WHO...? HOW...?
DID I NOT TELL YOU, APPRENTICE?
TRUST IN THE FORCE.
I WILL FIND YOU.

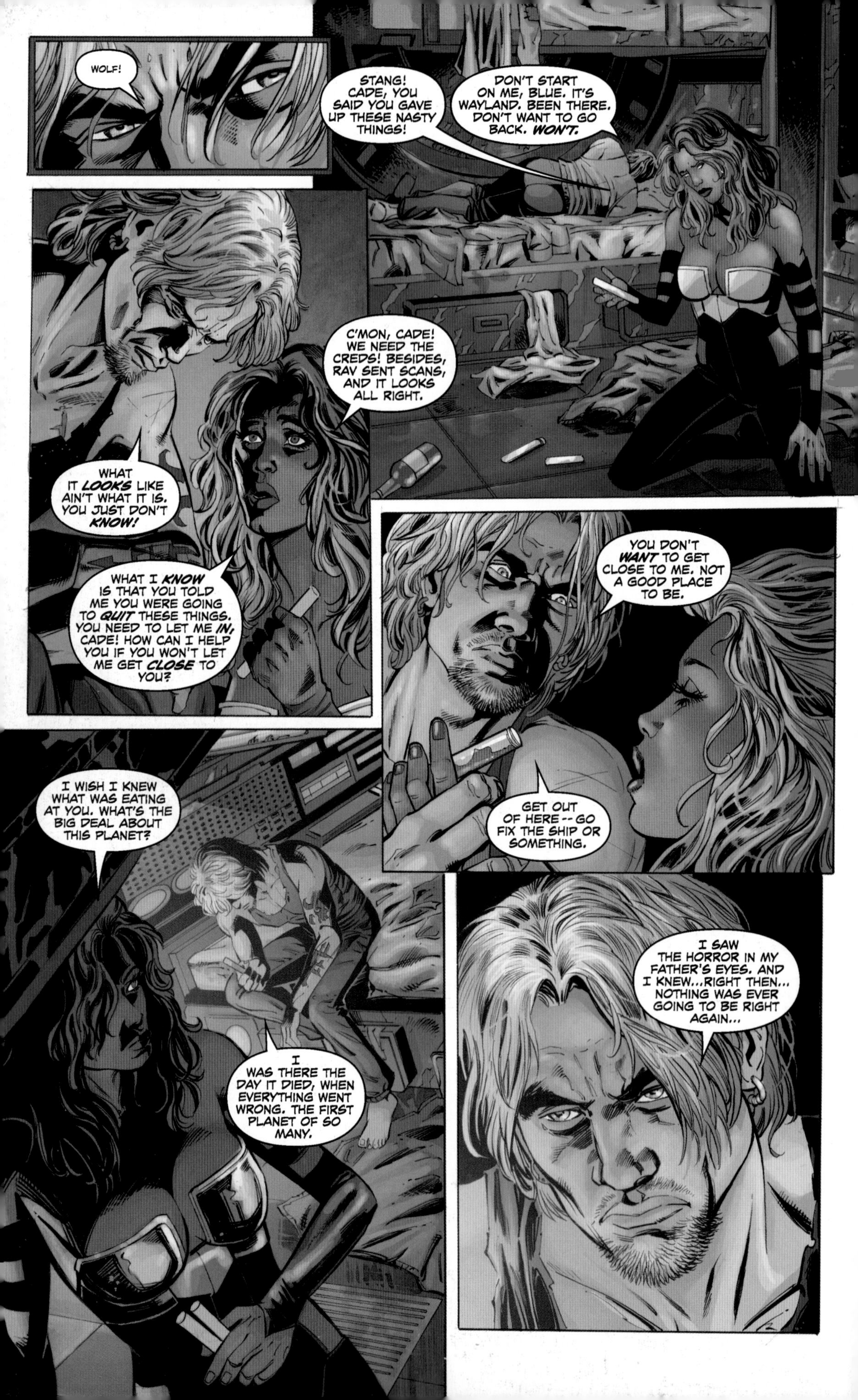
WOLF!
STANG! CADE, YOU SAID YOU GAVE UP THESE NASTY THINGS!
DON'T START ON ME, BLUE. IT'S WAYLAND. BEEN THERE. DON'T WANT TO GO BACK. WON'T.
C'MON, CADE! WE NEED THE CREDS! BESIDES, RAV SENT SCANS, AND IT LOOKS ALL RIGHT.
WHAT IT LOOKS LIKE AIN'T WHAT IT IS. YOU JUST DON'T KNOW!
WHAT I KNOW IS THAT YOU TOLD ME YOU WERE GOING TO QUIT THESE THINGS. YOU NEED TO LET ME IN, CADE! HOW CAN I HELP YOU IF YOU WON'T LET ME GET CLOSE TO YOU?
YOU DON'T WANT TO GET CLOSE TO ME. NOT A GOOD PLACE TO BE.
GET OUT OF HERE -- GO FIX THE SHIP OR SOMETHING.
I WISH I KNEW WHAT WAS EATING AT YOU. WHAT'S THE BIG DEAL ABOUT THIS PLANET?
I WAS THERE THE DAY IT DIED, WHEN EVERYTHING WENT WRONG. THE FIRST PLANET OF SO MANY.
I SAW THE HORROR IN MY FATHER'S EYES. AND I KNEW...RIGHT THEN... NOTHING WAS EVER GOING TO BE RIGHT AGAIN...

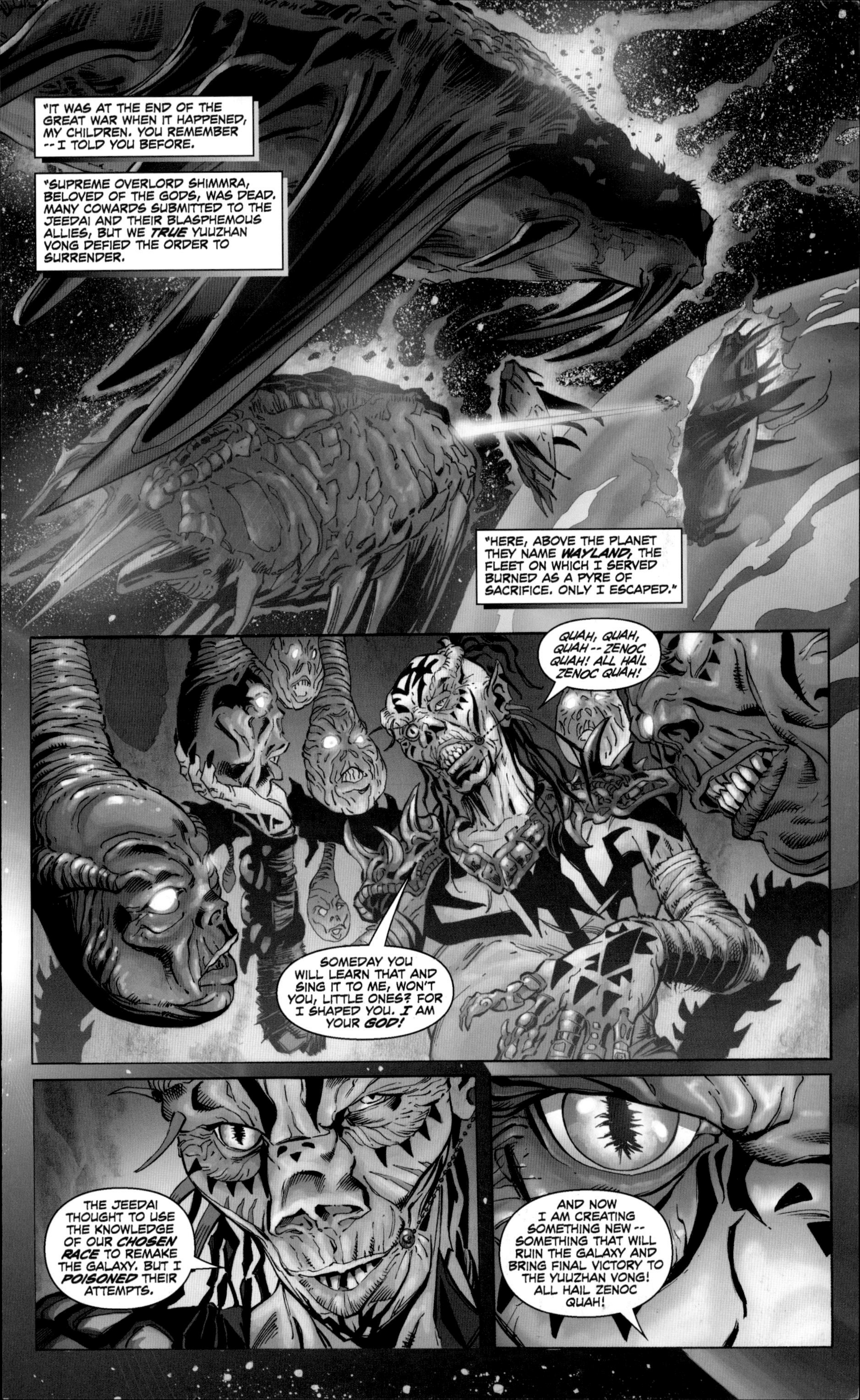
"IT WAS AT THE END OF THE GREAT WAR WHEN IT HAPPENED, MY CHILDREN. YOU REMEMBER -- I TOLD YOU BEFORE.
"SUPREME OVERLORD SHIMMRA, BELOVED OF THE GODS, WAS DEAD. MANY COWARDS SUBMITTED TO THE JEEDAI AND THEIR BLASPHEMOUS ALLIES, BUT WE TRUE YUUZHAN VONG DEFIED THE ORDER TO SURRENDER.
"HERE, ABOVE THE PLANET THEY NAME WAYLAND, THE FLEET ON WHICH I SERVED BURNED AS A PYRE OF SACRIFICE. ONLY I ESCAPED."
QUAH, QUAH, QUAH -- ZENOC QUAH! ALL HAIL ZENOC QUAH!
SOMEDAY YOU WILL LEARN THAT AND SING IT TO ME, WON'T YOU, LITTLE ONES? FOR I SHAPED YOU. I AM YOUR GOD!
THE JEEDAI THOUGHT TO USE THE KNOWLEDGE OF OUR CHOSEN RACE TO REMAKE THE GALAXY. BUT I POISONED THEIR ATTEMPTS.
AND NOW I AM CREATING SOMETHING NEW -- SOMETHING THAT WILL RUIN THE GALAXY AND BRING FINAL VICTORY TO THE YUUZHAN VONG! ALL HAIL ZENOC QUAH!

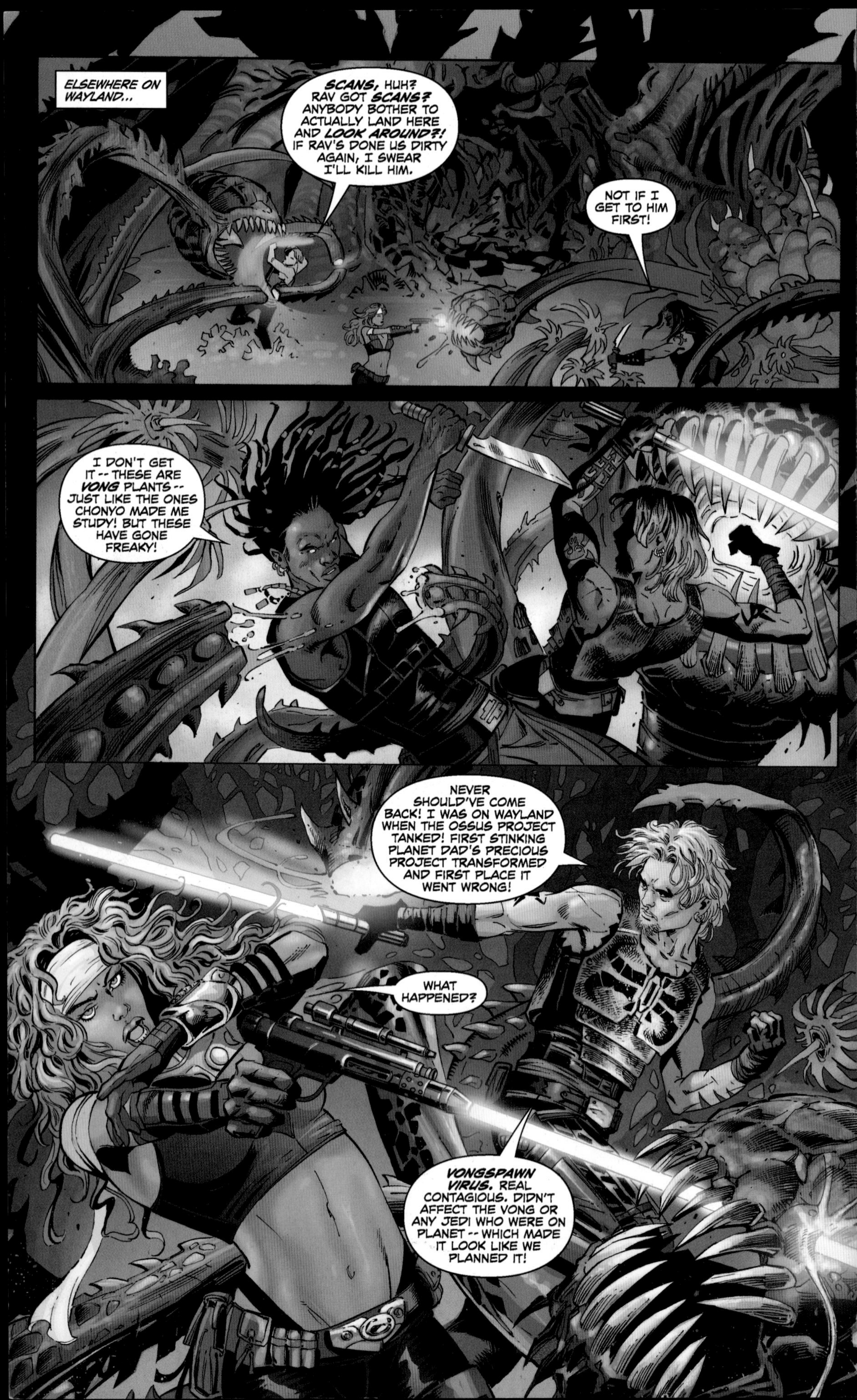
ELSEWHERE ON WAYLAND...
SCANS, HUH? RAV GOT SCANS? ANYBODY BOTHER TO ACTUALLY LAND HERE AND LOOK AROUND?! IF RAV'S DONE US DIRTY AGAIN, I SWEAR I'LL KILL HIM.
NOT IF I GET TO HIM FIRST!
I DON'T GET IT -- THESE ARE VONG PLANTS -- JUST LIKE THE ONES CHONYO MADE ME STUDY! BUT THESE HAVE GONE FREAKY!
NEVER SHOULD'VE COME BACK! I WAS ON WAYLAND WHEN THE OSSUS PROJECT TANKED! FIRST STINKING PLANET DAD'S PRECIOUS PROJECT TRANSFORMED AND FIRST PLACE IT WENT WRONG!
WHAT HAPPENED?
VONGSPAWN VIRUS. REAL CONTAGIOUS. DIDN'T AFFECT THE VONG OR ANY JEDI WHO WERE ON PLANET -- WHICH MADE IT LOOK LIKE WE PLANNED IT!

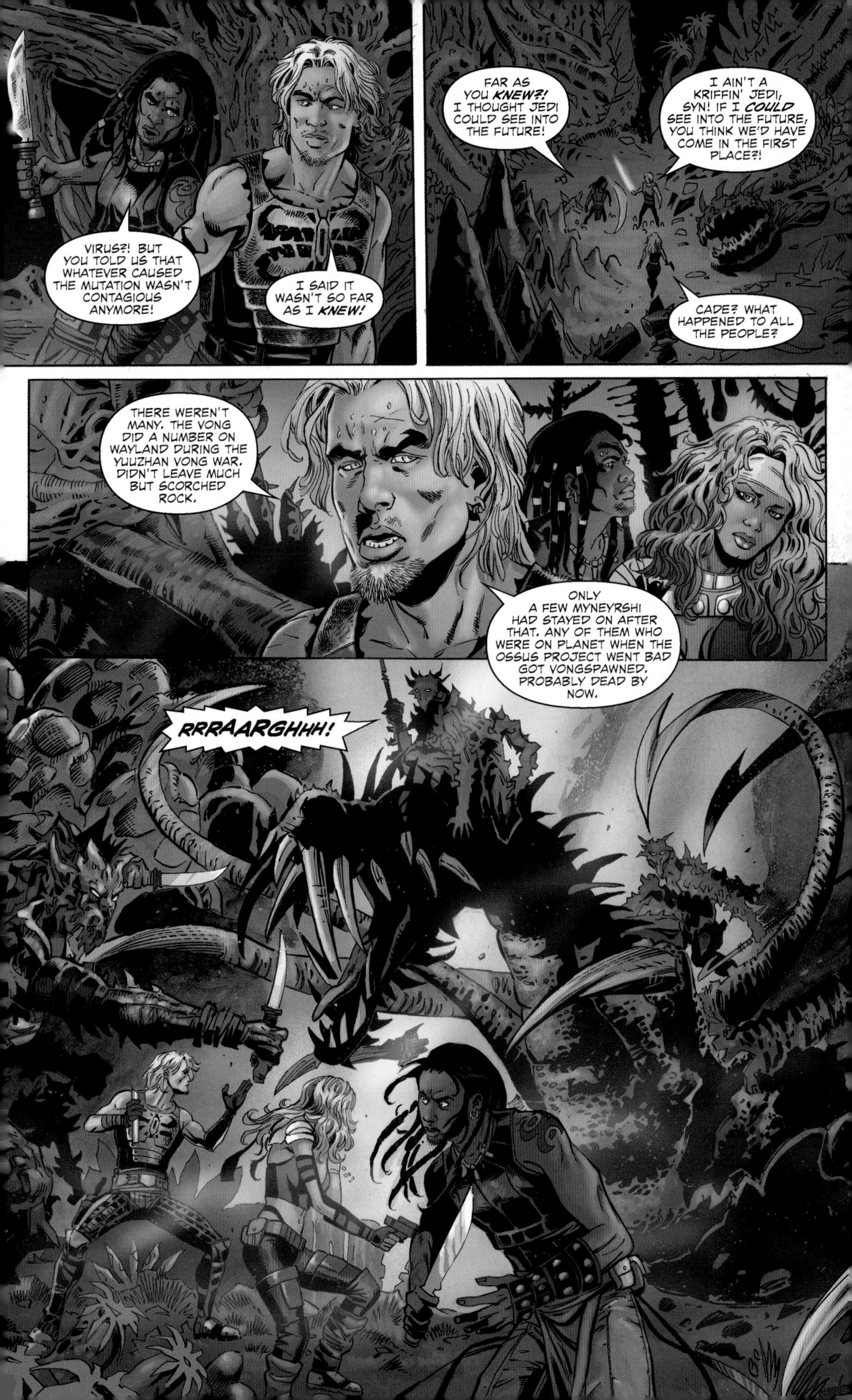
VIRUS?! BUT YOU TOLD US THAT WHATEVER CAUSED THE MUTATION WASN'T CONTAGIOUS ANYMORE!
I SAID IT WASN'T SO FAR AS I KNEW!
FAR AS YOU KNEW?! I THOUGHT JEDI COULD SEE INTO THE FUTURE!
I AIN'T A KRIFFIN' JEDI, SYN! IF I COULD SEE INTO THE FUTURE, YOU THINK WE'D HAVE COME IN THE FIRST PLACE?!
CADE? WHAT HAPPENED TO ALL THE PEOPLE?
THERE WEREN'T MANY. THE VONG DID A NUMBER ON WAYLAND DURING THE YUUZHAN VONG WAR. DIDN'T LEAVE MUCH BUT SCORCHED ROCK.
ONLY A FEW MYNEYRSHI HAD STAYED ON AFTER THAT. ANY OF THEM WHO WERE ON PLANET WHEN THE OSSUS PROJECT WENT BAD GOT VONGSPAWNED. PROBABLY DEAD BY NOW.
RRRAARGHHH!

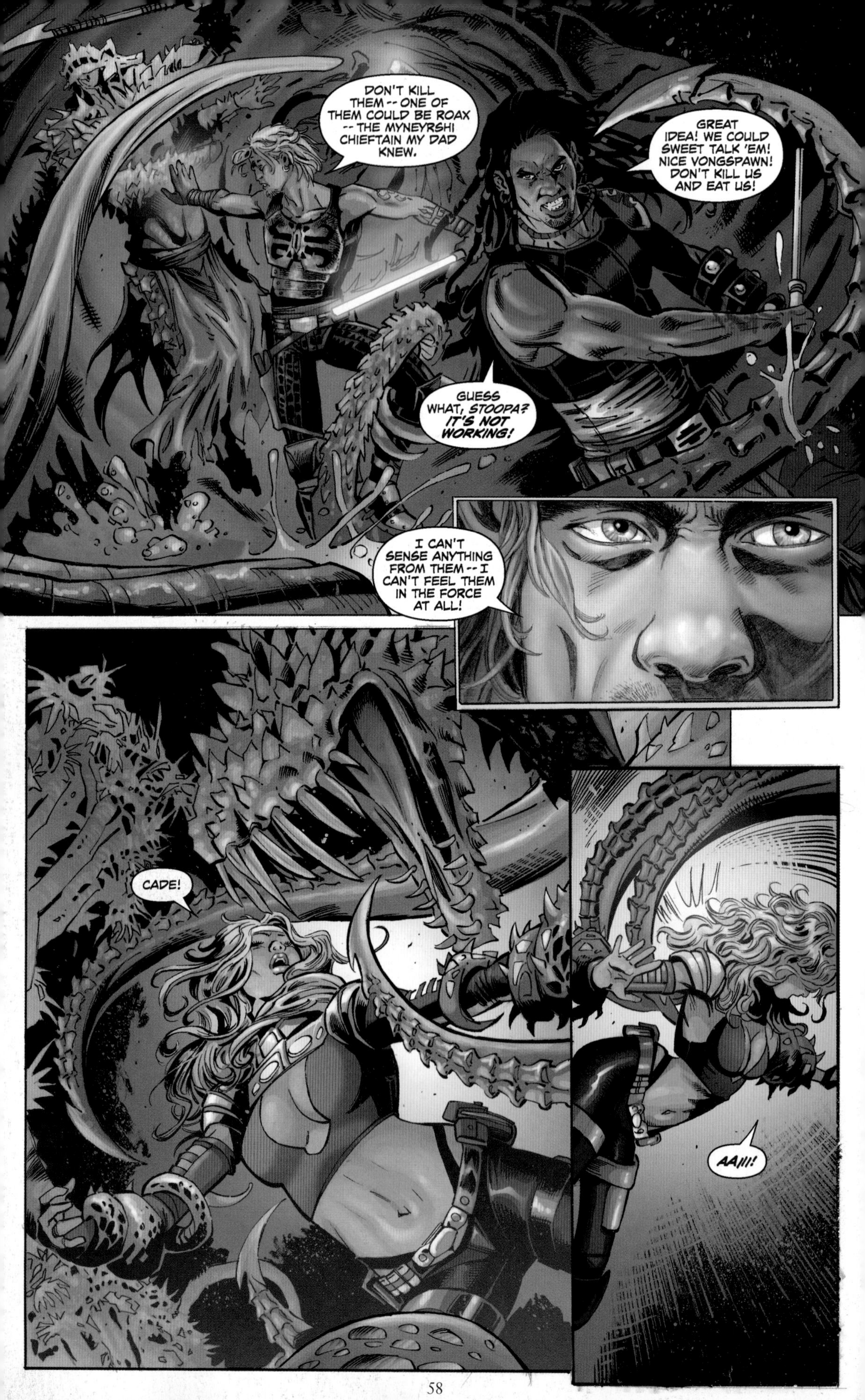
DON'T KILL THEM -- ONE OF THEM COULD BE ROAX -- THE MYNEYRSHI CHIEFTAIN MY DAD KNEW.
GREAT IDEA! WE COULD SWEET TALK 'EM! NICE VONGSPAWN! DON'T KILL US AND EAT US!
GUESS WHAT, STOOPA? IT'S NOT WORKING!
I CAN'T SENSE ANYTHING FROM THEM -- I CAN'T FEEL THEM IN THE FORCE AT ALL!
CADE!
AAIII!

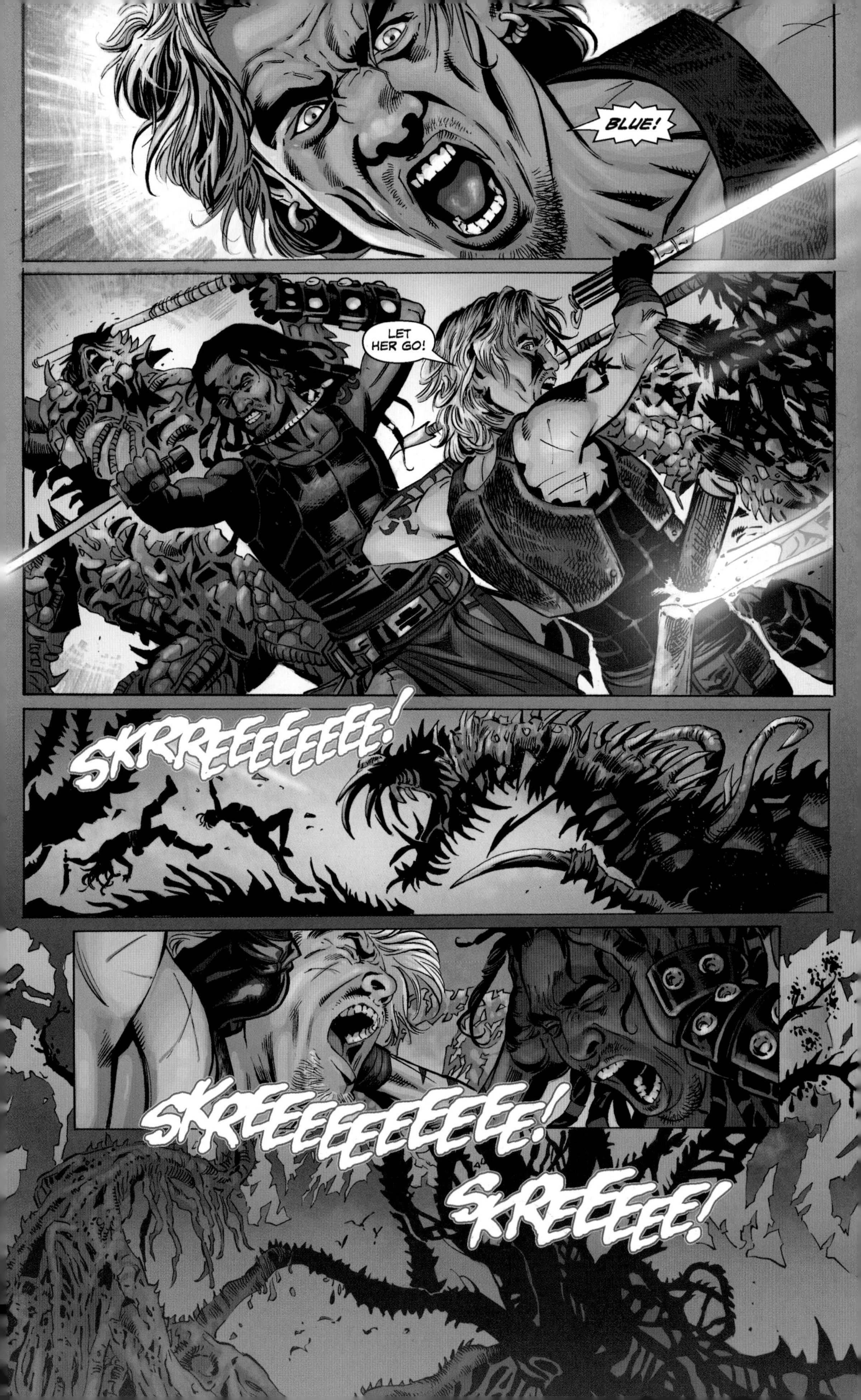
BLUE!
LET HER GO!
SKRREEEEEEEEE!
SKREEEEEEEEEEEE!
SKREEEEE!

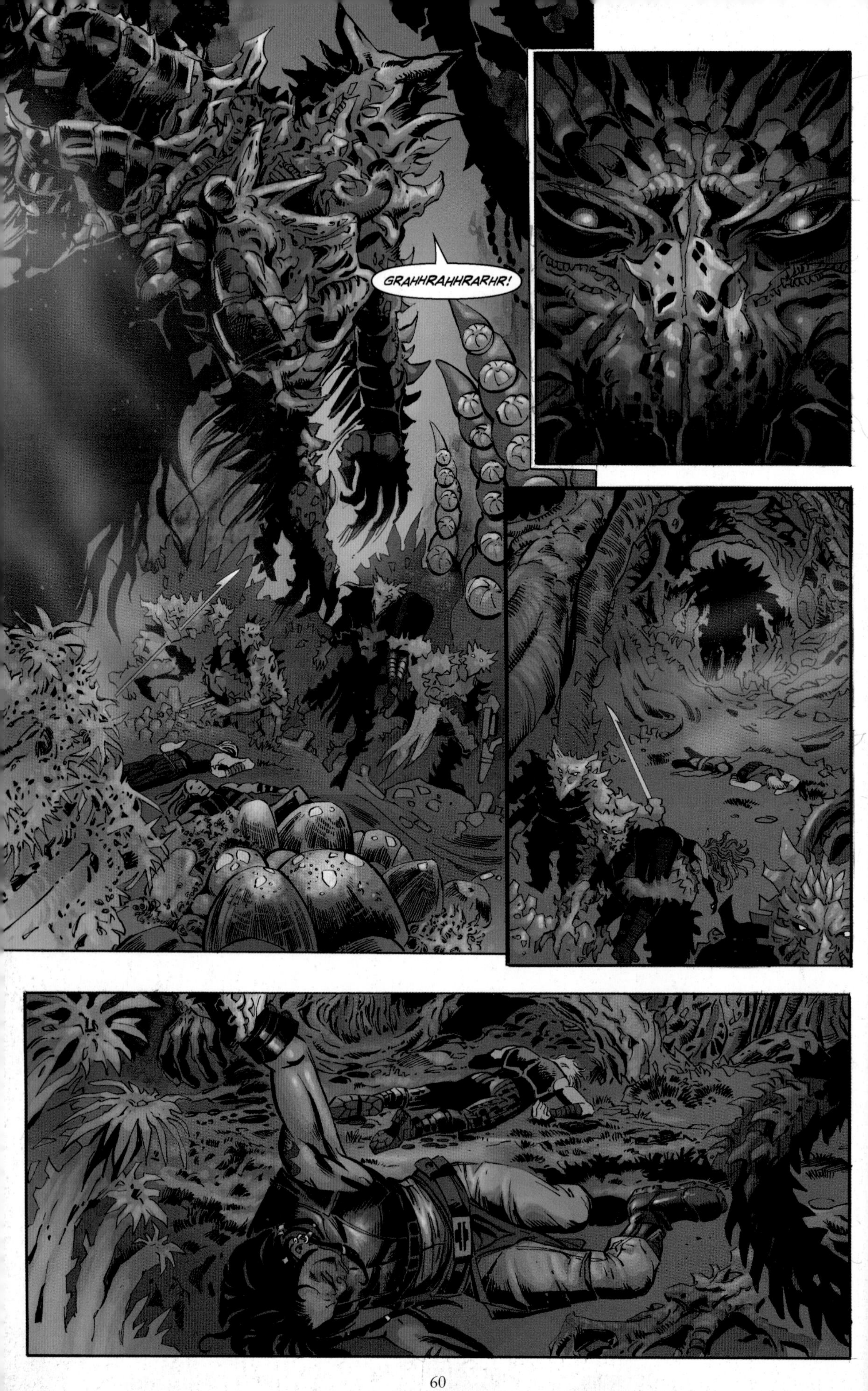
GRAHHRAHHRARHR!

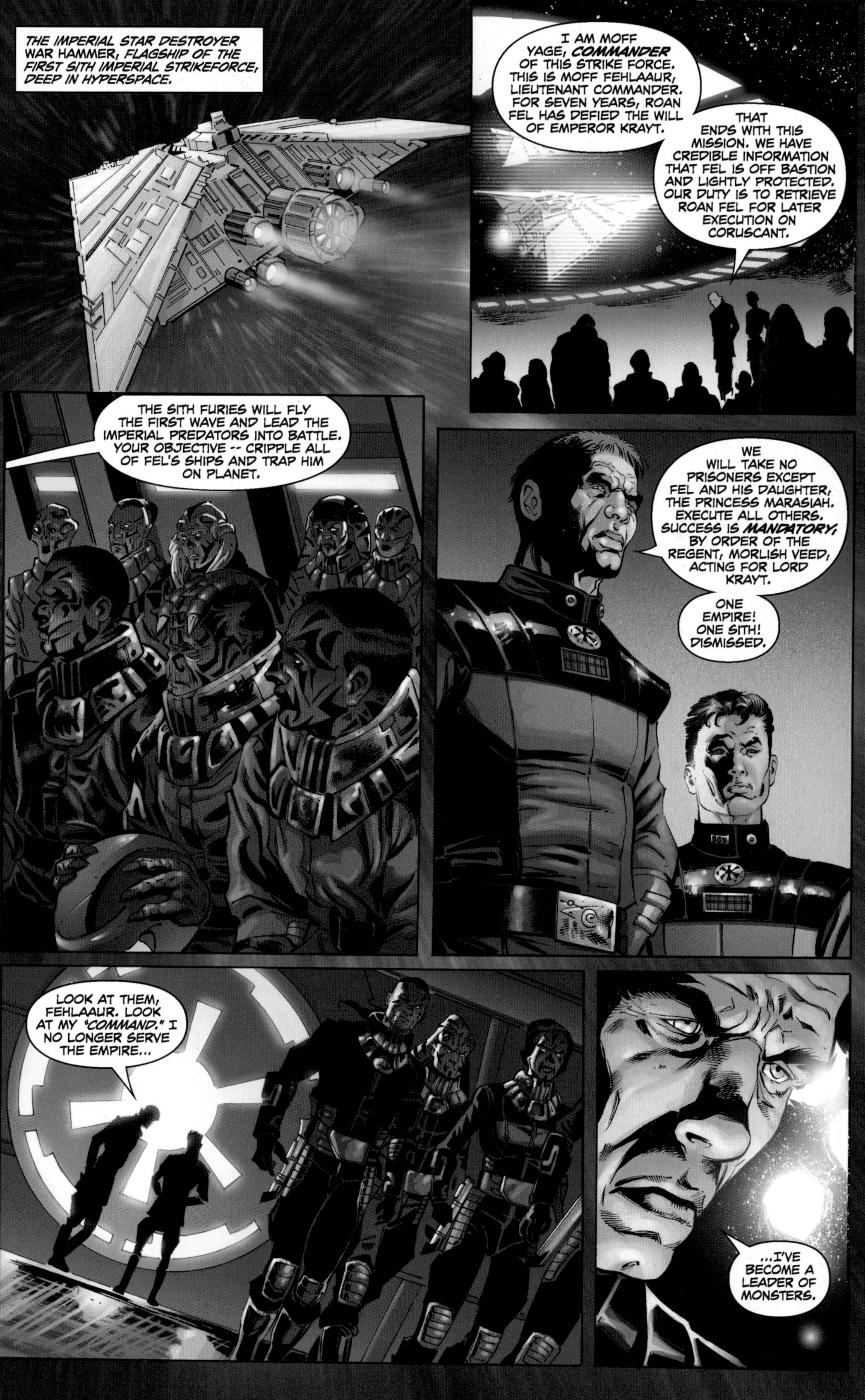
THE IMPERIAL STAR DESTROYER WAR HAMMER, FLAGSHIP OF THE FIRST SITH IMPERIAL STRIKEFORCE, DEEP IN HYPERSPACE.
I AM MOFF YAGE, COMMANDER OF THIS STRIKE FORCE. THIS IS MOFF FEHLAAUR, LIEUTENANT COMMANDER. FOR SEVEN YEARS, ROAN FEL HAS DEFIED THE WILL OF EMPEROR KRAYT.
THAT ENDS WITH THIS MISSION. WE HAVE CREDIBLE INFORMATION THAT FEL IS OFF BASTION AND LIGHTLY PROTECTED. OUR DUTY IS TO RETRIEVE ROAN FEL FOR LATER EXECUTION ON CORUSCANT.
THE SITH FURIES WILL FLY THE FIRST WAVE AND LEAD THE IMPERIAL PREDATORS INTO BATTLE. YOUR OBJECTIVE -- CRIPPLE ALL OF FEL'S SHIPS AND TRAP HIM ON PLANET.
WE WILL TAKE NO PRISONERS EXCEPT FEL AND HIS DAUGHTER, THE PRINCESS MARASIAH. EXECUTE ALL OTHERS. SUCCESS IS MANDATORY, BY ORDER OF THE REGENT, MORLISH VEED, ACTING FOR LORD KRAYT.
ONE EMPIRE! ONE SITH! DISMISSED.
LOOK AT THEM, FEHLAAUR. LOOK AT MY "COMMAND." I NO LONGER SERVE THE EMPIRE...
...I'VE BECOME A LEADER OF MONSTERS.

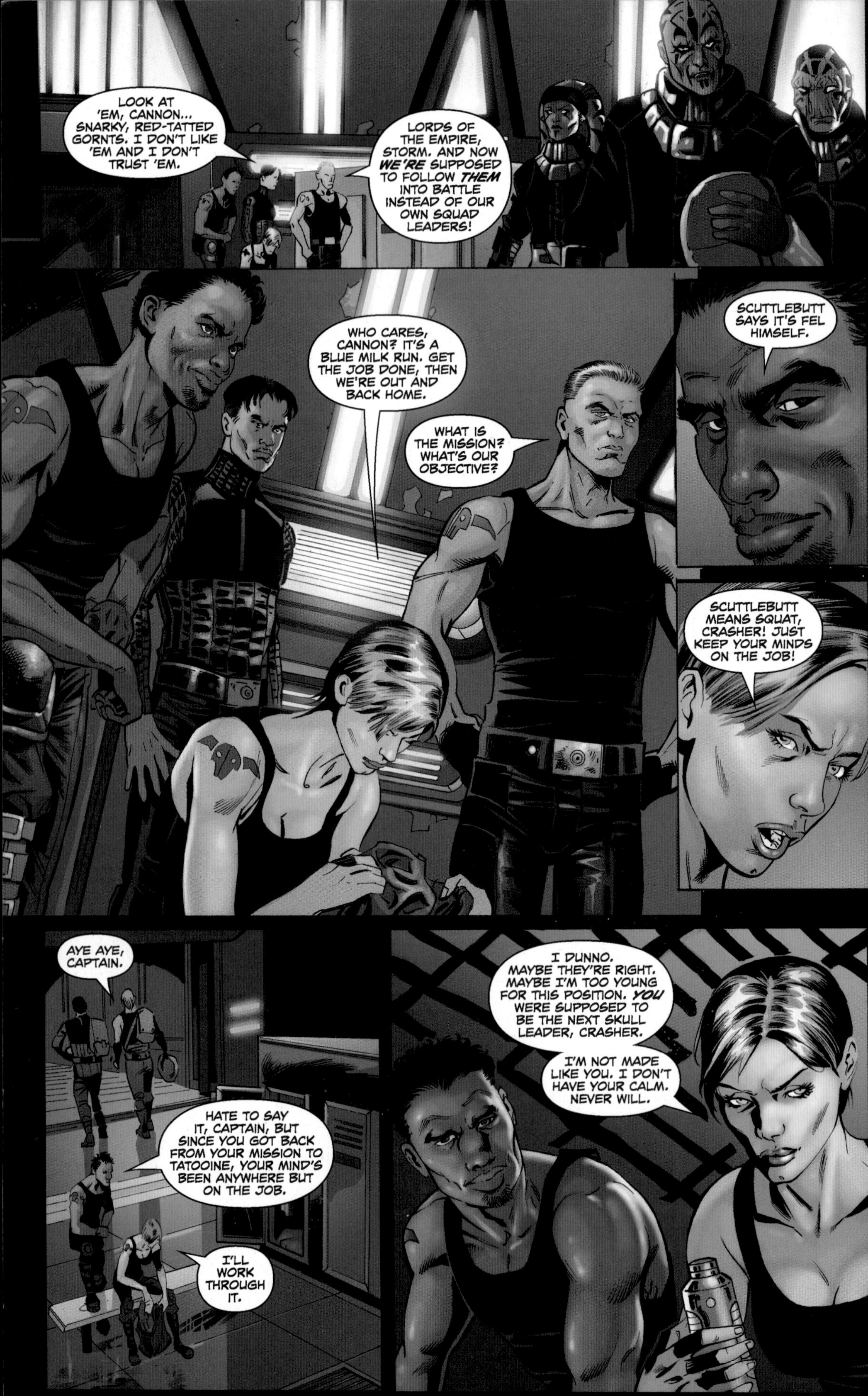
LOOK AT 'EM, CANNON... SNARKY, RED-TATTED GORNTS. I DON'T LIKE 'EM AND I DON'T TRUST 'EM.
LORDS OF THE EMPIRE, STORM. AND NOW *WE'RE* SUPPOSED TO FOLLOW *THEM* INTO BATTLE INSTEAD OF OUR OWN SQUAD LEADERS!
WHO CARES, CANNON? IT'S A BLUE MILK RUN. GET THE JOB DONE, THEN WE'RE OUT AND BACK HOME.
WHAT IS THE MISSION? WHAT'S OUR OBJECTIVE?
SCUTTLEBUTT SAYS IT'S FEL HIMSELF.
SCUTTLEBUTT MEANS SQUAT, CRASHER! JUST KEEP YOUR MINDS ON THE JOB!
AYE AYE, CAPTAIN.
HATE TO SAY IT, CAPTAIN, BUT SINCE YOU GOT BACK FROM YOUR MISSION TO TATOOINE, YOUR MIND'S BEEN ANYWHERE BUT ON THE JOB.
I'LL WORK THROUGH IT.
I DUNNO. MAYBE THEY'RE RIGHT. MAYBE I'M TOO YOUNG FOR THIS POSITION. *YOU* WERE SUPPOSED TO BE THE NEXT SKULL LEADER, CRASHER.
I'M NOT MADE LIKE YOU. I DON'T HAVE YOUR CALM. NEVER WILL.

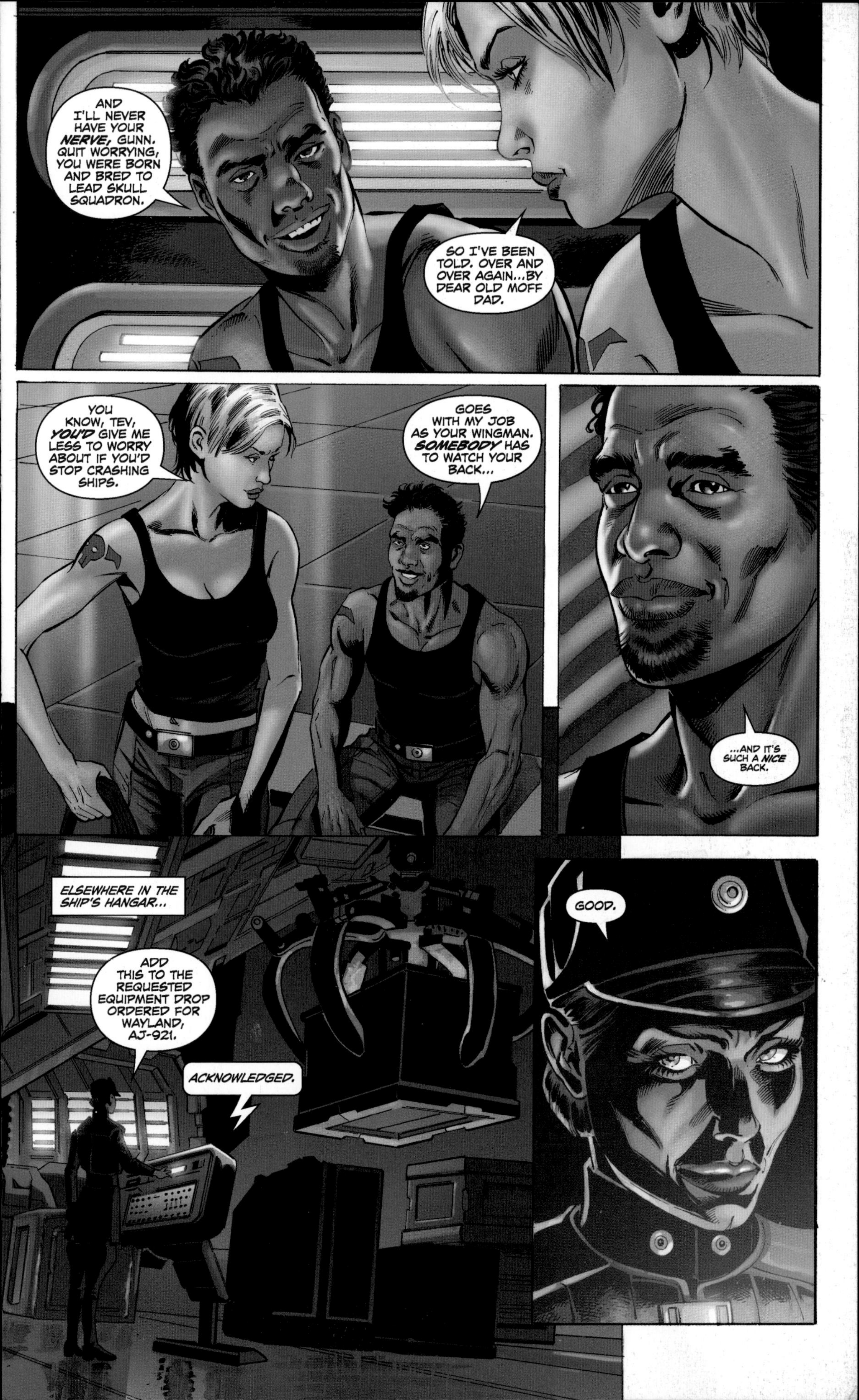
AND I'LL NEVER HAVE YOUR NERVE, GUNN. QUIT WORRYING, YOU WERE BORN AND BRED TO LEAD SKULL SQUADRON.
SO I'VE BEEN TOLD. OVER AND OVER AGAIN...BY DEAR OLD MOFF DAD.
YOU KNOW, TEV, YOU'D GIVE ME LESS TO WORRY ABOUT IF YOU'D STOP CRASHING SHIPS.
GOES WITH MY JOB AS YOUR WINGMAN. SOMEBODY HAS TO WATCH YOUR BACK...
...AND IT'S SUCH A NICE BACK.
ELSEWHERE IN THE SHIP'S HANGAR...
ADD THIS TO THE REQUESTED EQUIPMENT DROP ORDERED FOR WAYLAND, AJ-921.
ACKNOWLEDGED.
GOOD.

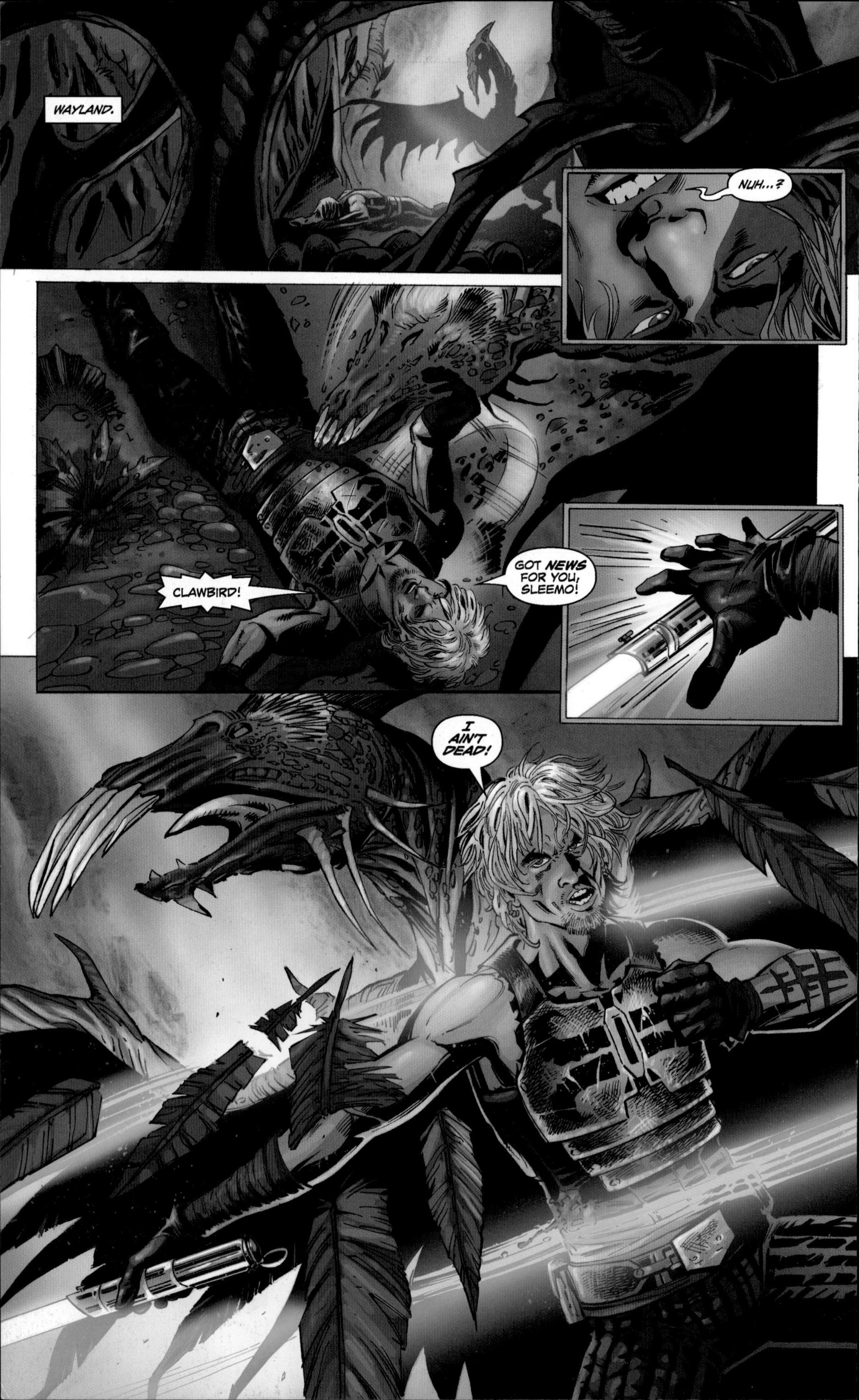
WAYLAND.
NUH...?
CLAWBIRD!
GOT **NEWS** FOR YOU, SLEEMO!
I AIN'T DEAD!

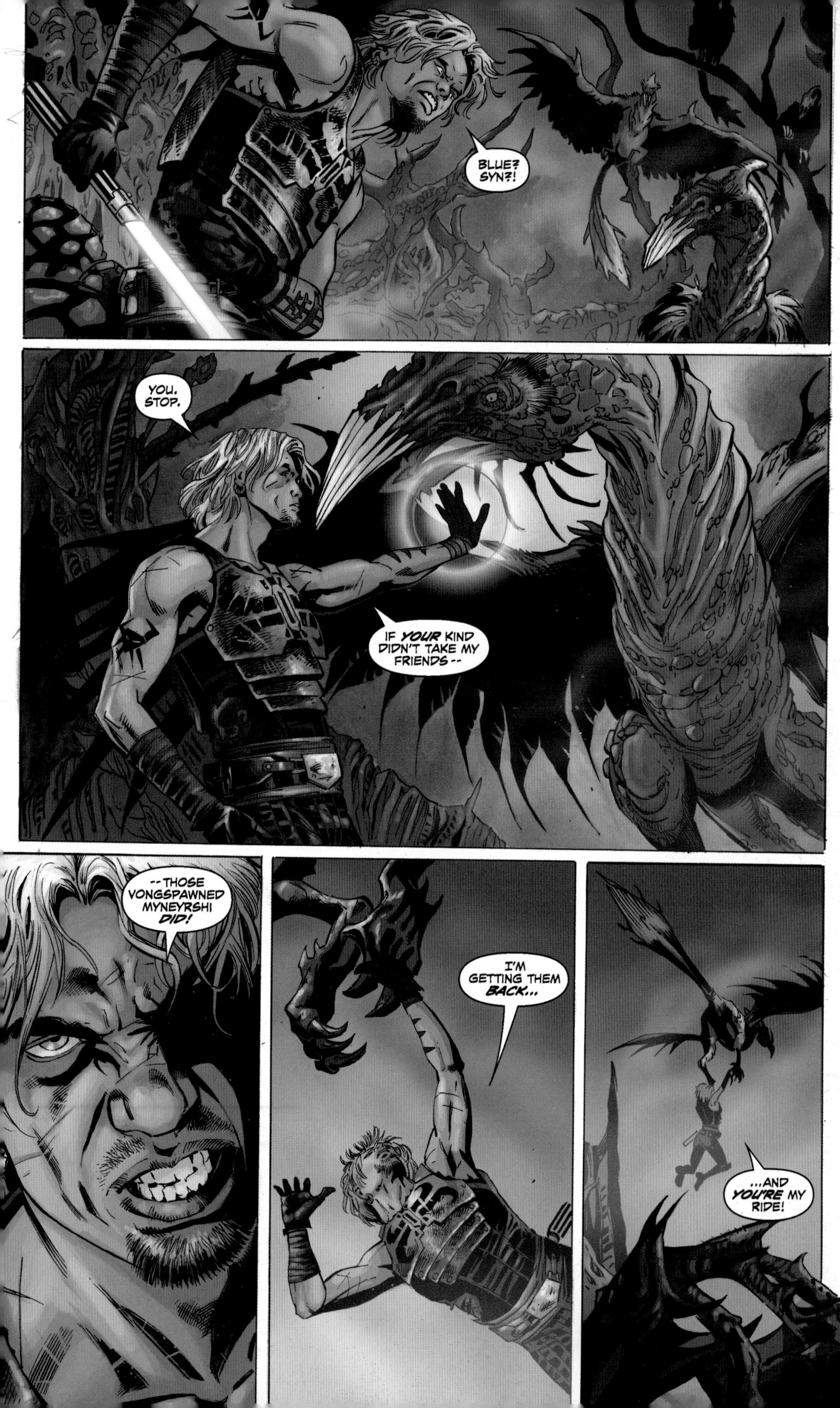
BLUE? SYN?!
YOU. STOP.
IF *YOUR* KIND DIDN'T TAKE MY FRIENDS --
-- THOSE VONGSPAWNED MYNEYRSHI *DID!*
I'M GETTING THEM *BACK*...
...AND *YOU'RE* MY RIDE!

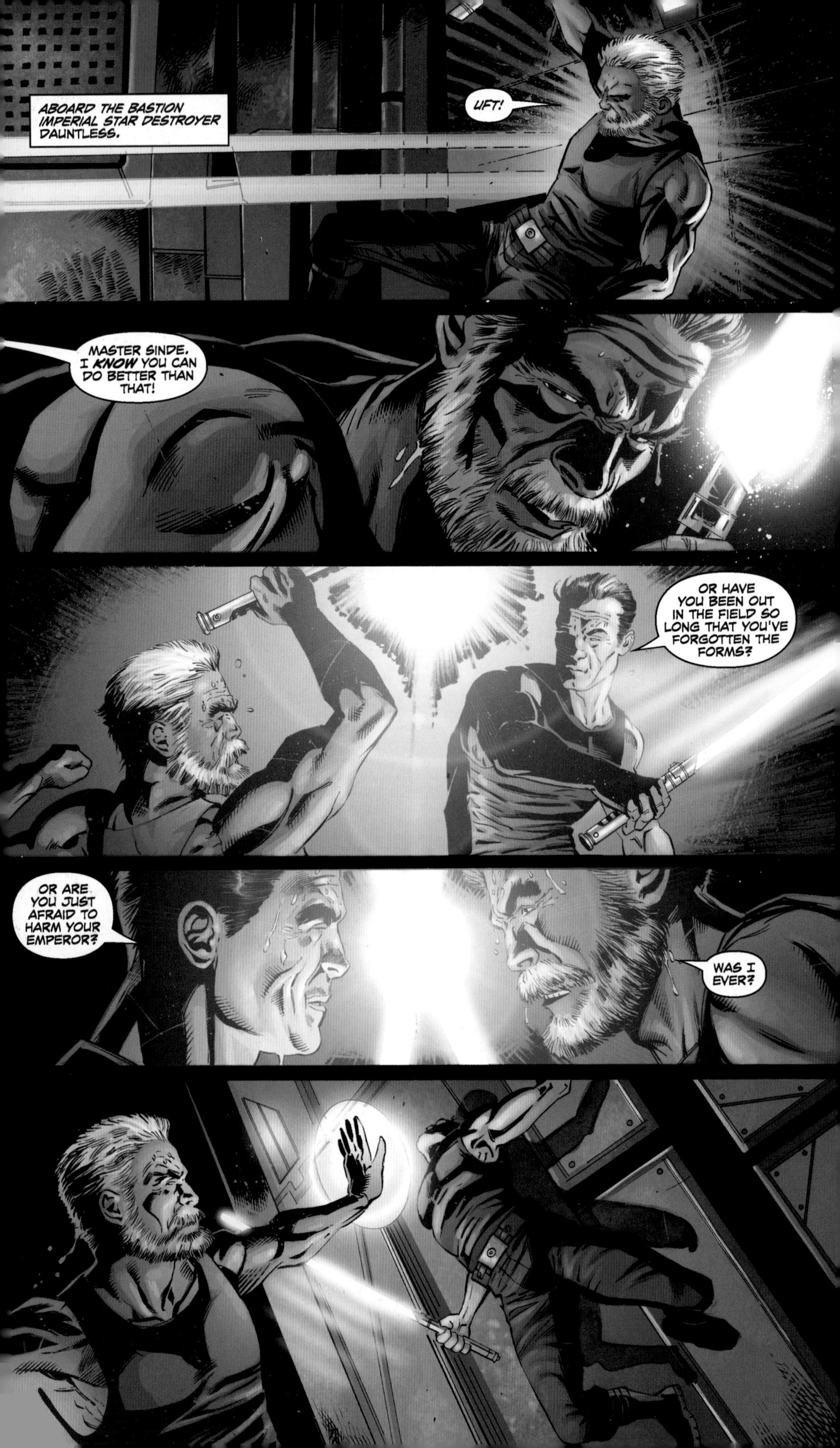
ABOARD THE BASTION IMPERIAL STAR DESTROYER DAUNTLESS.
UFT!
MASTER SINDE. I KNOW YOU CAN DO BETTER THAN THAT!
OR HAVE YOU BEEN OUT IN THE FIELD SO LONG THAT YOU'VE FORGOTTEN THE FORMS?
OR ARE YOU JUST AFRAID TO HARM YOUR EMPEROR?
WAS I EVER?

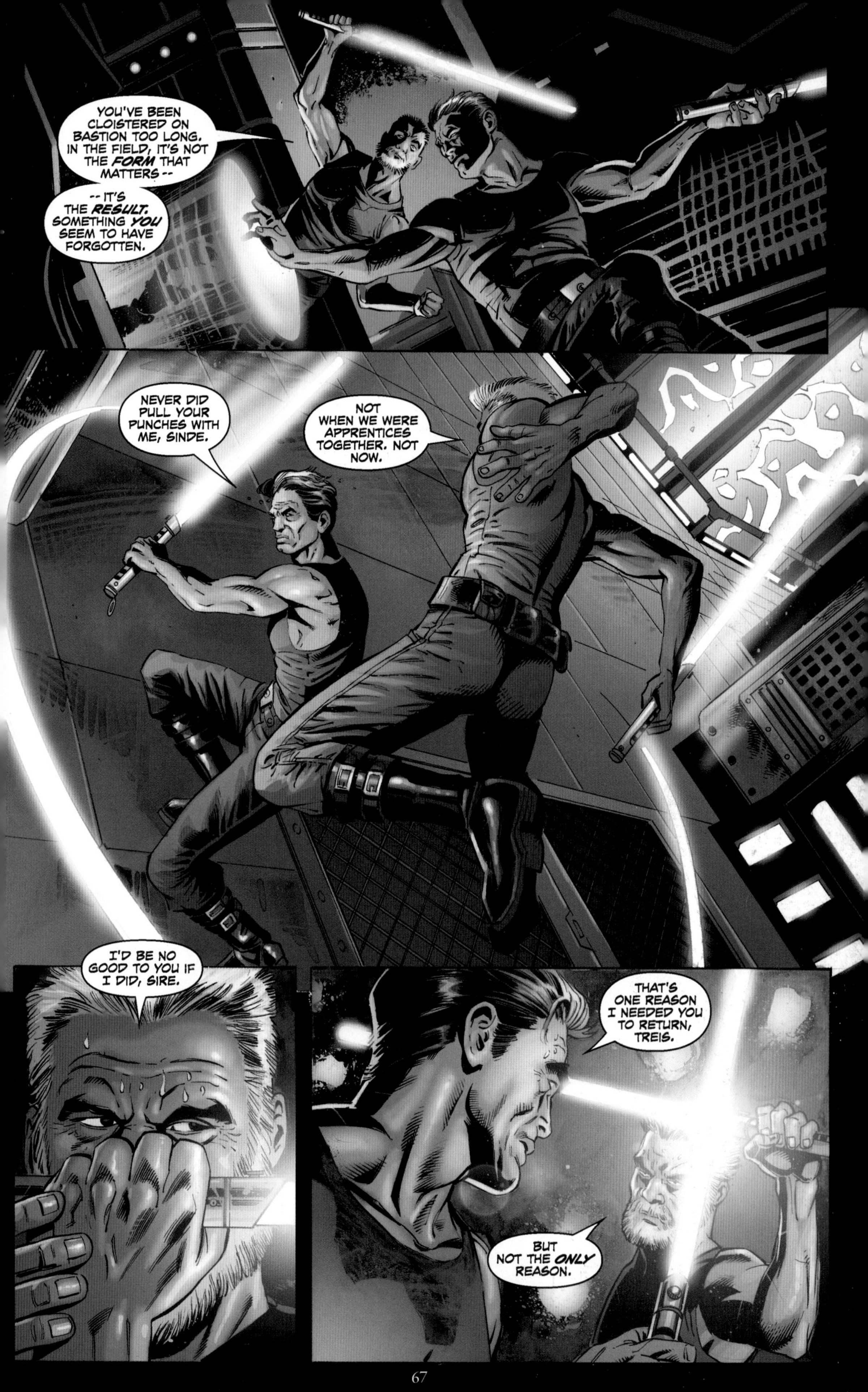
YOU'VE BEEN CLOISTERED ON BASTION TOO LONG. IN THE FIELD, IT'S NOT THE *FORM* THAT MATTERS --
-- IT'S THE *RESULT.* SOMETHING *YOU* SEEM TO HAVE FORGOTTEN.
NEVER DID PULL YOUR PUNCHES WITH ME, SINDE.
NOT WHEN WE WERE APPRENTICES TOGETHER. NOT NOW.
I'D BE NO GOOD TO YOU IF I DID, SIRE.
THAT'S ONE REASON I NEEDED YOU TO RETURN, TREIS.
BUT NOT THE *ONLY* REASON.

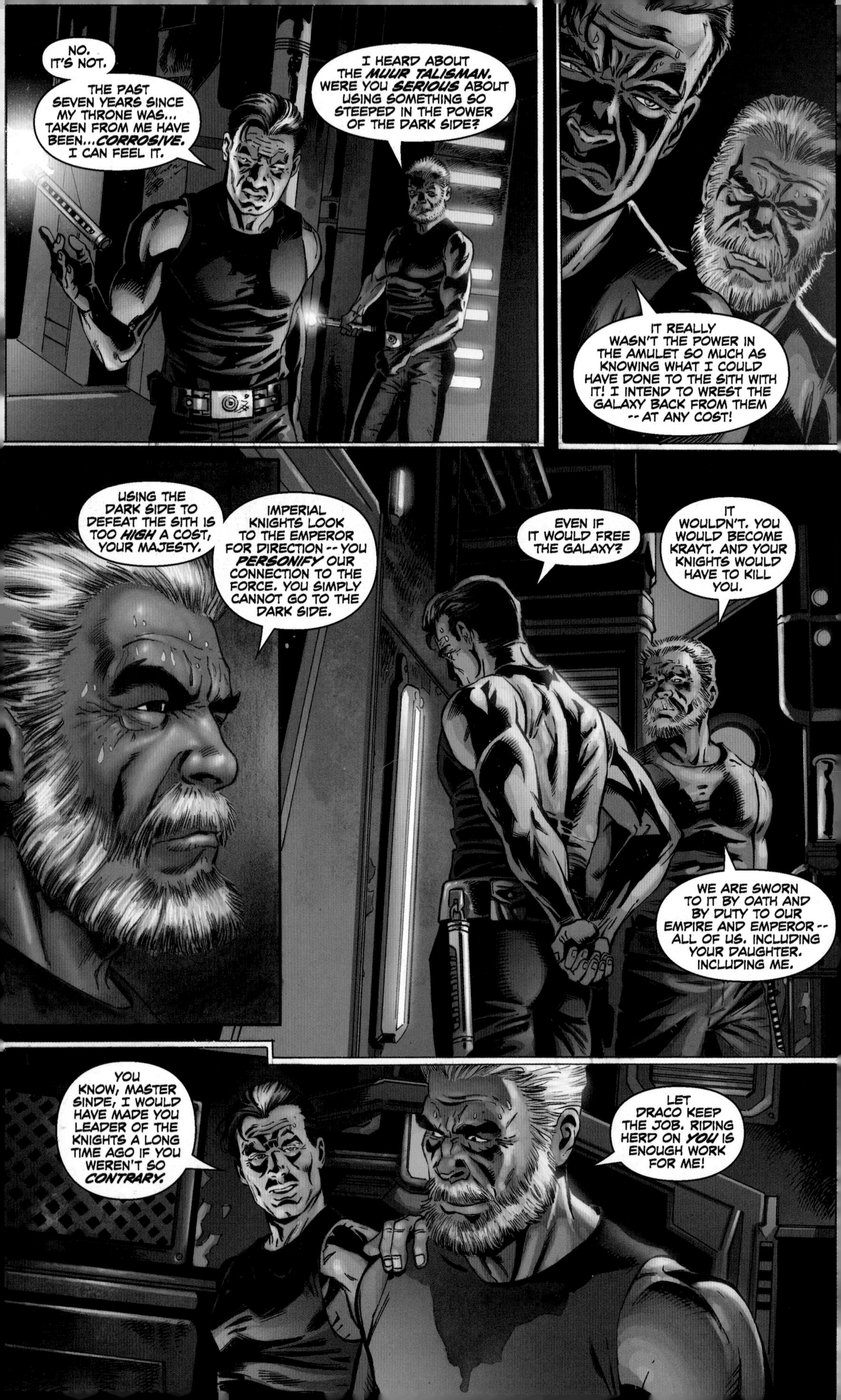

NO. IT'S NOT.
THE PAST SEVEN YEARS SINCE MY THRONE WAS... TAKEN FROM ME HAVE BEEN...CORROSIVE. I CAN FEEL IT.
I HEARD ABOUT THE MUUR TALISMAN. WERE YOU SERIOUS ABOUT USING SOMETHING SO STEEPED IN THE POWER OF THE DARK SIDE?
IT REALLY WASN'T THE POWER IN THE AMULET SO MUCH AS KNOWING WHAT I COULD HAVE DONE TO THE SITH WITH IT! I INTEND TO WREST THE GALAXY BACK FROM THEM -- AT ANY COST!
USING THE DARK SIDE TO DEFEAT THE SITH IS TOO HIGH A COST, YOUR MAJESTY.
IMPERIAL KNIGHTS LOOK TO THE EMPEROR FOR DIRECTION -- YOU PERSONIFY OUR CONNECTION TO THE FORCE. YOU SIMPLY CANNOT GO TO THE DARK SIDE.
EVEN IF IT WOULD FREE THE GALAXY?
IT WOULDN'T. YOU WOULD BECOME KRAYT. AND YOUR KNIGHTS WOULD HAVE TO KILL YOU.
WE ARE SWORN TO IT BY OATH AND BY DUTY TO OUR EMPIRE AND EMPEROR -- ALL OF US. INCLUDING YOUR DAUGHTER. INCLUDING ME.
YOU KNOW, MASTER SINDE, I WOULD HAVE MADE YOU LEADER OF THE KNIGHTS A LONG TIME AGO IF YOU WEREN'T SO CONTRARY.
LET DRACO KEEP THE JOB. RIDING HERD ON YOU IS ENOUGH WORK FOR ME!

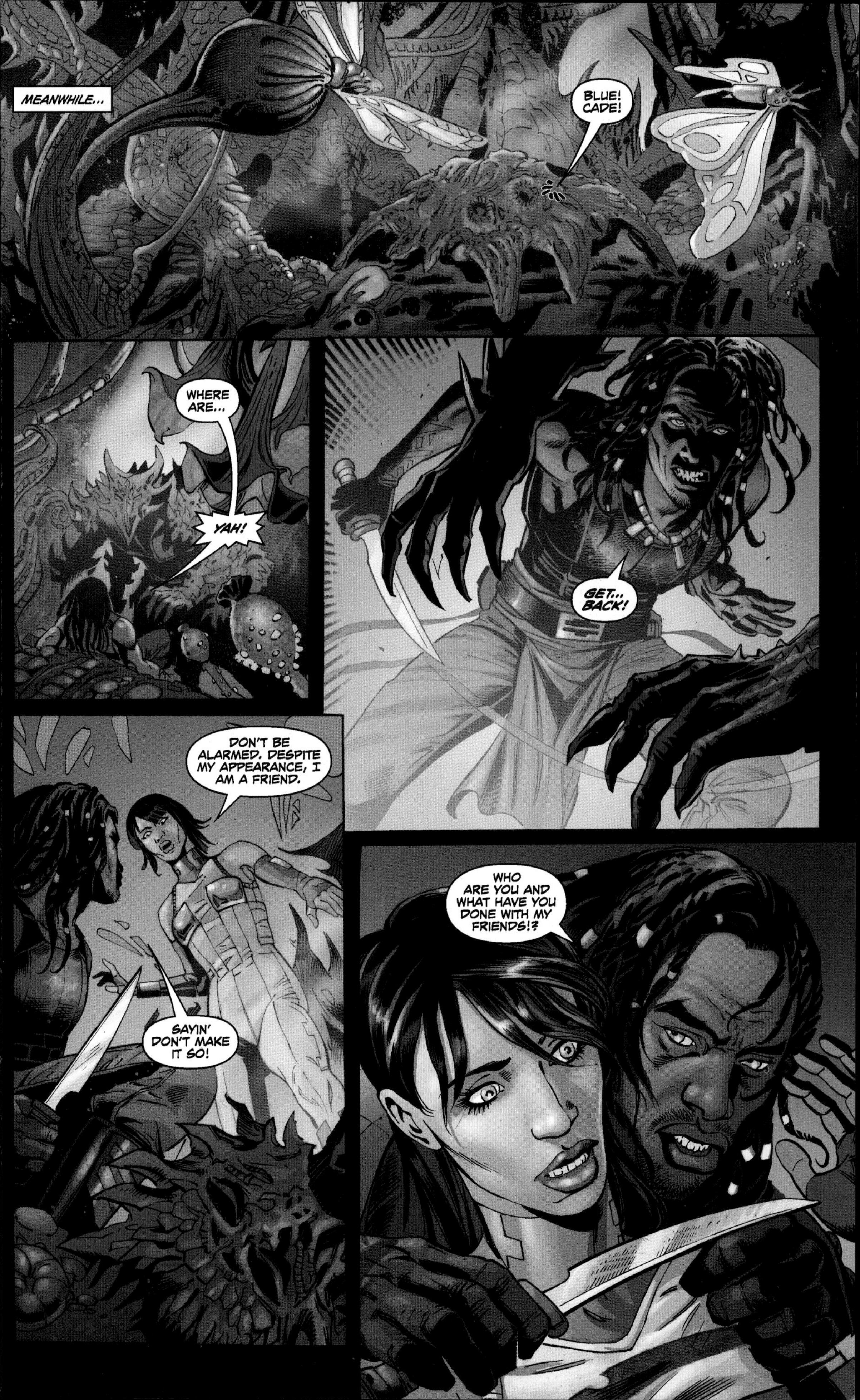
MEANWHILE...
BLUE! CADE!
WHERE ARE...
YAH!
GET... BACK!
DON'T BE ALARMED. DESPITE MY APPEARANCE, I AM A FRIEND.
SAYIN' DON'T MAKE IT SO!
WHO ARE YOU AND WHAT HAVE YOU DONE WITH MY FRIENDS!?

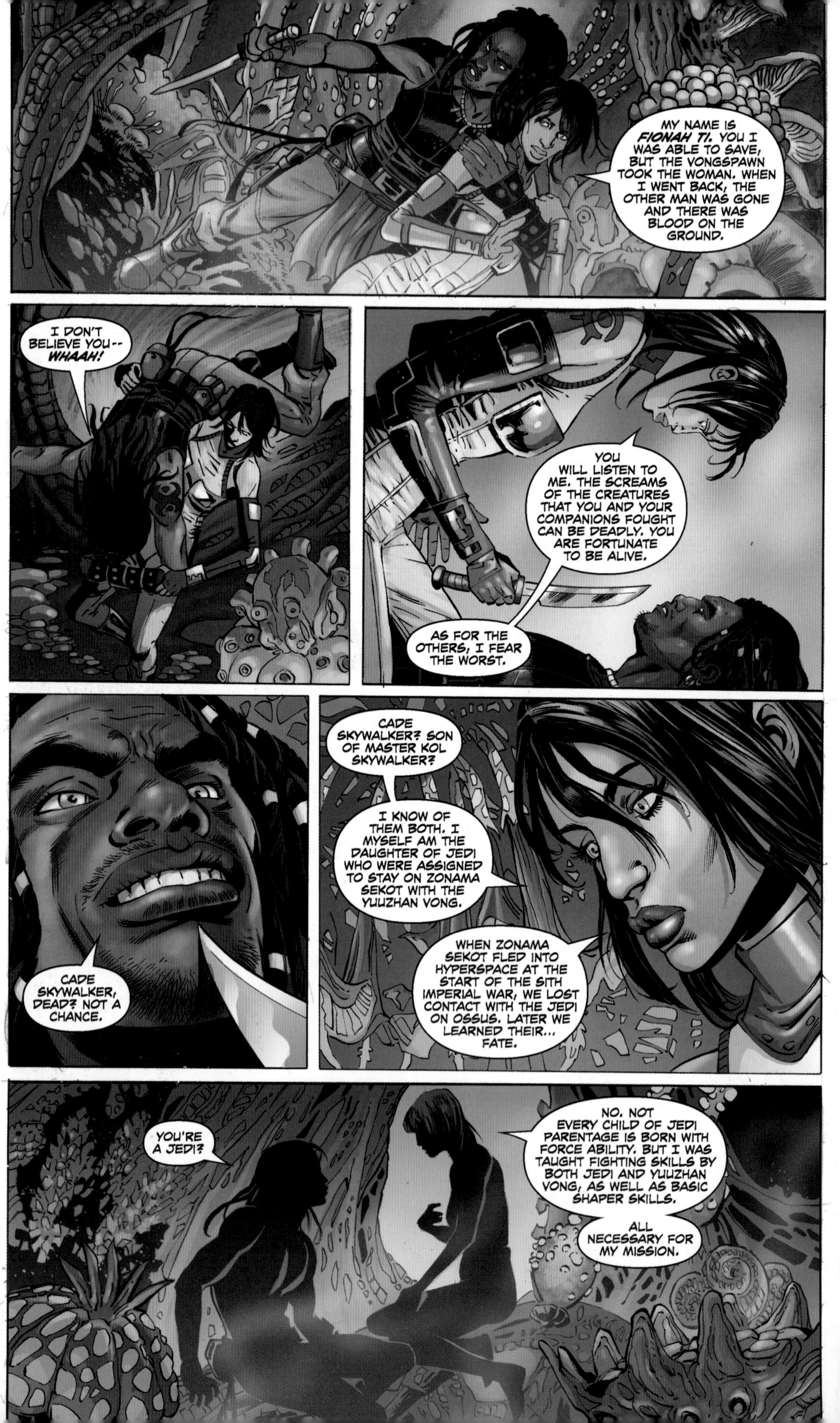
MY NAME IS *FIONAH TI.* YOU I WAS ABLE TO SAVE, BUT THE VONGSPAWN TOOK THE WOMAN. WHEN I WENT BACK, THE OTHER MAN WAS GONE AND THERE WAS BLOOD ON THE GROUND.
I DON'T BELIEVE YOU-- *WHAAH!*
YOU WILL LISTEN TO ME. THE SCREAMS OF THE CREATURES THAT YOU AND YOUR COMPANIONS FOUGHT CAN BE DEADLY. YOU ARE FORTUNATE TO BE ALIVE.
AS FOR THE OTHERS, I FEAR THE WORST.
CADE SKYWALKER, DEAD? NOT A CHANCE.
CADE SKYWALKER? SON OF MASTER KOL SKYWALKER?
I KNOW OF THEM BOTH. I MYSELF AM THE DAUGHTER OF JEDI WHO WERE ASSIGNED TO STAY ON ZONAMA SEKOT WITH THE YUUZHAN VONG.
WHEN ZONAMA SEKOT FLED INTO HYPERSPACE AT THE START OF THE SITH IMPERIAL WAR, WE LOST CONTACT WITH THE JEDI ON OSSUS. LATER WE LEARNED THEIR... FATE.
YOU'RE A JEDI?
NO. NOT EVERY CHILD OF JEDI PARENTAGE IS BORN WITH FORCE ABILITY. BUT I WAS TAUGHT FIGHTING SKILLS BY BOTH JEDI AND YUUZHAN VONG, AS WELL AS BASIC SHAPER SKILLS.
ALL NECESSARY FOR MY MISSION.

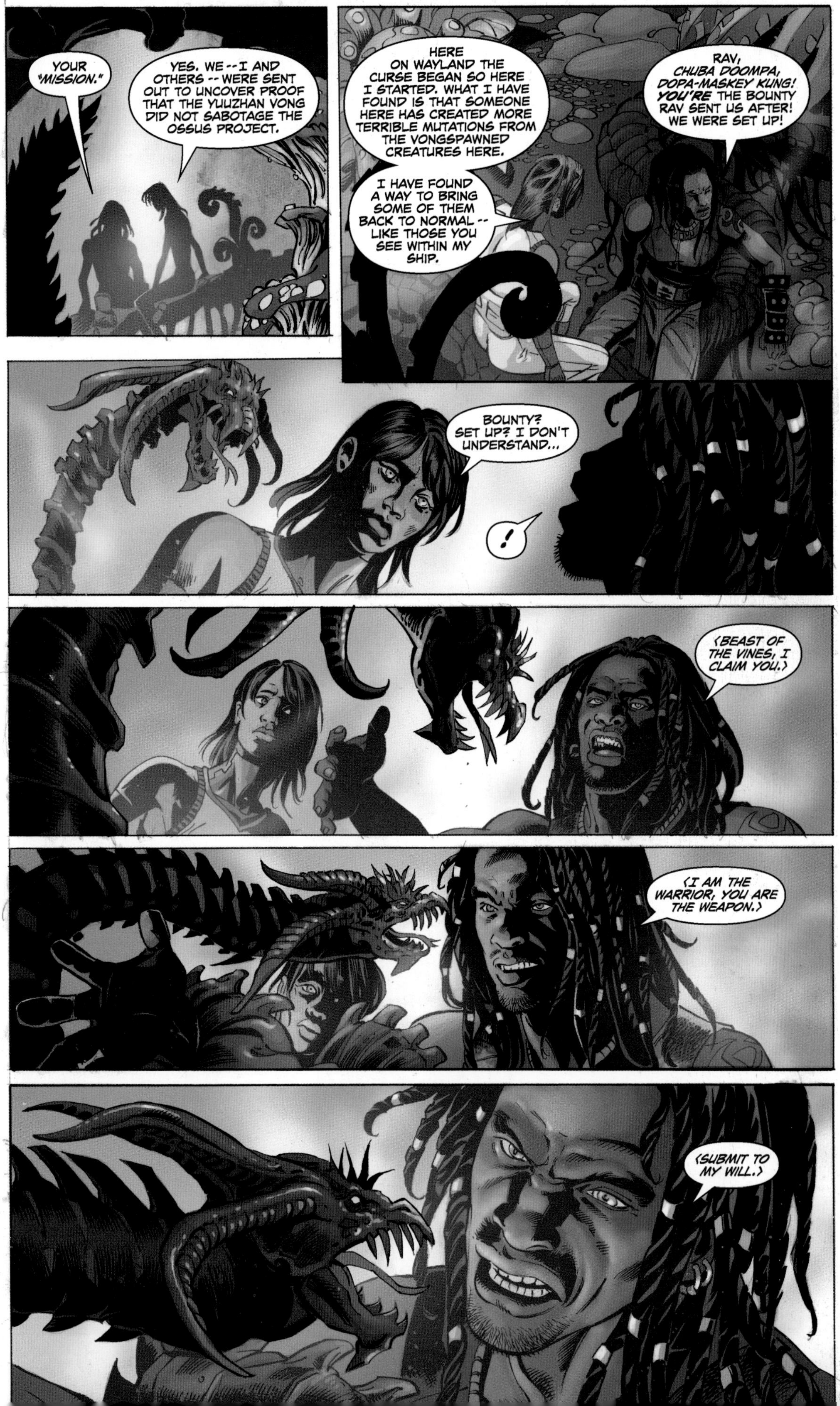
YOUR "MISSION."
YES. WE -- I AND OTHERS -- WERE SENT OUT TO UNCOVER PROOF THAT THE YUUZHAN VONG DID NOT SABOTAGE THE OSSUS PROJECT.
HERE ON WAYLAND THE CURSE BEGAN SO HERE I STARTED. WHAT I HAVE FOUND IS THAT SOMEONE HERE HAS CREATED MORE TERRIBLE MUTATIONS FROM THE VONGSPAWNED CREATURES HERE.
I HAVE FOUND A WAY TO BRING SOME OF THEM BACK TO NORMAL -- LIKE THOSE YOU SEE WITHIN MY SHIP.
RAV, CHUBA DOOMPA, DOPA-MASKEY KUNG! YOU'RE THE BOUNTY RAV SENT US AFTER! WE WERE SET UP!
BOUNTY? SET UP? I DON'T UNDERSTAND...
!
‹BEAST OF THE VINES, I CLAIM YOU.›
‹I AM THE WARRIOR, YOU ARE THE WEAPON.›
‹SUBMIT TO MY WILL.›

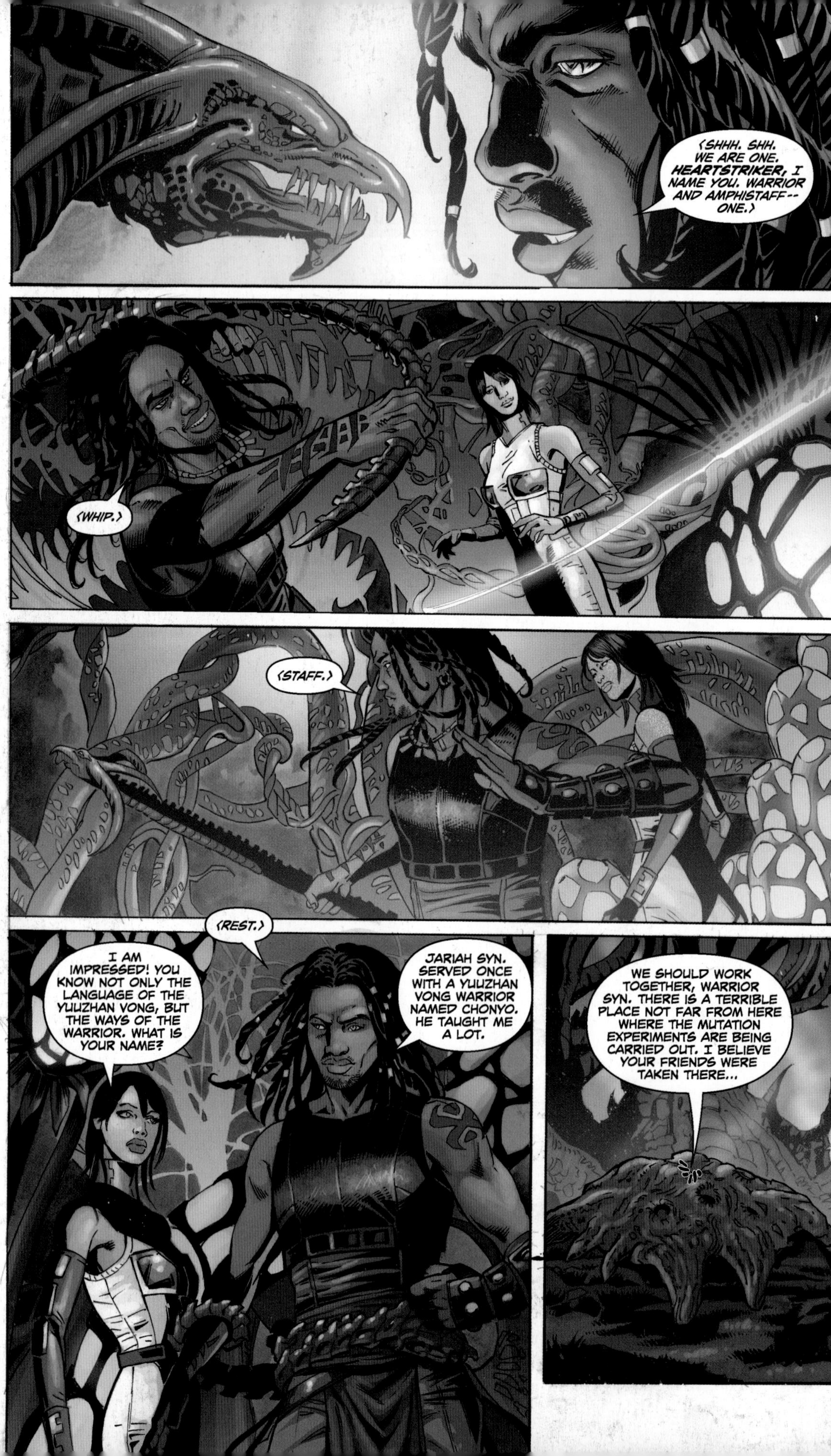
⟨SHHH. SHH. WE ARE ONE. HEARTSTRIKER, I NAME YOU. WARRIOR AND AMPHISTAFF-- ONE.⟩
⟨WHIP.⟩
⟨STAFF.⟩
⟨REST.⟩
I AM IMPRESSED! YOU KNOW NOT ONLY THE LANGUAGE OF THE YUUZHAN VONG, BUT THE WAYS OF THE WARRIOR. WHAT IS YOUR NAME?
JARIAH SYN. SERVED ONCE WITH A YUUZHAN VONG WARRIOR NAMED CHONYO. HE TAUGHT ME A LOT.
WE SHOULD WORK TOGETHER, WARRIOR SYN. THERE IS A TERRIBLE PLACE NOT FAR FROM HERE WHERE THE MUTATION EXPERIMENTS ARE BEING CARRIED OUT. I BELIEVE YOUR FRIENDS WERE TAKEN THERE...

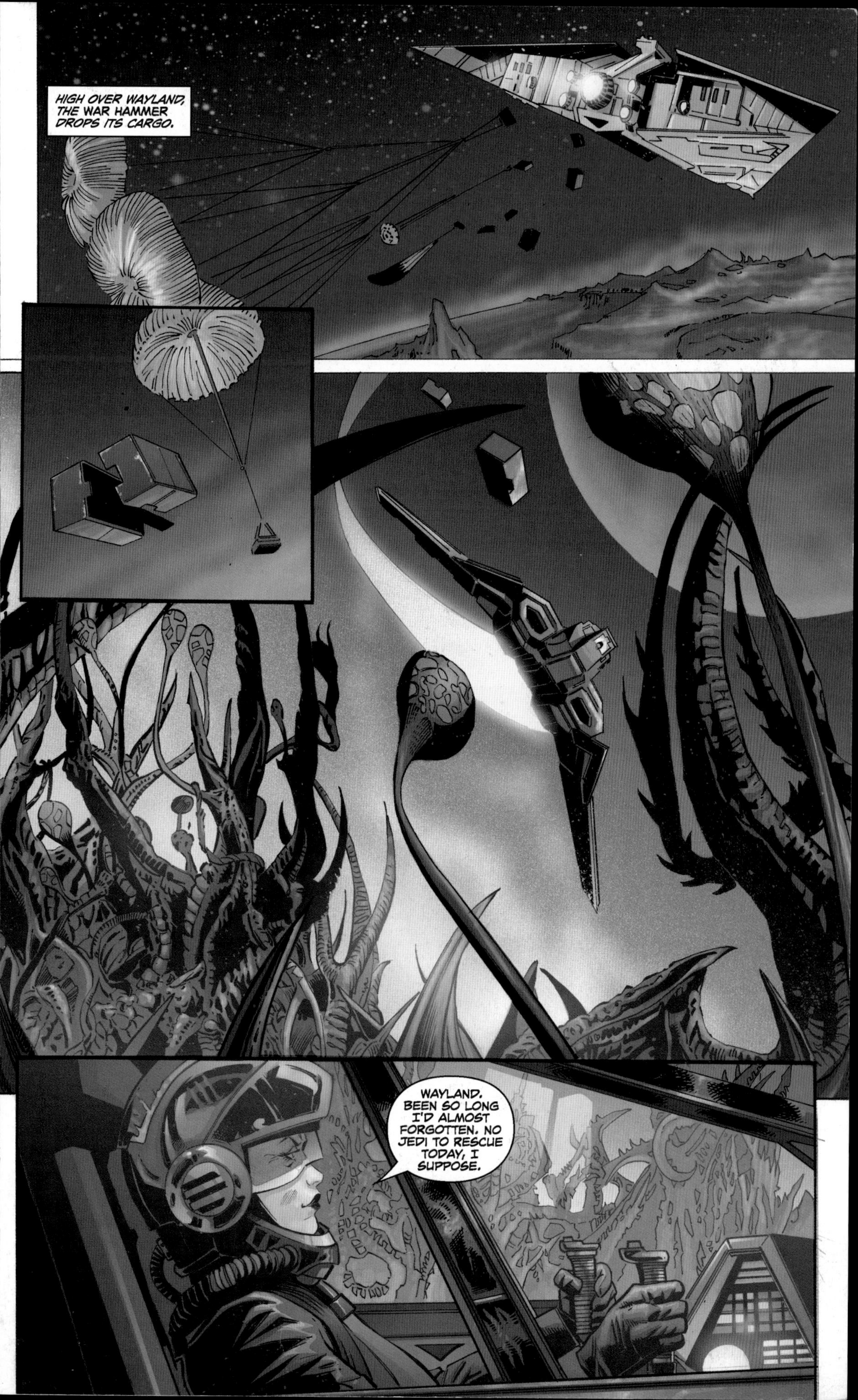
HIGH OVER WAYLAND, THE WAR HAMMER DROPS ITS CARGO.
WAYLAND. BEEN SO LONG I'D ALMOST FORGOTTEN. NO JEDI TO RESCUE TODAY, I SUPPOSE.

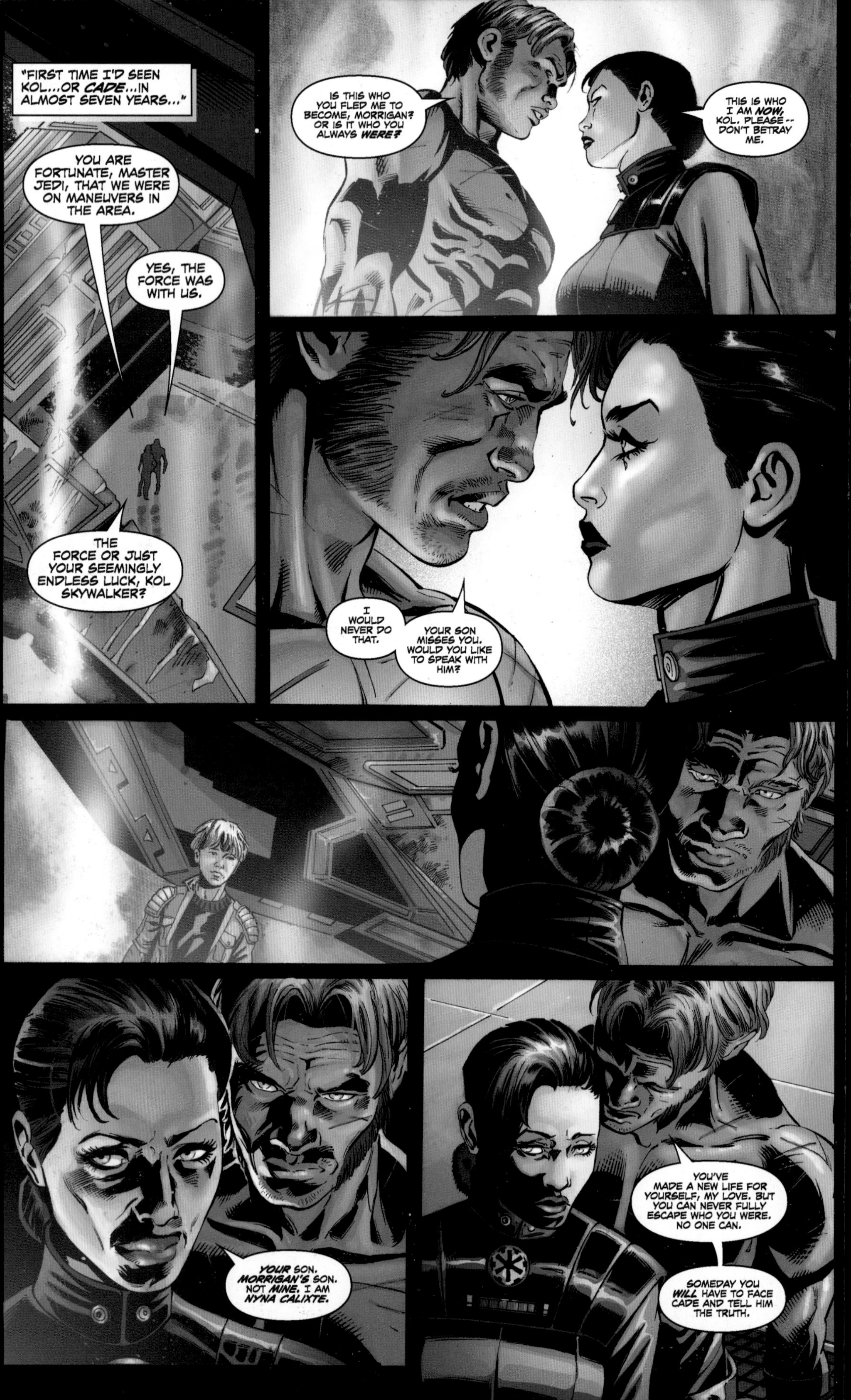
"FIRST TIME I'D SEEN KOL...OR CADE...IN ALMOST SEVEN YEARS..."
YOU ARE FORTUNATE, MASTER JEDI, THAT WE WERE ON MANEUVERS IN THE AREA.
YES, THE FORCE WAS WITH US.
THE FORCE OR JUST YOUR SEEMINGLY ENDLESS LUCK, KOL SKYWALKER?
IS THIS WHO YOU FLED ME TO BECOME, MORRIGAN? OR IS IT WHO YOU ALWAYS WERE?
THIS IS WHO I AM NOW, KOL. PLEASE-- DON'T BETRAY ME.
I WOULD NEVER DO THAT.
YOUR SON MISSES YOU. WOULD YOU LIKE TO SPEAK WITH HIM?
YOUR SON. MORRIGAN'S SON. NOT MINE. I AM NYNA CALIXTE.
YOU'VE MADE A NEW LIFE FOR YOURSELF, MY LOVE. BUT YOU CAN NEVER FULLY ESCAPE WHO YOU WERE. NO ONE CAN.
SOMEDAY YOU WILL HAVE TO FACE CADE AND TELL HIM THE TRUTH.

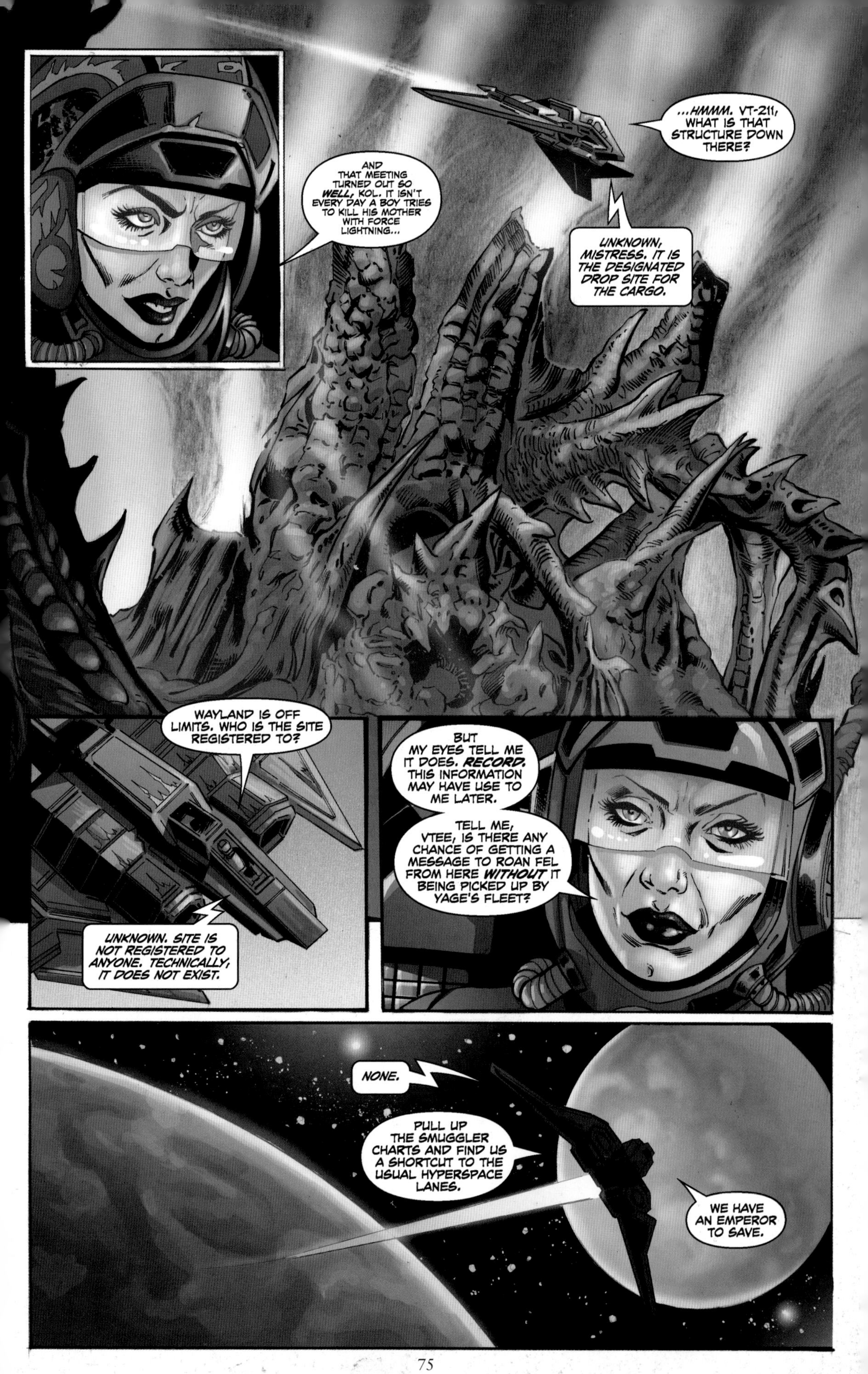
AND THAT MEETING TURNED OUT SO WELL, KOL. IT ISN'T EVERY DAY A BOY TRIES TO KILL HIS MOTHER WITH FORCE LIGHTNING...
...HMMM. VT-211, WHAT IS THAT STRUCTURE DOWN THERE?
UNKNOWN, MISTRESS. IT IS THE DESIGNATED DROP SITE FOR THE CARGO.
WAYLAND IS OFF LIMITS. WHO IS THE SITE REGISTERED TO?
UNKNOWN. SITE IS NOT REGISTERED TO ANYONE. TECHNICALLY, IT DOES NOT EXIST.
BUT MY EYES TELL ME IT DOES. RECORD. THIS INFORMATION MAY HAVE USE TO ME LATER.
TELL ME, VTEE, IS THERE ANY CHANCE OF GETTING A MESSAGE TO ROAN FEL FROM HERE WITHOUT IT BEING PICKED UP BY YAGE'S FLEET?
NONE.
PULL UP THE SMUGGLER CHARTS AND FIND US A SHORTCUT TO THE USUAL HYPERSPACE LANES.
WE HAVE AN EMPEROR TO SAVE.

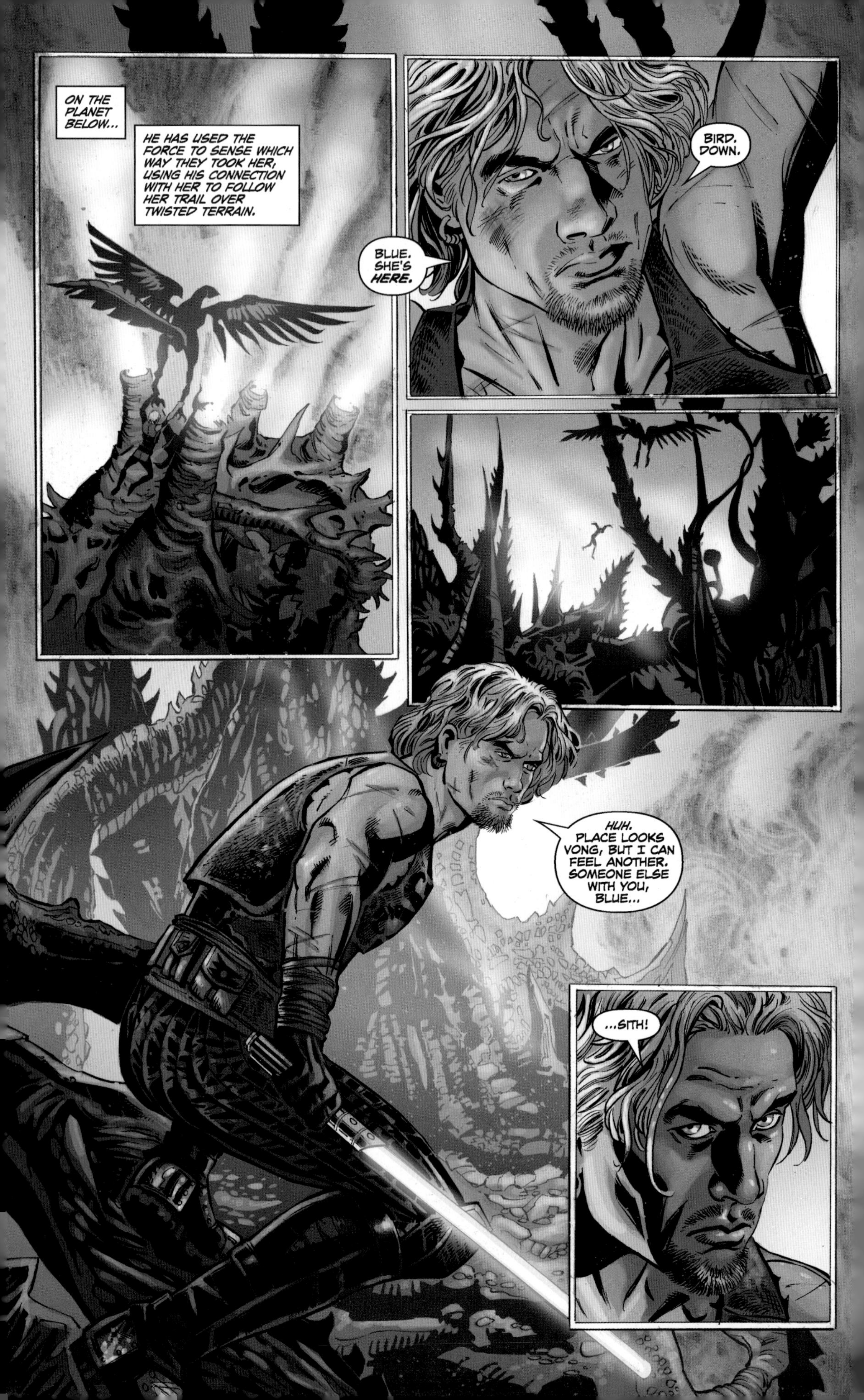
ON THE PLANET BELOW...
HE HAS USED THE FORCE TO SENSE WHICH WAY THEY TOOK HER, USING HIS CONNECTION WITH HER TO FOLLOW HER TRAIL OVER TWISTED TERRAIN.
BLUE. SHE'S *HERE.*
BIRD. DOWN.
HUH. PLACE LOOKS VONG, BUT I CAN FEEL ANOTHER. SOMEONE ELSE WITH YOU, BLUE...
...SITH!

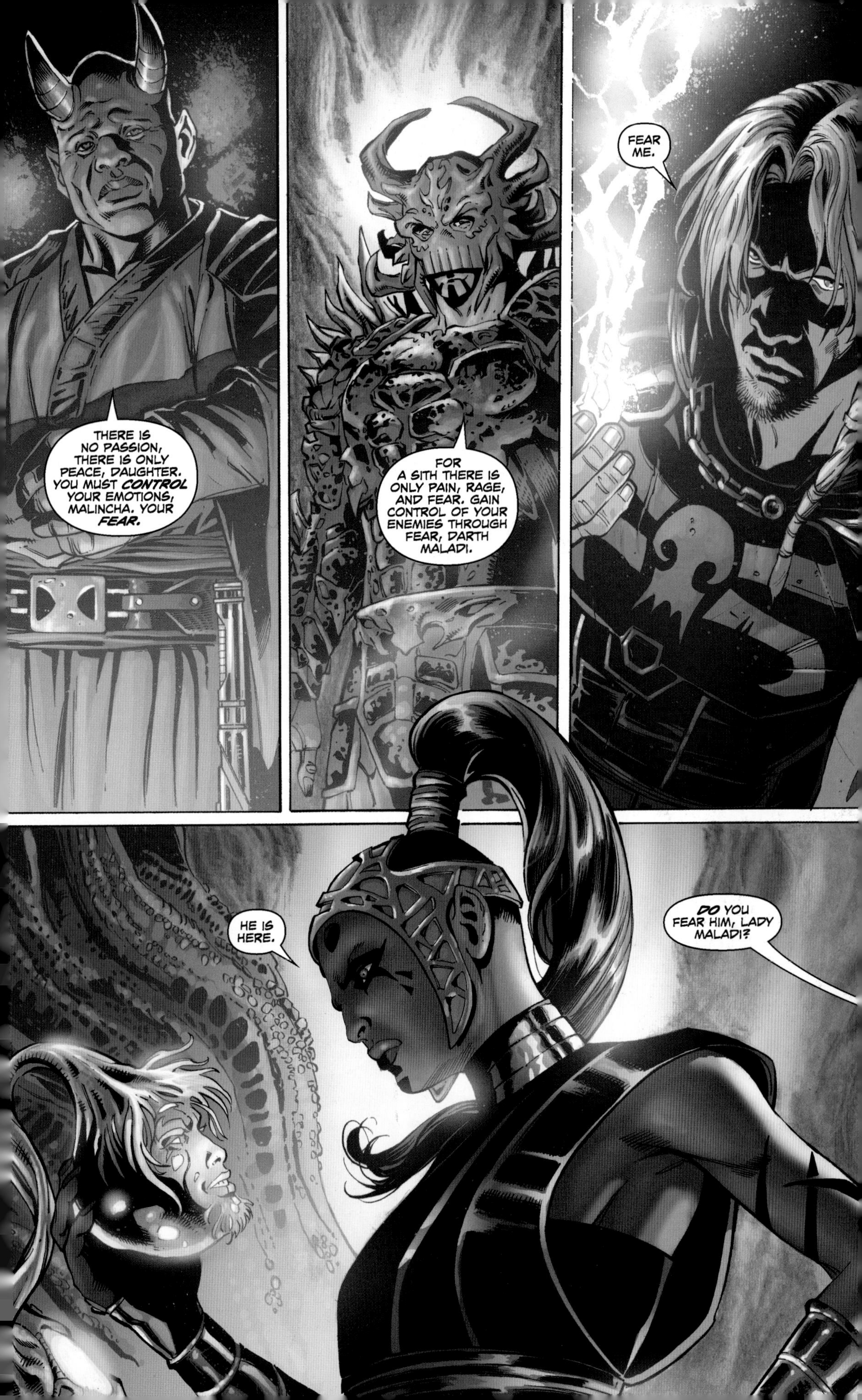
THERE IS NO PASSION, THERE IS ONLY PEACE, DAUGHTER. YOU MUST CONTROL YOUR EMOTIONS, MALINCHA. YOUR FEAR.
FOR A SITH THERE IS ONLY PAIN, RAGE, AND FEAR. GAIN CONTROL OF YOUR ENEMIES THROUGH FEAR, DARTH MALADI.
FEAR ME.
HE IS HERE.
DO YOU FEAR HIM, LADY MALADI?

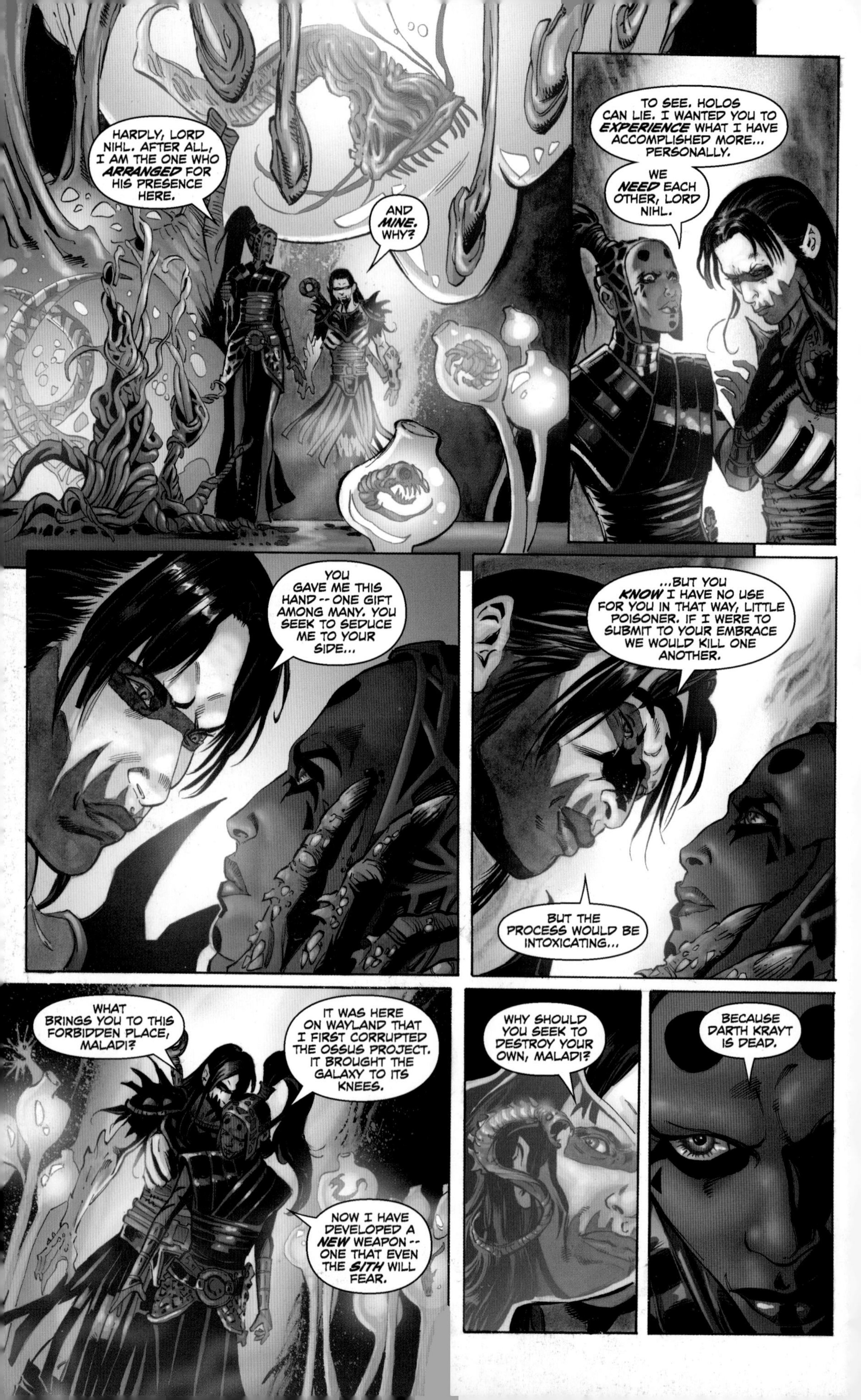
HARDLY, LORD NIHL. AFTER ALL, I AM THE ONE WHO ARRANGED FOR HIS PRESENCE HERE.
AND MINE. WHY?
TO SEE. HOLOS CAN LIE. I WANTED YOU TO EXPERIENCE WHAT I HAVE ACCOMPLISHED MORE... PERSONALLY.
WE NEED EACH OTHER, LORD NIHL.
YOU GAVE ME THIS HAND -- ONE GIFT AMONG MANY. YOU SEEK TO SEDUCE ME TO YOUR SIDE...
...BUT YOU KNOW I HAVE NO USE FOR YOU IN THAT WAY, LITTLE POISONER. IF I WERE TO SUBMIT TO YOUR EMBRACE WE WOULD KILL ONE ANOTHER.
BUT THE PROCESS WOULD BE INTOXICATING...
WHAT BRINGS YOU TO THIS FORBIDDEN PLACE, MALADI?
IT WAS HERE ON WAYLAND THAT I FIRST CORRUPTED THE OSSUS PROJECT. IT BROUGHT THE GALAXY TO ITS KNEES.
NOW I HAVE DEVELOPED A NEW WEAPON -- ONE THAT EVEN THE SITH WILL FEAR.
WHY SHOULD YOU SEEK TO DESTROY YOUR OWN, MALADI?
BECAUSE DARTH KRAYT IS DEAD.

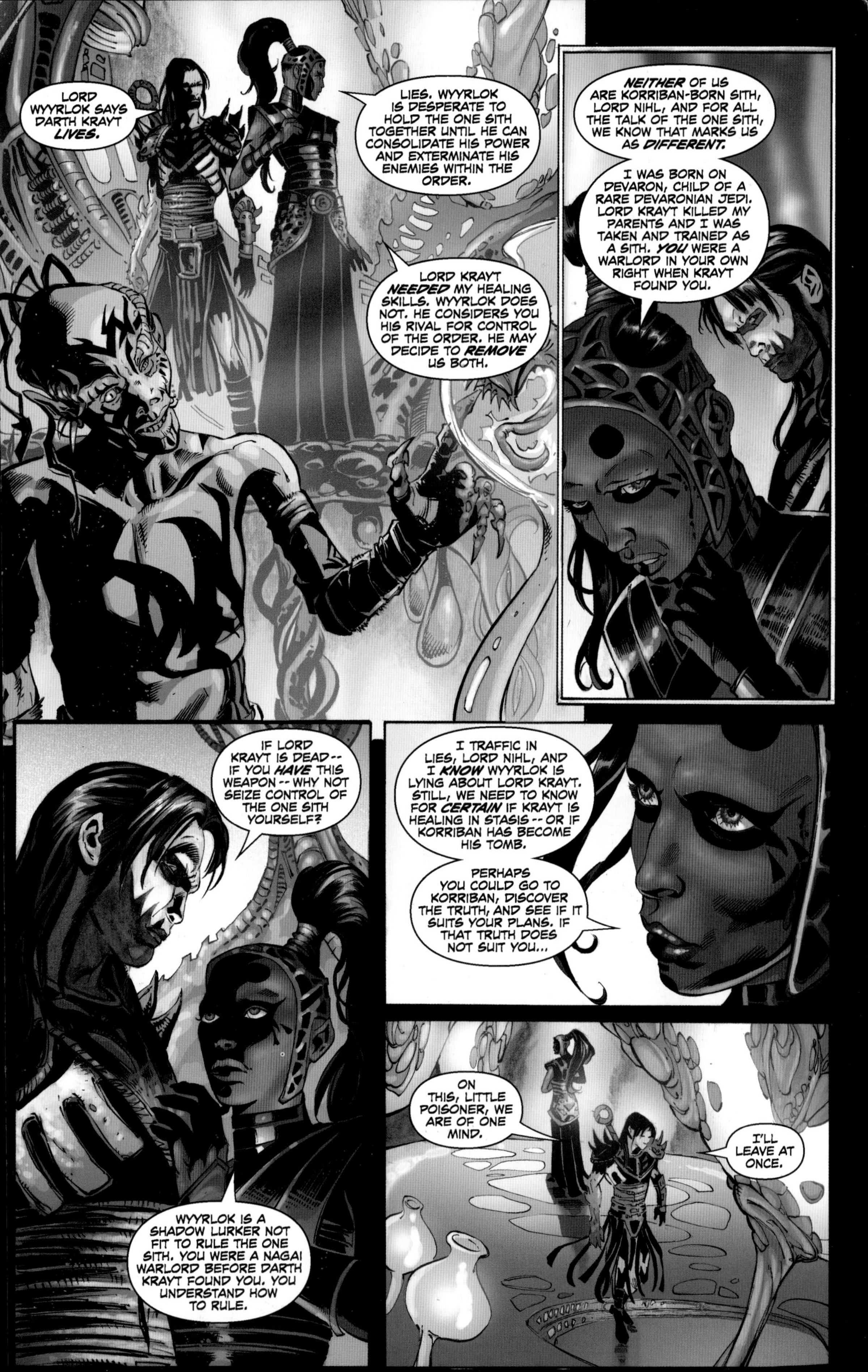
LORD WYYRLOK SAYS DARTH KRAYT *LIVES.*
LIES. WYYRLOK IS DESPERATE TO HOLD THE ONE SITH TOGETHER UNTIL HE CAN CONSOLIDATE HIS POWER AND EXTERMINATE HIS ENEMIES WITHIN THE ORDER.
LORD KRAYT *NEEDED* MY HEALING SKILLS. WYYRLOK DOES NOT. HE CONSIDERS YOU HIS RIVAL FOR CONTROL OF THE ORDER. HE MAY DECIDE TO *REMOVE* US BOTH.
NEITHER OF US ARE KORRIBAN-BORN SITH, LORD NIHL, AND FOR ALL THE TALK OF THE ONE SITH, WE KNOW THAT MARKS US AS *DIFFERENT.*
I WAS BORN ON DEVARON, CHILD OF A RARE DEVARONIAN JEDI. LORD KRAYT KILLED MY PARENTS AND I WAS TAKEN AND TRAINED AS A SITH. *YOU* WERE A WARLORD IN YOUR OWN RIGHT WHEN KRAYT FOUND YOU.
IF LORD KRAYT IS DEAD-- IF YOU *HAVE* THIS WEAPON -- WHY NOT SEIZE CONTROL OF THE ONE SITH YOURSELF?
WYYRLOK IS A SHADOW LURKER NOT FIT TO RULE THE ONE SITH. YOU WERE A NAGAI WARLORD BEFORE DARTH KRAYT FOUND YOU. YOU UNDERSTAND HOW TO RULE.
I TRAFFIC IN LIES, LORD NIHL, AND I *KNOW* WYYRLOK IS LYING ABOUT LORD KRAYT. STILL, WE NEED TO KNOW FOR *CERTAIN* IF KRAYT IS HEALING IN STASIS -- OR IF KORRIBAN HAS BECOME HIS TOMB.
PERHAPS YOU COULD GO TO KORRIBAN, DISCOVER THE TRUTH, AND SEE IF IT SUITS YOUR PLANS. IF THAT TRUTH DOES NOT SUIT YOU...
ON THIS, LITTLE POISONER, WE ARE OF ONE MIND.
I'LL LEAVE AT ONCE.

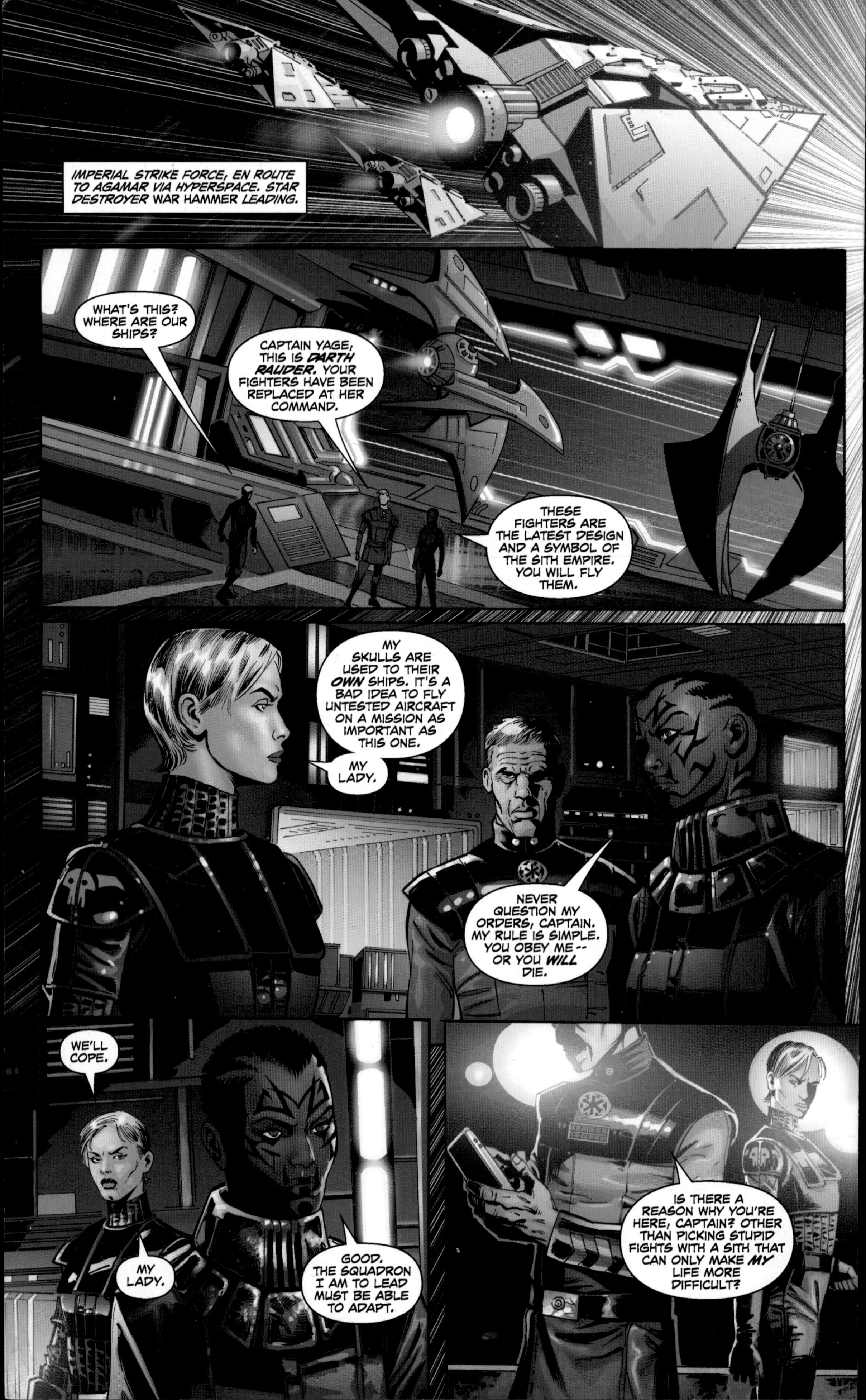
IMPERIAL STRIKE FORCE, EN ROUTE TO AGAMAR VIA HYPERSPACE. STAR DESTROYER WAR HAMMER LEADING.
WHAT'S THIS? WHERE ARE OUR SHIPS?
CAPTAIN YAGE, THIS IS DARTH RAUDER. YOUR FIGHTERS HAVE BEEN REPLACED AT HER COMMAND.
THESE FIGHTERS ARE THE LATEST DESIGN AND A SYMBOL OF THE SITH EMPIRE. YOU WILL FLY THEM.
MY SKULLS ARE USED TO THEIR OWN SHIPS. IT'S A BAD IDEA TO FLY UNTESTED AIRCRAFT ON A MISSION AS IMPORTANT AS THIS ONE.
MY LADY.
NEVER QUESTION MY ORDERS, CAPTAIN. MY RULE IS SIMPLE. YOU OBEY ME -- OR YOU WILL DIE.
WE'LL COPE.
MY LADY.
GOOD. THE SQUADRON I AM TO LEAD MUST BE ABLE TO ADAPT.
IS THERE A REASON WHY YOU'RE HERE, CAPTAIN? OTHER THAN PICKING STUPID FIGHTS WITH A SITH THAT CAN ONLY MAKE MY LIFE MORE DIFFICULT?

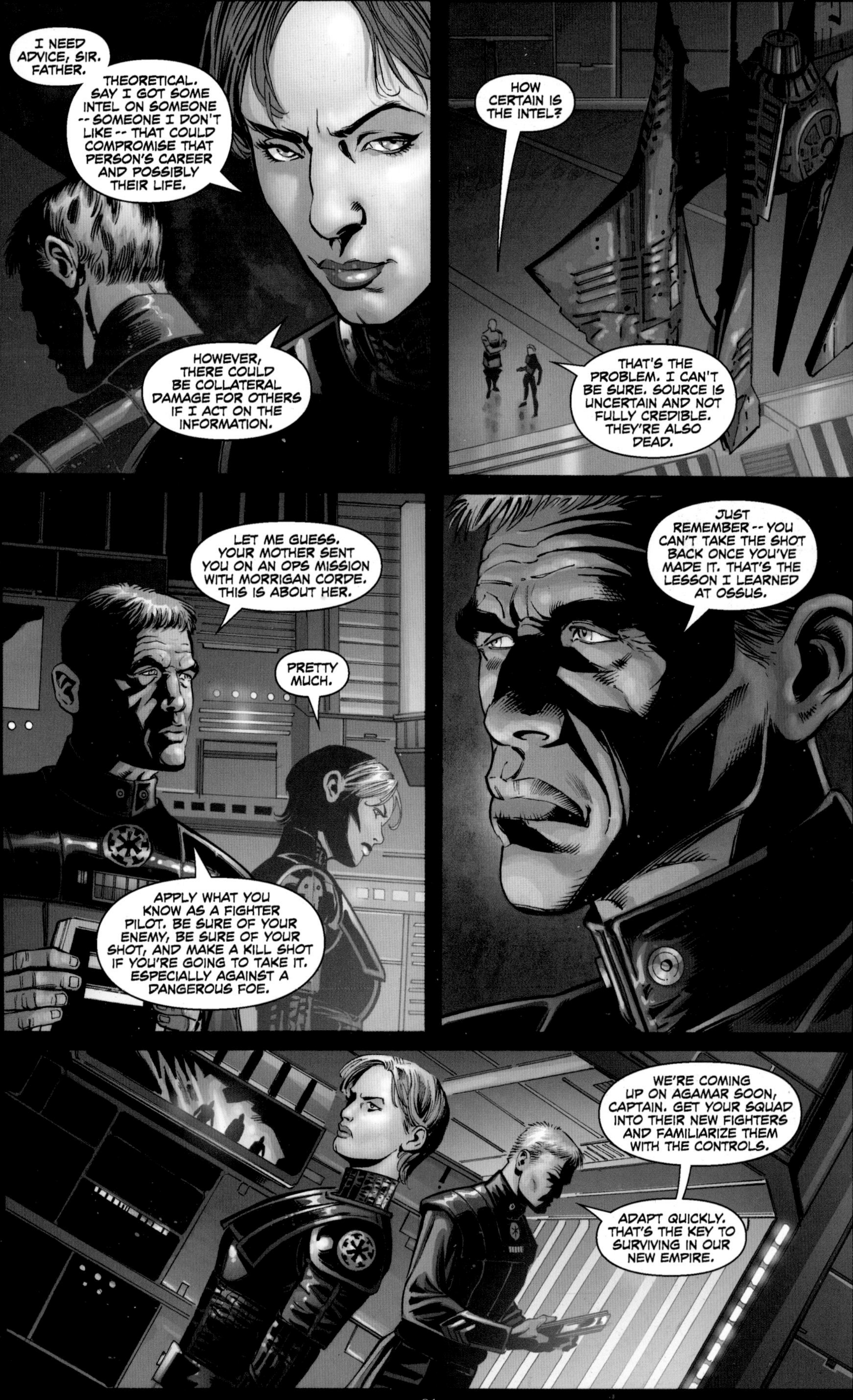
I NEED ADVICE, SIR. FATHER.
THEORETICAL. SAY I GOT SOME INTEL ON SOMEONE -- SOMEONE I DON'T LIKE -- THAT COULD COMPROMISE THAT PERSON'S CAREER AND POSSIBLY THEIR LIFE.
HOWEVER, THERE COULD BE COLLATERAL DAMAGE FOR OTHERS IF I ACT ON THE INFORMATION.
HOW CERTAIN IS THE INTEL?
THAT'S THE PROBLEM. I CAN'T BE SURE. SOURCE IS UNCERTAIN AND NOT FULLY CREDIBLE. THEY'RE ALSO DEAD.
LET ME GUESS. YOUR MOTHER SENT YOU ON AN OPS MISSION WITH MORRIGAN CORDE. THIS IS ABOUT HER.
PRETTY MUCH.
APPLY WHAT YOU KNOW AS A FIGHTER PILOT. BE SURE OF YOUR ENEMY, BE SURE OF YOUR SHOT, AND MAKE A KILL SHOT IF YOU'RE GOING TO TAKE IT. ESPECIALLY AGAINST A DANGEROUS FOE.
JUST REMEMBER -- YOU CAN'T TAKE THE SHOT BACK ONCE YOU'VE MADE IT. THAT'S THE LESSON I LEARNED AT OSSUS.
WE'RE COMING UP ON AGAMAR SOON, CAPTAIN. GET YOUR SQUAD INTO THEIR NEW FIGHTERS AND FAMILIARIZE THEM WITH THE CONTROLS.
ADAPT QUICKLY. THAT'S THE KEY TO SURVIVING IN OUR NEW EMPIRE.

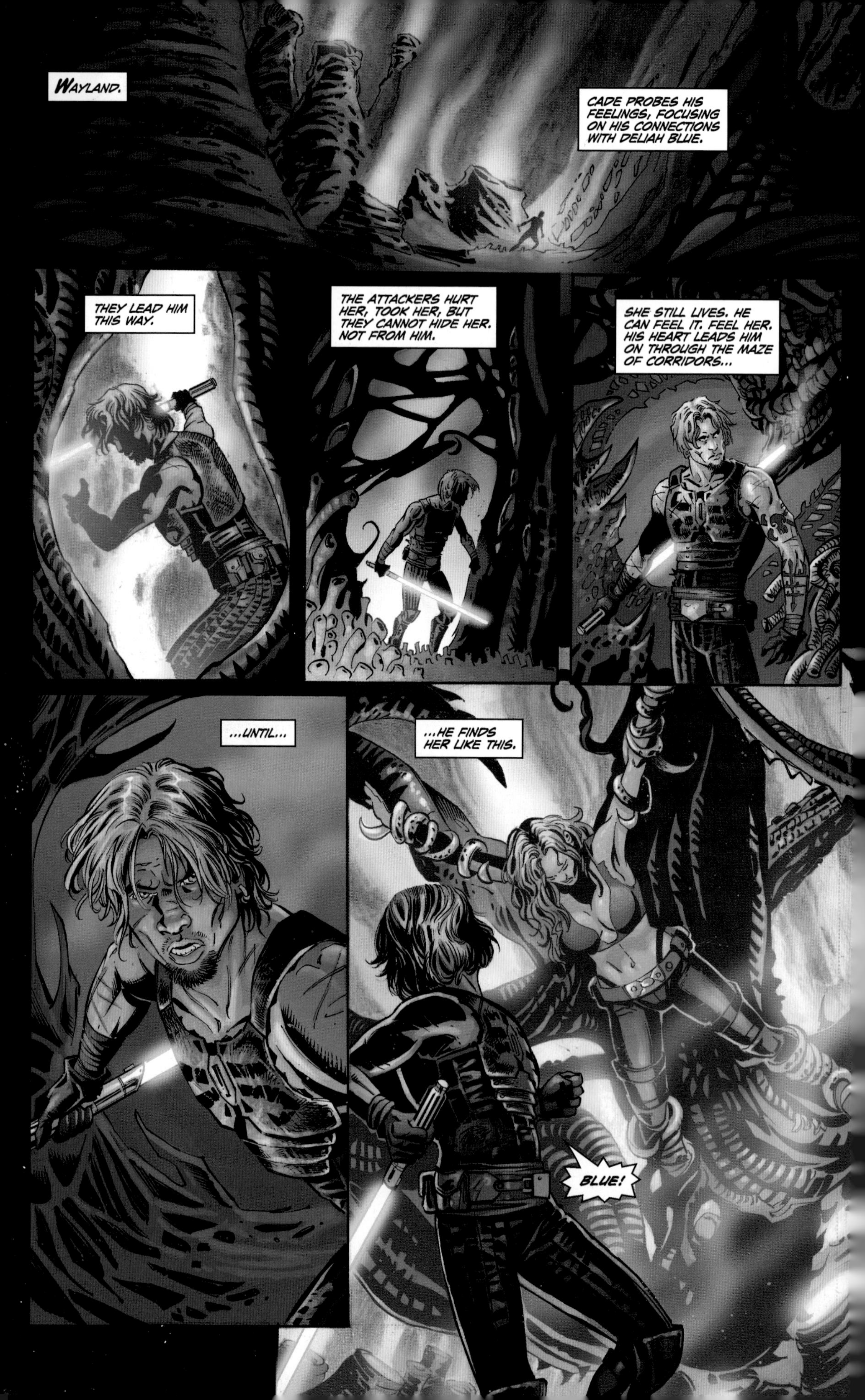
WAYLAND.
CADE PROBES HIS FEELINGS, FOCUSING ON HIS CONNECTIONS WITH DELIAH BLUE.
THEY LEAD HIM THIS WAY.
THE ATTACKERS HURT HER, TOOK HER, BUT THEY CANNOT HIDE HER. NOT FROM HIM.
SHE STILL LIVES. HE CAN FEEL IT. FEEL HER. HIS HEART LEADS HIM ON THROUGH THE MAZE OF CORRIDORS...
...UNTIL...
...HE FINDS HER LIKE THIS.
BLUE!

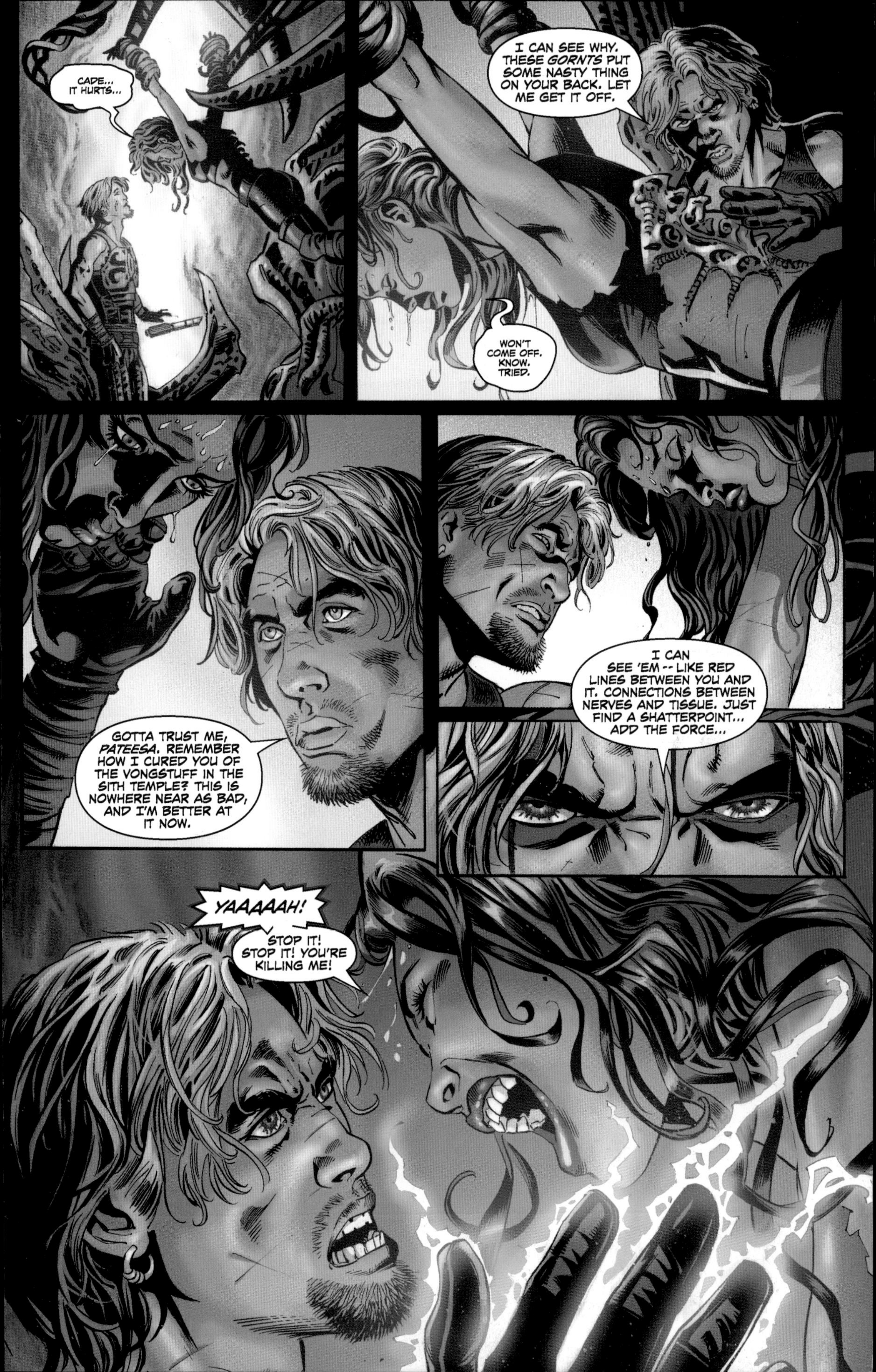
CADE... IT HURTS...
I CAN SEE WHY. THESE GORNTS PUT SOME NASTY THING ON YOUR BACK. LET ME GET IT OFF.
WON'T COME OFF. KNOW. TRIED.
GOTTA TRUST ME, PATEESA. REMEMBER HOW I CURED YOU OF THE VONGSTUFF IN THE SITH TEMPLE? THIS IS NOWHERE NEAR AS BAD, AND I'M BETTER AT IT NOW.
I CAN SEE 'EM -- LIKE RED LINES BETWEEN YOU AND IT. CONNECTIONS BETWEEN NERVES AND TISSUE. JUST FIND A SHATTERPOINT... ADD THE FORCE...
YAAAAAH!
STOP IT! STOP IT! YOU'RE KILLING ME!

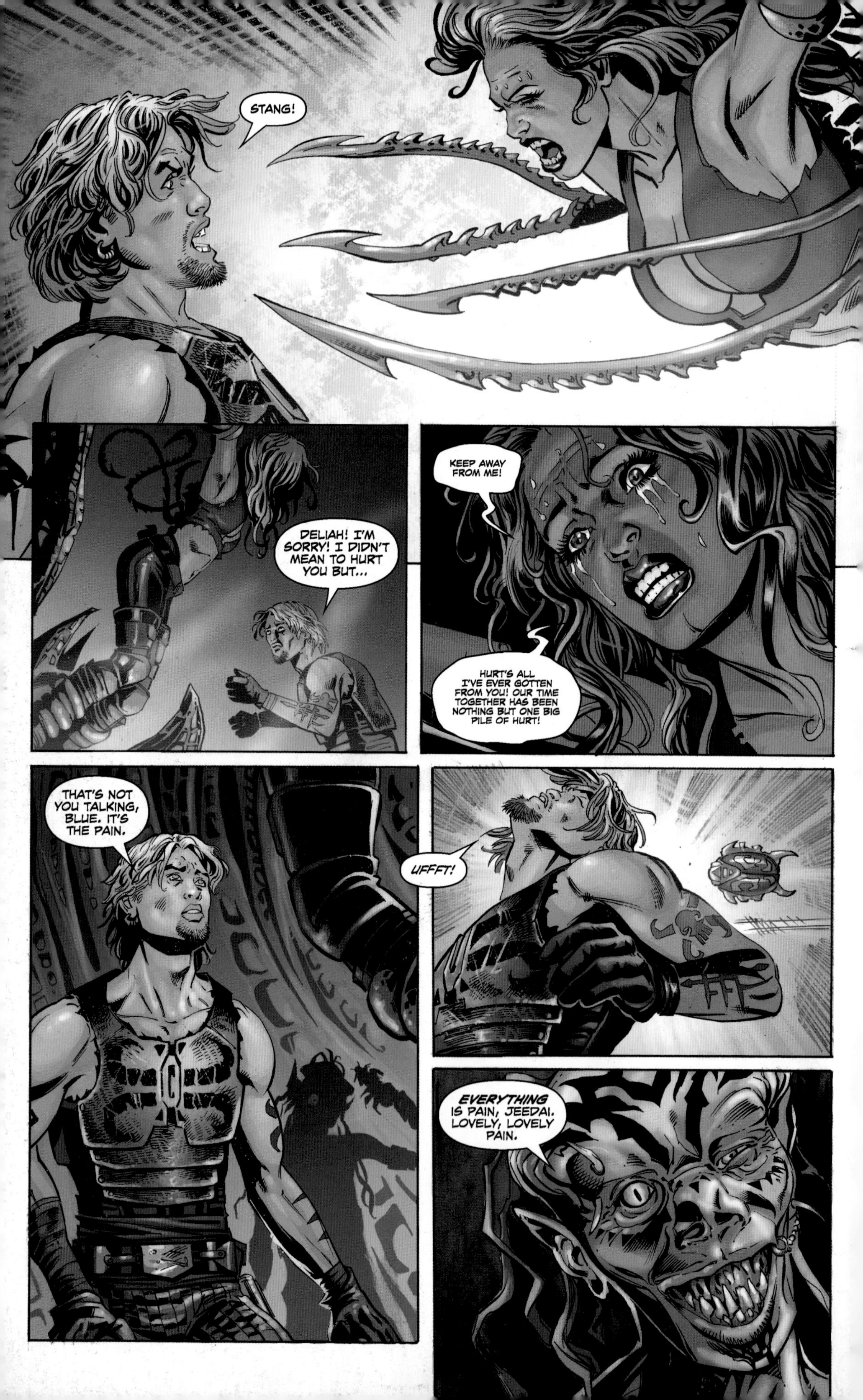
STANG!
DELIAH! I'M SORRY! I DIDN'T MEAN TO HURT YOU BUT...
KEEP AWAY FROM ME!
HURT'S ALL I'VE EVER GOTTEN FROM YOU! OUR TIME TOGETHER HAS BEEN NOTHING BUT ONE BIG PILE OF HURT!
THAT'S NOT YOU TALKING, BLUE. IT'S THE PAIN.
UFFFT!
EVERYTHING IS PAIN, JEEDAI. LOVELY, LOVELY PAIN.

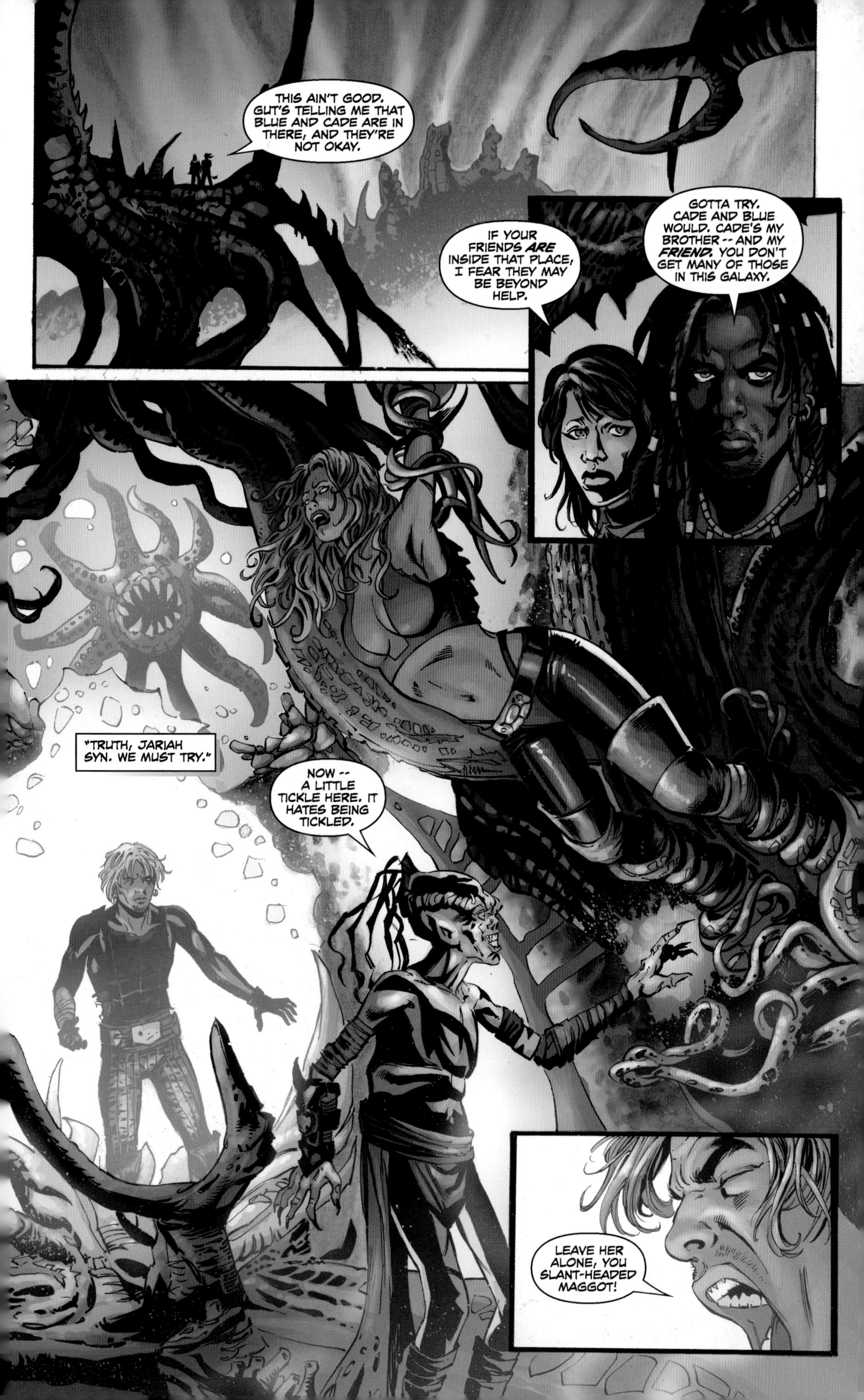
THIS AIN'T GOOD. GUT'S TELLING ME THAT BLUE AND CADE ARE IN THERE, AND THEY'RE NOT OKAY.
IF YOUR FRIENDS ARE INSIDE THAT PLACE, I FEAR THEY MAY BE BEYOND HELP.
GOTTA TRY. CADE AND BLUE WOULD. CADE'S MY BROTHER -- AND MY FRIEND. YOU DON'T GET MANY OF THOSE IN THIS GALAXY.
"TRUTH, JARIAH SYN. WE MUST TRY."
NOW -- A LITTLE TICKLE HERE. IT HATES BEING TICKLED.
LEAVE HER ALONE, YOU SLANT-HEADED MAGGOT!

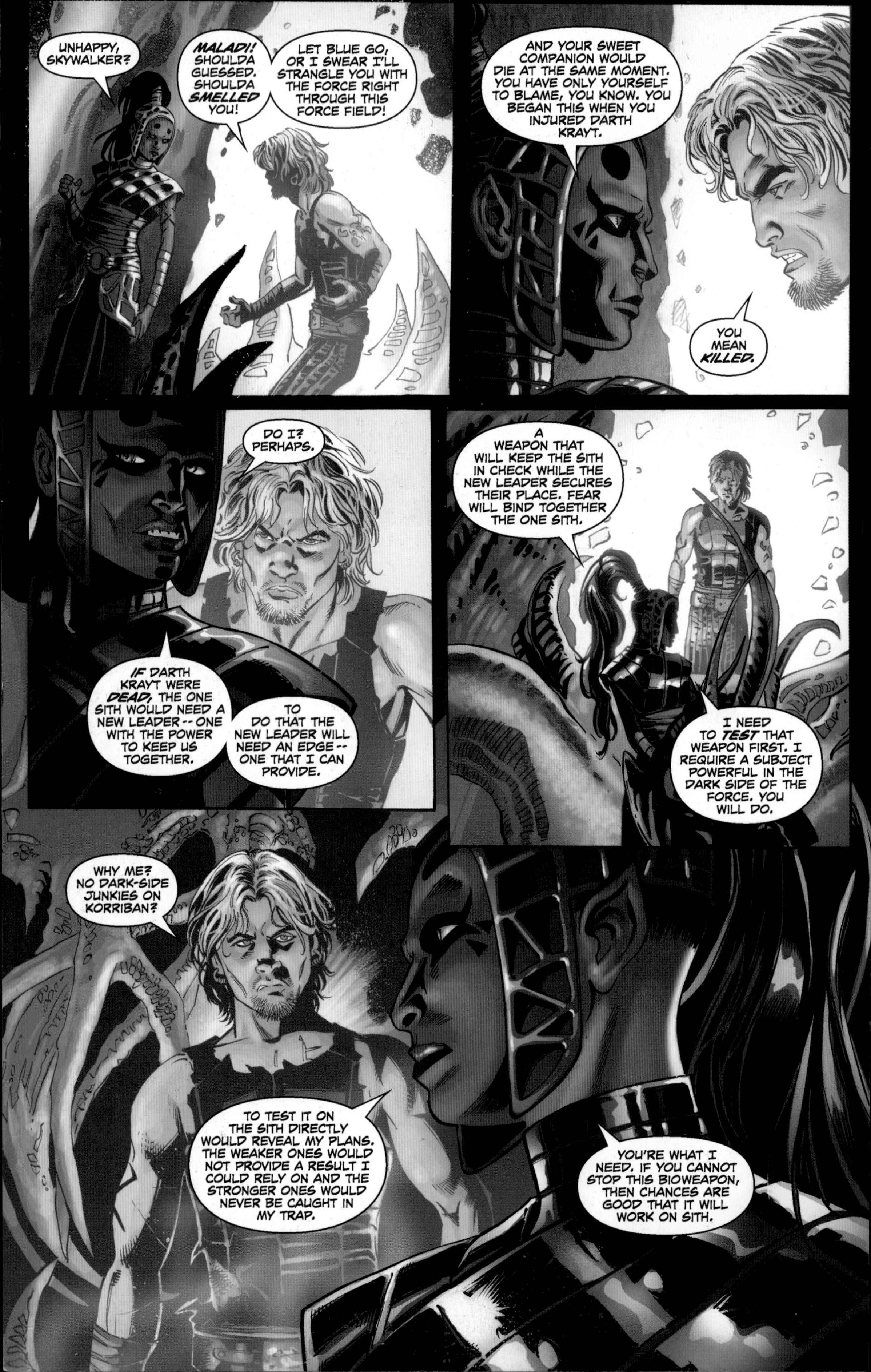
UNHAPPY, SKYWALKER?
MALADI! SHOULDA GUESSED. SHOULDA SMELLED YOU!
LET BLUE GO, OR I SWEAR I'LL STRANGLE YOU WITH THE FORCE RIGHT THROUGH THIS FORCE FIELD!
AND YOUR SWEET COMPANION WOULD DIE AT THE SAME MOMENT. YOU HAVE ONLY YOURSELF TO BLAME, YOU KNOW. YOU BEGAN THIS WHEN YOU INJURED DARTH KRAYT.
YOU MEAN KILLED.
DO I? PERHAPS.
IF DARTH KRAYT WERE DEAD, THE ONE SITH WOULD NEED A NEW LEADER -- ONE WITH THE POWER TO KEEP US TOGETHER.
TO DO THAT THE NEW LEADER WILL NEED AN EDGE -- ONE THAT I CAN PROVIDE.
A WEAPON THAT WILL KEEP THE SITH IN CHECK WHILE THE NEW LEADER SECURES THEIR PLACE. FEAR WILL BIND TOGETHER THE ONE SITH.
I NEED TO TEST THAT WEAPON FIRST. I REQUIRE A SUBJECT POWERFUL IN THE DARK SIDE OF THE FORCE. YOU WILL DO.
WHY ME? NO DARK-SIDE JUNKIES ON KORRIBAN?
TO TEST IT ON THE SITH DIRECTLY WOULD REVEAL MY PLANS. THE WEAKER ONES WOULD NOT PROVIDE A RESULT I COULD RELY ON AND THE STRONGER ONES WOULD NEVER BE CAUGHT IN MY TRAP.
YOU'RE WHAT I NEED. IF YOU CANNOT STOP THIS BIOWEAPON, THEN CHANCES ARE GOOD THAT IT WILL WORK ON SITH.

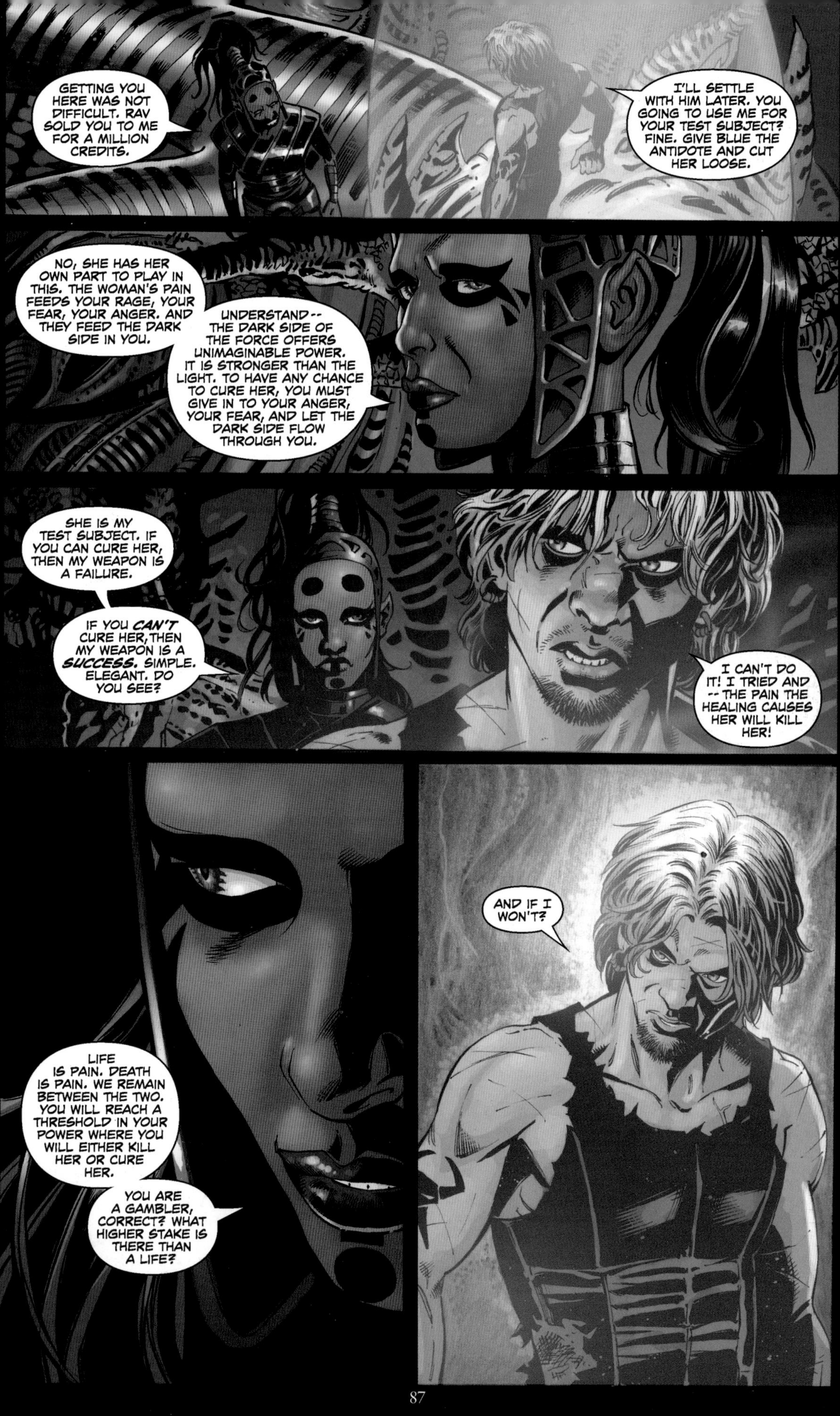
GETTING YOU HERE WAS NOT DIFFICULT. RAV SOLD YOU TO ME FOR A MILLION CREDITS.
I'LL SETTLE WITH HIM LATER. YOU GOING TO USE ME FOR YOUR TEST SUBJECT? FINE. GIVE BLUE THE ANTIDOTE AND CUT HER LOOSE.
NO, SHE HAS HER OWN PART TO PLAY IN THIS. THE WOMAN'S PAIN FEEDS YOUR RAGE, YOUR FEAR, YOUR ANGER. AND THEY FEED THE DARK SIDE IN YOU.
UNDERSTAND-- THE DARK SIDE OF THE FORCE OFFERS UNIMAGINABLE POWER. IT IS STRONGER THAN THE LIGHT. TO HAVE ANY CHANCE TO CURE HER, YOU MUST GIVE IN TO YOUR ANGER, YOUR FEAR, AND LET THE DARK SIDE FLOW THROUGH YOU.
SHE IS MY TEST SUBJECT. IF YOU CAN CURE HER, THEN MY WEAPON IS A FAILURE.
IF YOU *CAN'T* CURE HER, THEN MY WEAPON IS A ***SUCCESS.*** SIMPLE. ELEGANT. DO YOU SEE?
I CAN'T DO IT! I TRIED AND -- THE PAIN THE HEALING CAUSES HER WILL KILL HER!
LIFE IS PAIN. DEATH IS PAIN. WE REMAIN BETWEEN THE TWO. YOU WILL REACH A THRESHOLD IN YOUR POWER WHERE YOU WILL EITHER KILL HER OR CURE HER.
YOU ARE A GAMBLER, CORRECT? WHAT HIGHER STAKE IS THERE THAN A LIFE?
AND IF I WON'T?

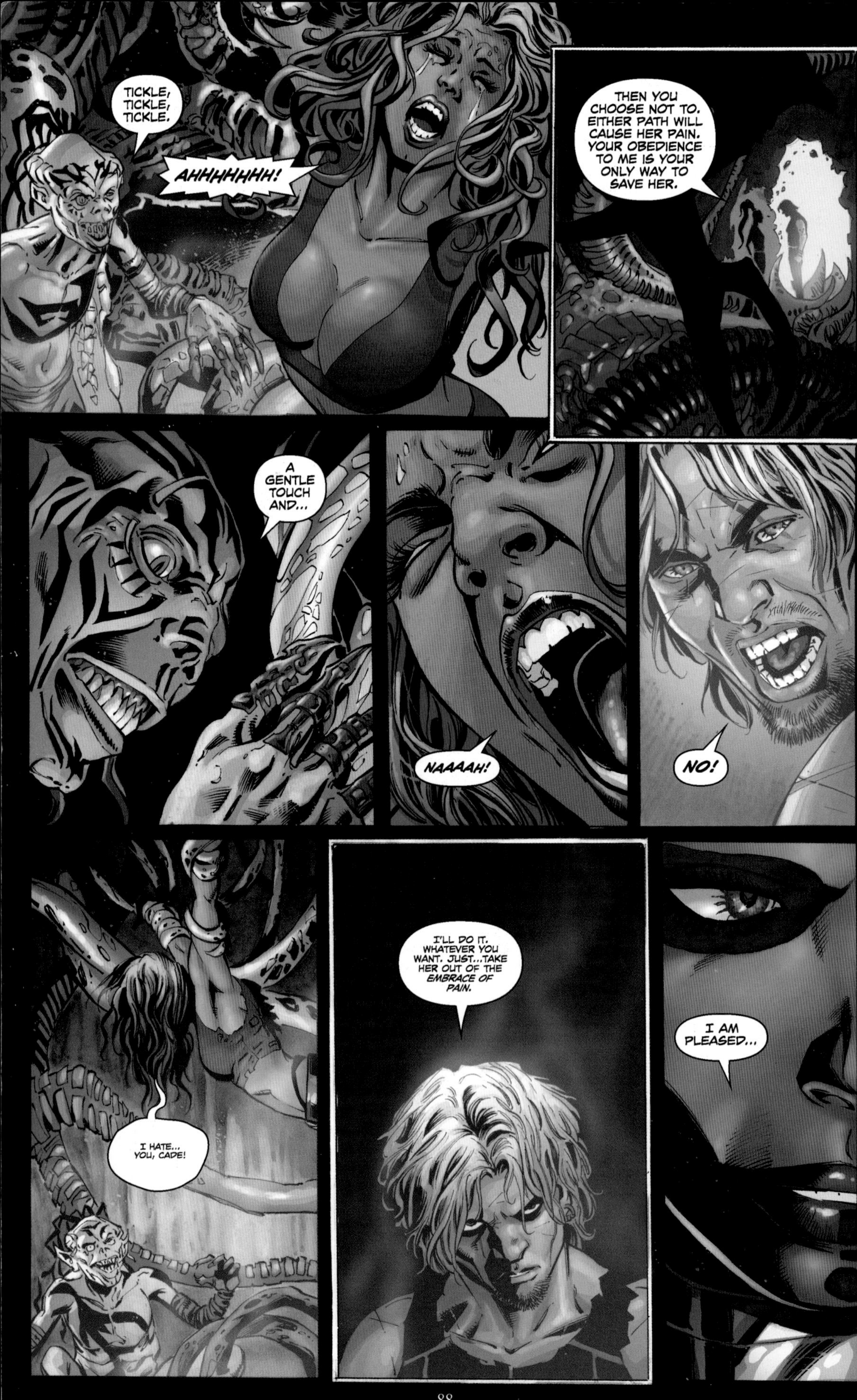
TICKLE, TICKLE, TICKLE.
AHHHHHHH!
THEN YOU CHOOSE NOT TO. EITHER PATH WILL CAUSE HER PAIN. YOUR OBEDIENCE TO ME IS YOUR ONLY WAY TO SAVE HER.
A GENTLE TOUCH AND...
NAAAAH!
NO!
I HATE... YOU, CADE!
I'LL DO IT. WHATEVER YOU WANT. JUST...TAKE HER OUT OF THE EMBRACE OF PAIN.
I AM PLEASED...

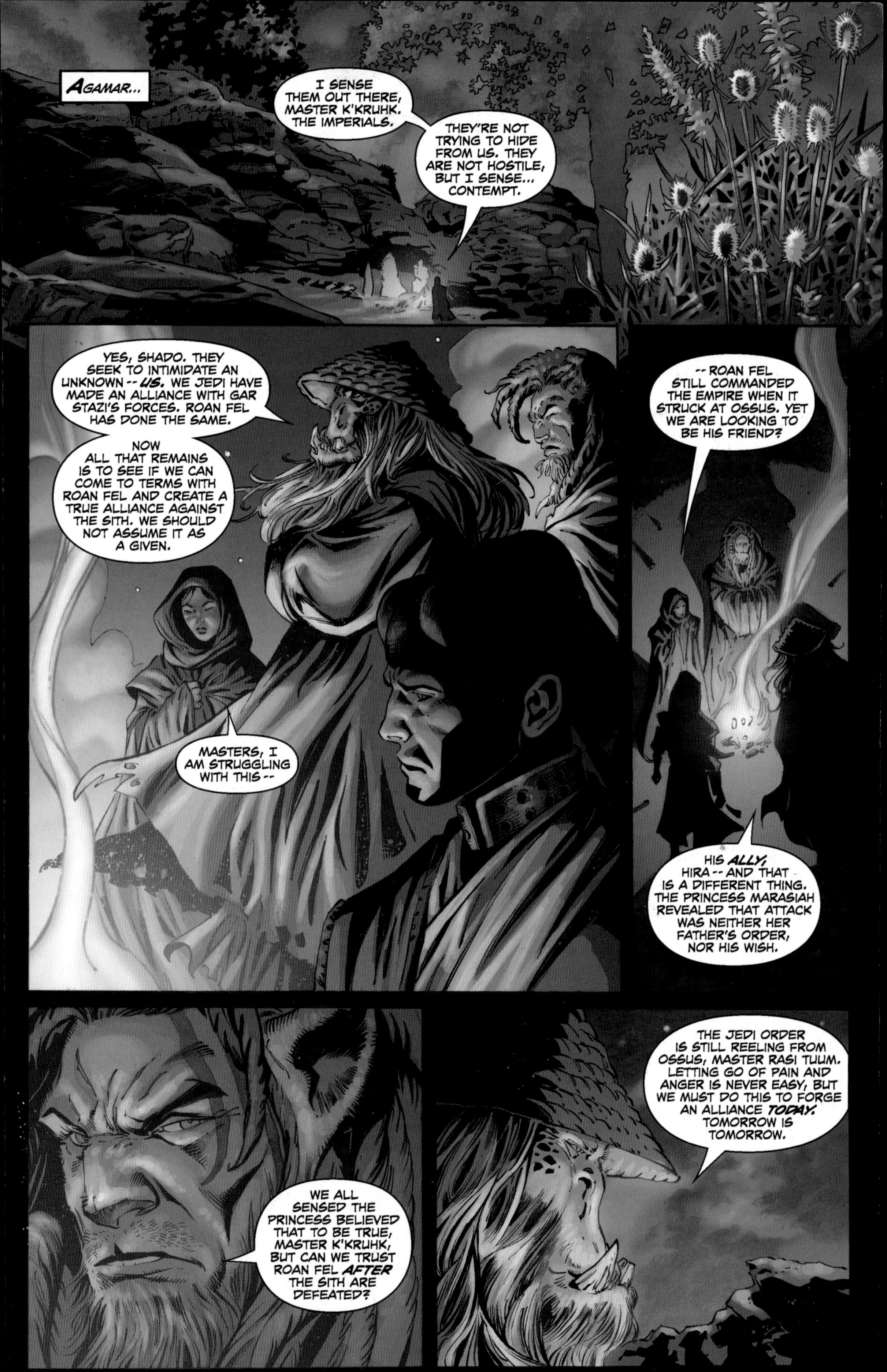

AGAMAR...
I SENSE THEM OUT THERE, MASTER K'KRUHK. THE IMPERIALS.
THEY'RE NOT TRYING TO HIDE FROM US. THEY ARE NOT HOSTILE, BUT I SENSE... CONTEMPT.
YES, SHADO. THEY SEEK TO INTIMIDATE AN UNKNOWN -- US. WE JEDI HAVE MADE AN ALLIANCE WITH GAR STAZI'S FORCES. ROAN FEL HAS DONE THE SAME.
NOW ALL THAT REMAINS IS TO SEE IF WE CAN COME TO TERMS WITH ROAN FEL AND CREATE A TRUE ALLIANCE AGAINST THE SITH. WE SHOULD NOT ASSUME IT AS A GIVEN.
MASTERS, I AM STRUGGLING WITH THIS --
-- ROAN FEL STILL COMMANDED THE EMPIRE WHEN IT STRUCK AT OSSUS. YET WE ARE LOOKING TO BE HIS FRIEND?
HIS ALLY, HIRA -- AND THAT IS A DIFFERENT THING. THE PRINCESS MARASIAH REVEALED THAT ATTACK WAS NEITHER HER FATHER'S ORDER, NOR HIS WISH.
WE ALL SENSED THE PRINCESS BELIEVED THAT TO BE TRUE, MASTER K'KRUHK, BUT CAN WE TRUST ROAN FEL AFTER THE SITH ARE DEFEATED?
THE JEDI ORDER IS STILL REELING FROM OSSUS, MASTER RASI TUUM. LETTING GO OF PAIN AND ANGER IS NEVER EASY, BUT WE MUST DO THIS TO FORGE AN ALLIANCE TODAY. TOMORROW IS TOMORROW.

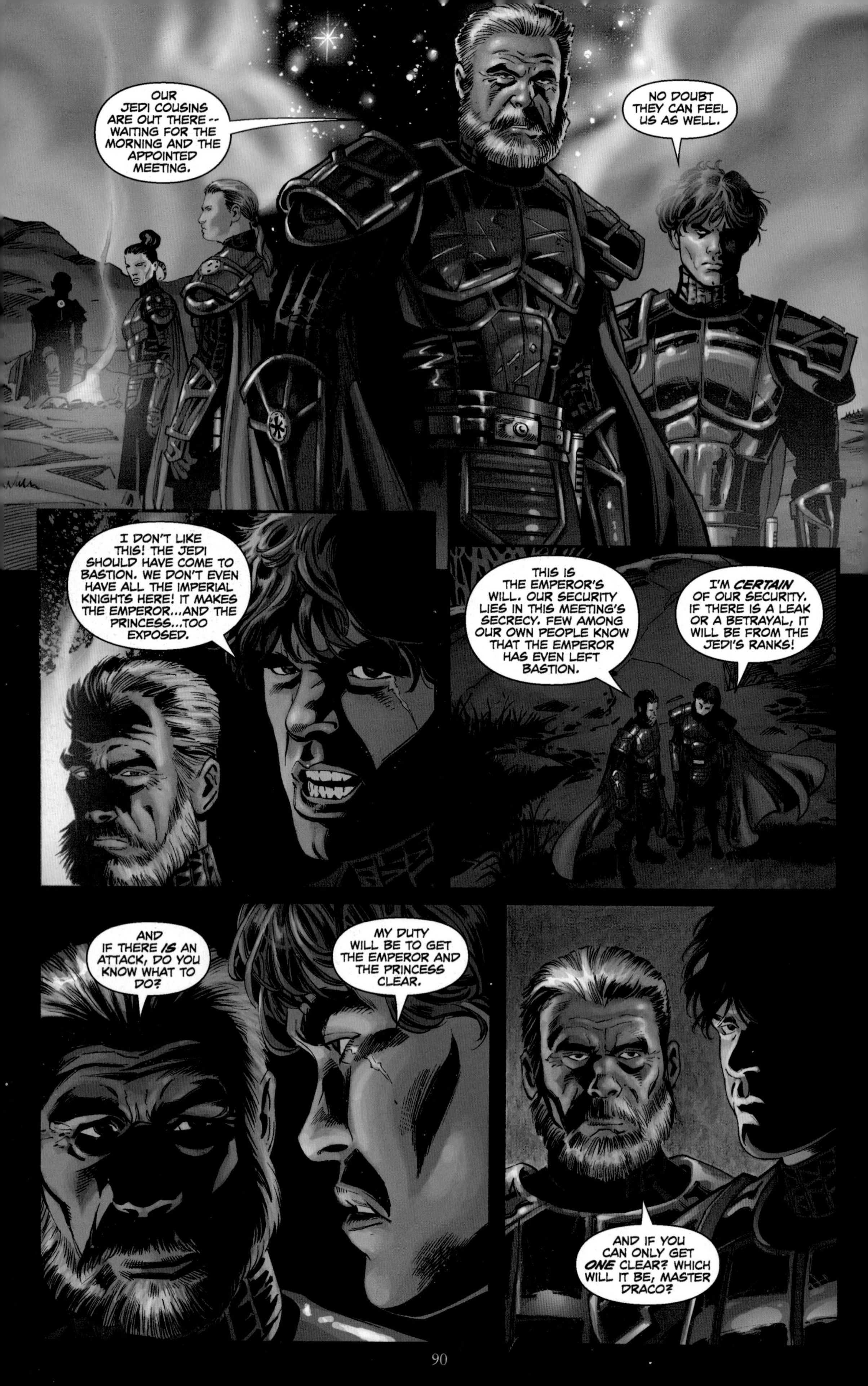
OUR JEDI COUSINS ARE OUT THERE -- WAITING FOR THE MORNING AND THE APPOINTED MEETING.
NO DOUBT THEY CAN FEEL US AS WELL.
I DON'T LIKE THIS! THE JEDI SHOULD HAVE COME TO BASTION. WE DON'T EVEN HAVE ALL THE IMPERIAL KNIGHTS HERE! IT MAKES THE EMPEROR...AND THE PRINCESS...TOO EXPOSED.
THIS IS THE EMPEROR'S WILL. OUR SECURITY LIES IN THIS MEETING'S SECRECY. FEW AMONG OUR OWN PEOPLE KNOW THAT THE EMPEROR HAS EVEN LEFT BASTION.
I'M *CERTAIN* OF OUR SECURITY. IF THERE IS A LEAK OR A BETRAYAL, IT WILL BE FROM THE JEDI'S RANKS!
AND IF THERE *IS* AN ATTACK, DO YOU KNOW WHAT TO DO?
MY DUTY WILL BE TO GET THE EMPEROR AND THE PRINCESS CLEAR.
AND IF YOU CAN ONLY GET *ONE* CLEAR? WHICH WILL IT BE, MASTER DRACO?

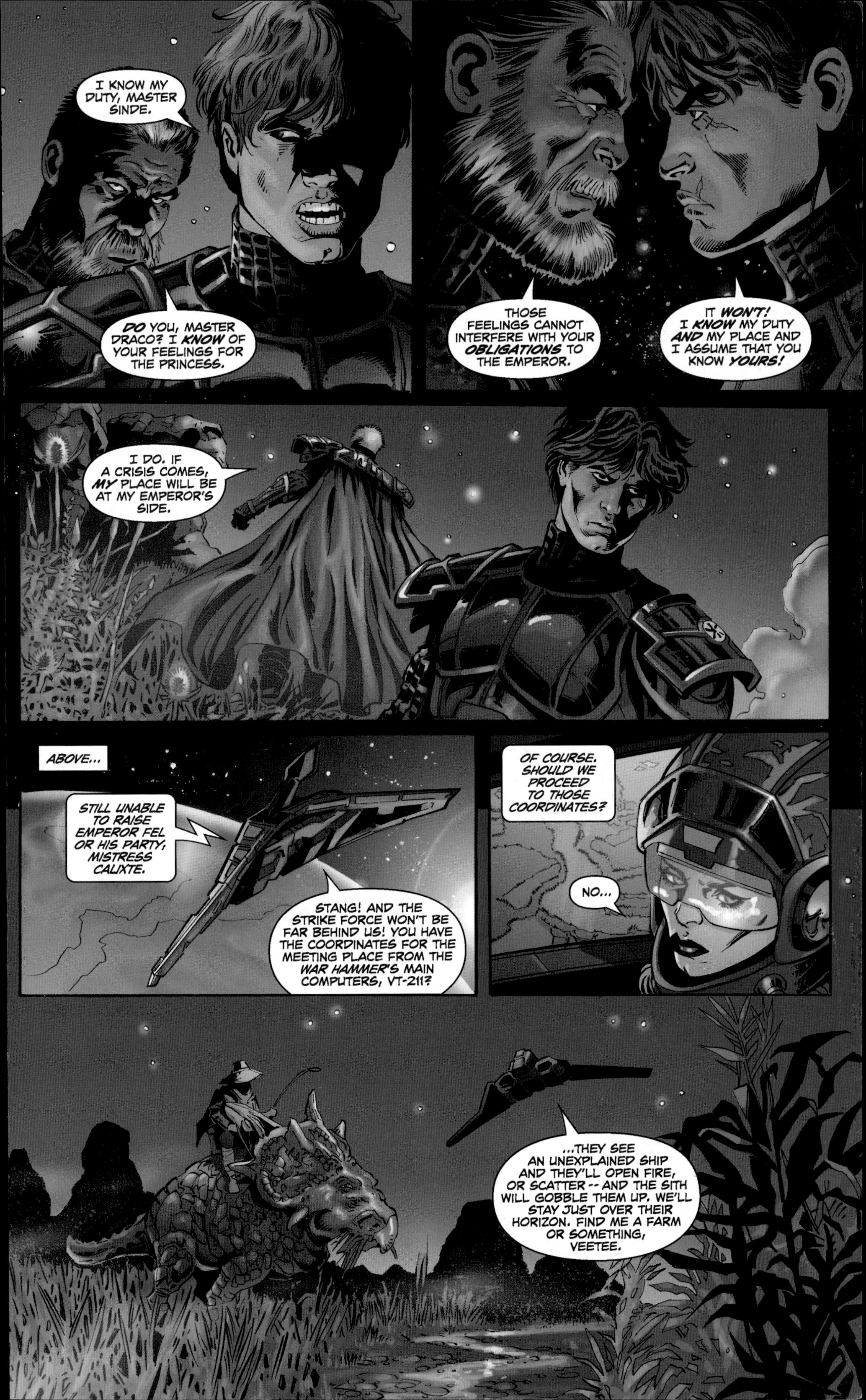
I KNOW MY DUTY, MASTER SINDE.
DO YOU, MASTER DRACO? I KNOW OF YOUR FEELINGS FOR THE PRINCESS.
THOSE FEELINGS CANNOT INTERFERE WITH YOUR OBLIGATIONS TO THE EMPEROR.
IT WON'T! I KNOW MY DUTY AND MY PLACE AND I ASSUME THAT YOU KNOW YOURS!
I DO. IF A CRISIS COMES, MY PLACE WILL BE AT MY EMPEROR'S SIDE.
ABOVE...
STILL UNABLE TO RAISE EMPEROR FEL OR HIS PARTY, MISTRESS CALIXTE.
STANG! AND THE STRIKE FORCE WON'T BE FAR BEHIND US! YOU HAVE THE COORDINATES FOR THE MEETING PLACE FROM THE WAR HAMMER'S MAIN COMPUTERS, VT-211?
OF COURSE. SHOULD WE PROCEED TO THOSE COORDINATES?
NO...
...THEY SEE AN UNEXPLAINED SHIP AND THEY'LL OPEN FIRE, OR SCATTER -- AND THE SITH WILL GOBBLE THEM UP. WE'LL STAY JUST OVER THEIR HORIZON. FIND ME A FARM OR SOMETHING, VEETEE.

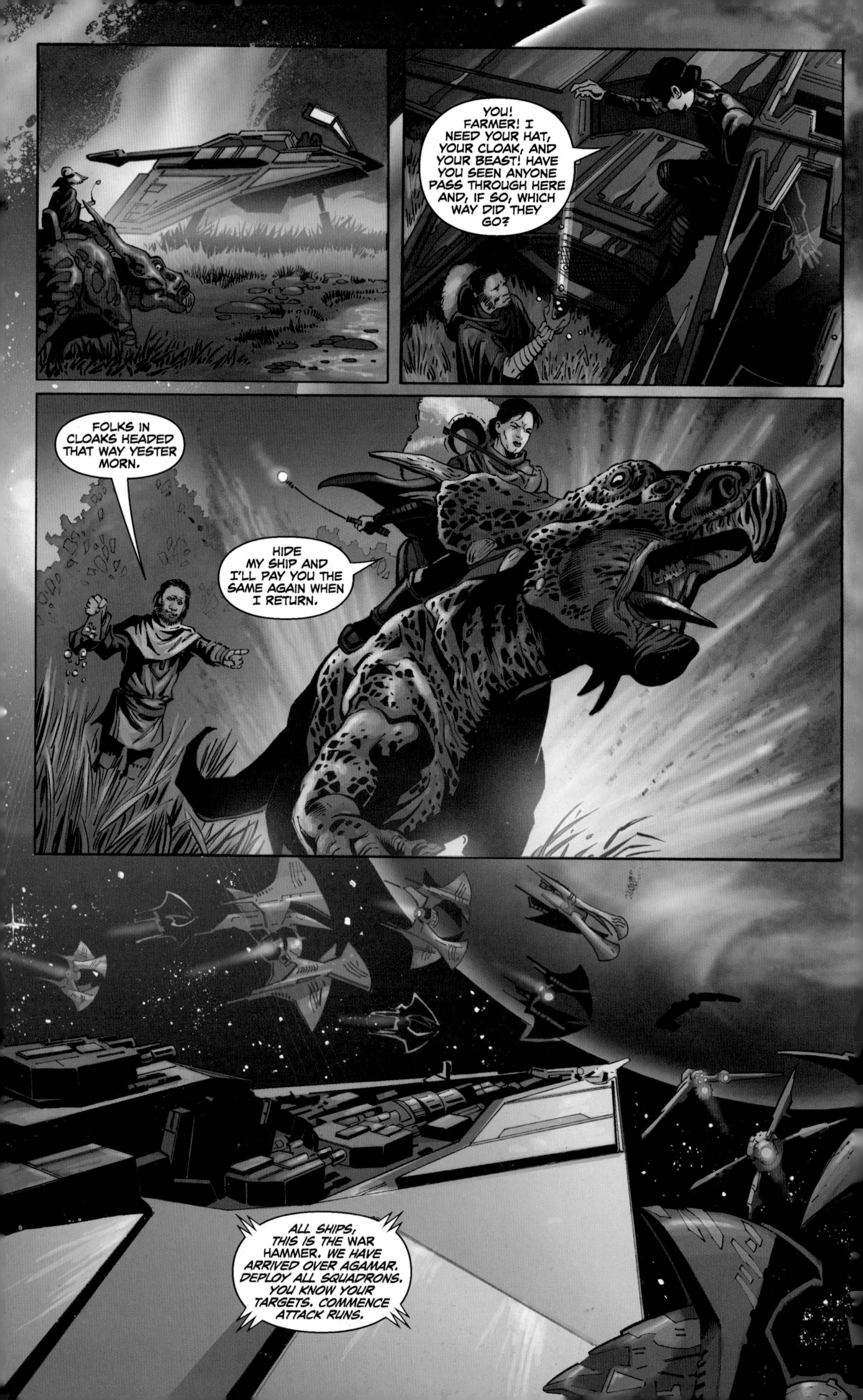
YOU! FARMER! I NEED YOUR HAT, YOUR CLOAK, AND YOUR BEAST! HAVE YOU SEEN ANYONE PASS THROUGH HERE AND, IF SO, WHICH WAY DID THEY GO?
FOLKS IN CLOAKS HEADED THAT WAY YESTER MORN.
HIDE MY SHIP AND I'LL PAY YOU THE SAME AGAIN WHEN I RETURN.
ALL SHIPS, THIS IS THE WAR HAMMER. WE HAVE ARRIVED OVER AGAMAR. DEPLOY ALL SQUADRONS. YOU KNOW YOUR TARGETS. COMMENCE ATTACK RUNS.

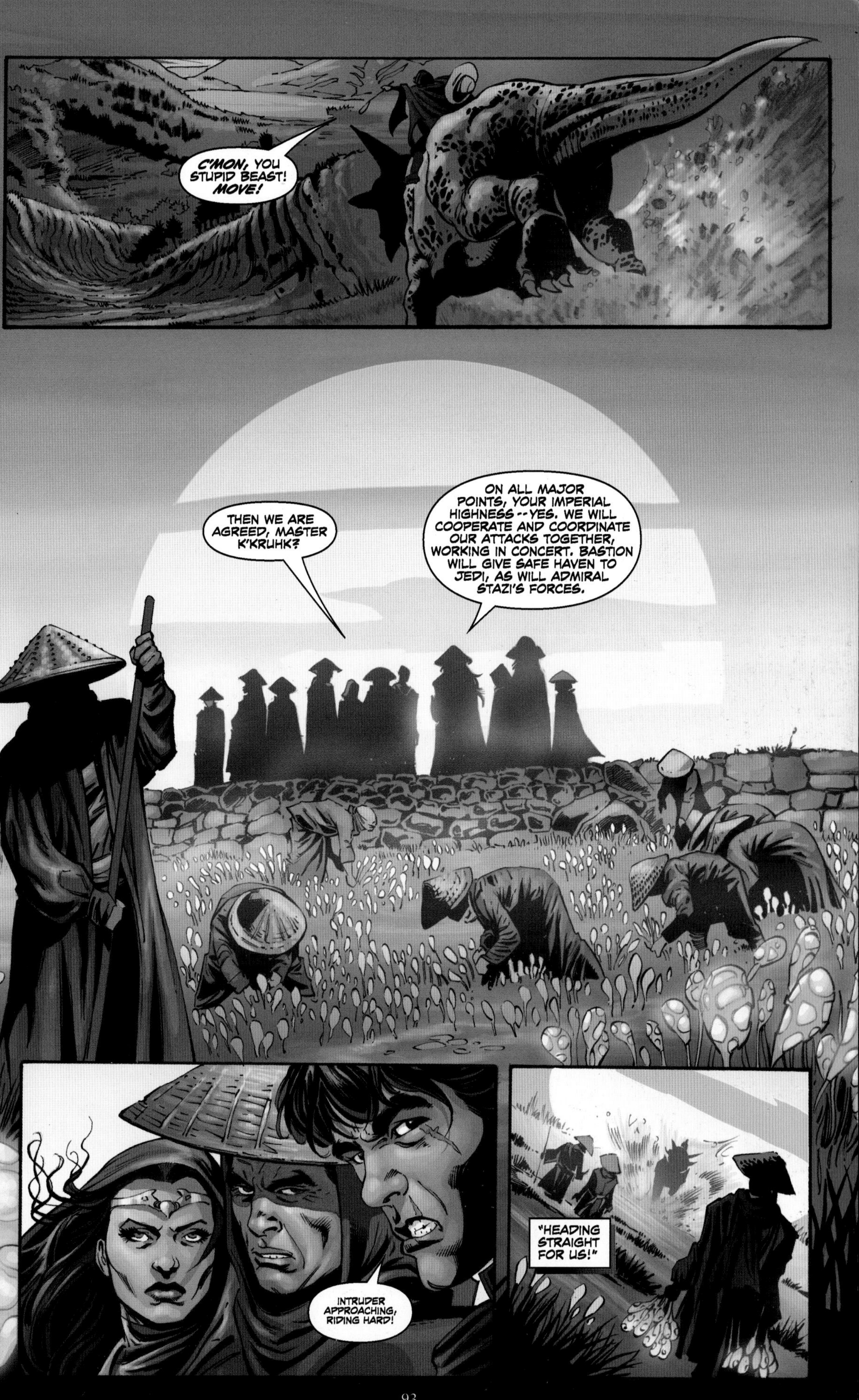
C'MON, YOU STUPID BEAST! MOVE!
THEN WE ARE AGREED, MASTER K'KRUHK?
ON ALL MAJOR POINTS, YOUR IMPERIAL HIGHNESS--YES. WE WILL COOPERATE AND COORDINATE OUR ATTACKS TOGETHER, WORKING IN CONCERT. BASTION WILL GIVE SAFE HAVEN TO JEDI, AS WILL ADMIRAL STAZI'S FORCES.
INTRUDER APPROACHING, RIDING HARD!
"HEADING STRAIGHT FOR US!"

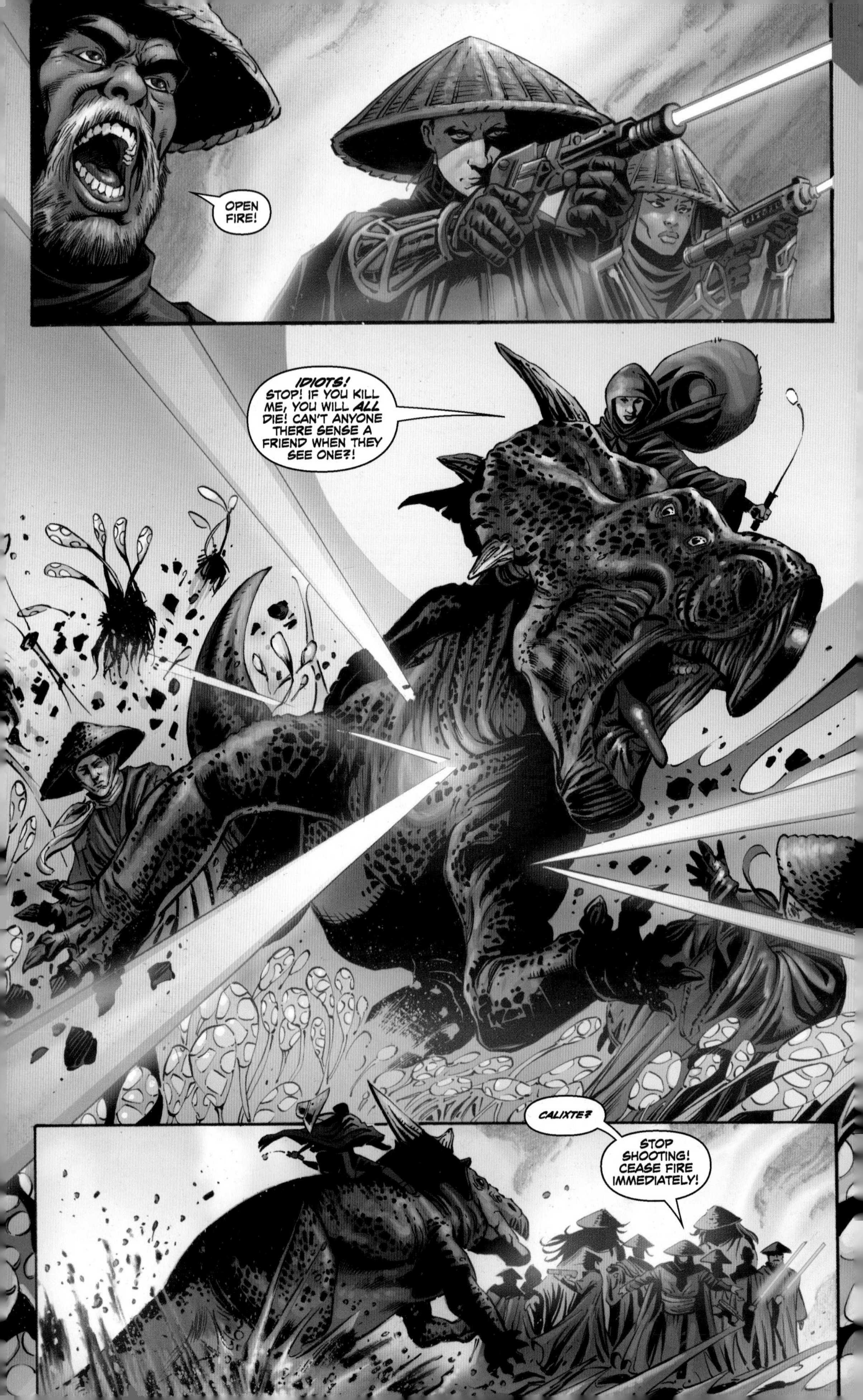
OPEN FIRE!
IDIOTS! STOP! IF YOU KILL ME, YOU WILL ALL DIE! CAN'T ANYONE THERE SENSE A FRIEND WHEN THEY SEE ONE?!
CALIXTE?
STOP SHOOTING! CEASE FIRE IMMEDIATELY!

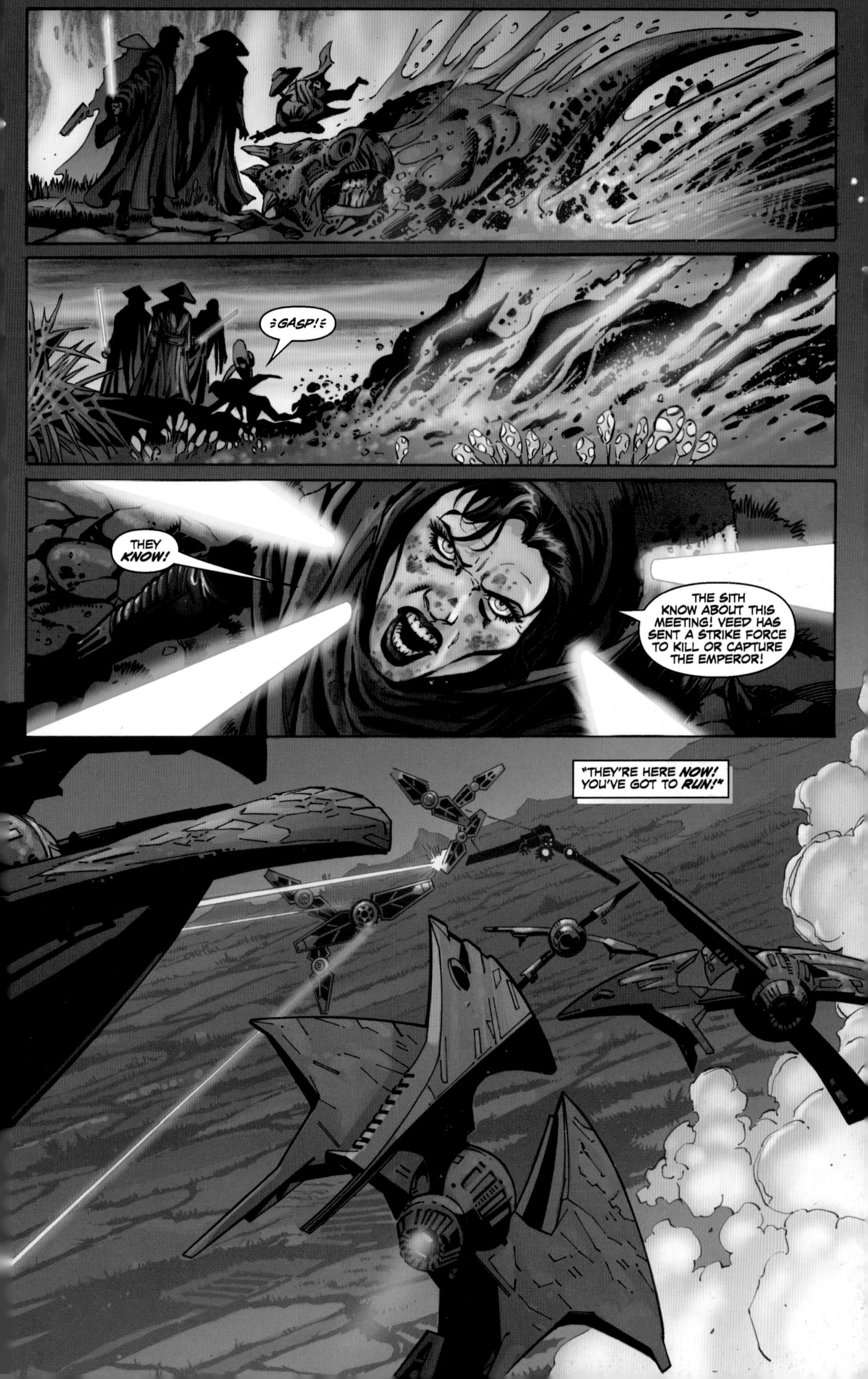

GASP!
THEY KNOW!
THE SITH KNOW ABOUT THIS MEETING! VEED HAS SENT A STRIKE FORCE TO KILL OR CAPTURE THE EMPEROR!
"THEY'RE HERE NOW! YOU'VE GOT TO RUN!"

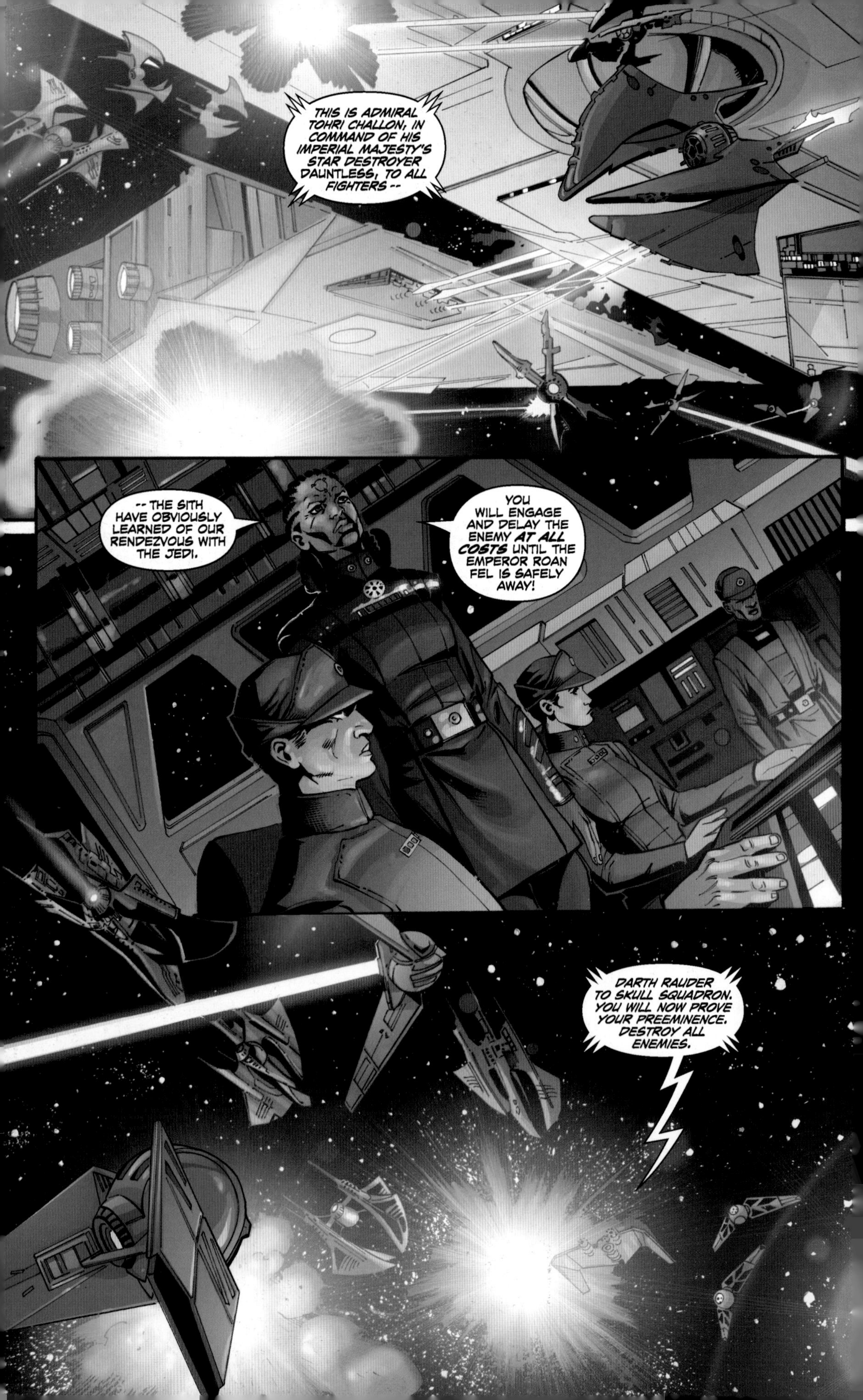
THIS IS ADMIRAL TOHRI CHALLON, IN COMMAND OF HIS IMPERIAL MAJESTY'S STAR DESTROYER DAUNTLESS, TO ALL FIGHTERS --
-- THE SITH HAVE OBVIOUSLY LEARNED OF OUR RENDEZVOUS WITH THE JEDI.
YOU WILL ENGAGE AND DELAY THE ENEMY AT ALL COSTS UNTIL THE EMPEROR ROAN FEL IS SAFELY AWAY!
DARTH RAUDER TO SKULL SQUADRON. YOU WILL NOW PROVE YOUR PREEMINENCE. DESTROY ALL ENEMIES.

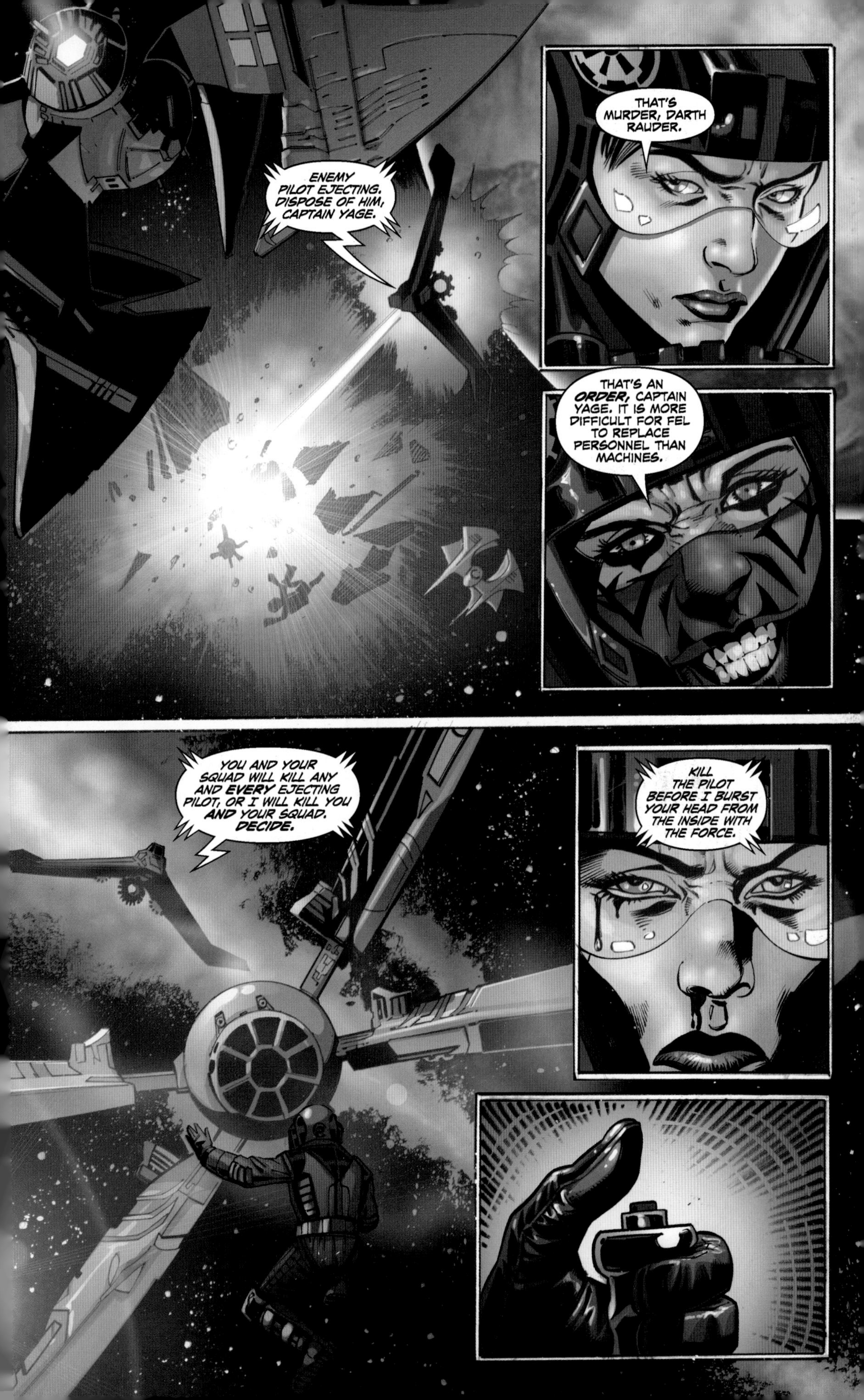
ENEMY PILOT EJECTING. DISPOSE OF HIM, CAPTAIN YAGE.
THAT'S MURDER, DARTH RAUDER.
THAT'S AN ORDER, CAPTAIN YAGE. IT IS MORE DIFFICULT FOR FEL TO REPLACE PERSONNEL THAN MACHINES.
YOU AND YOUR SQUAD WILL KILL ANY AND EVERY EJECTING PILOT, OR I WILL KILL YOU AND YOUR SQUAD. DECIDE.
KILL THE PILOT BEFORE I BURST YOUR HEAD FROM THE INSIDE WITH THE FORCE.

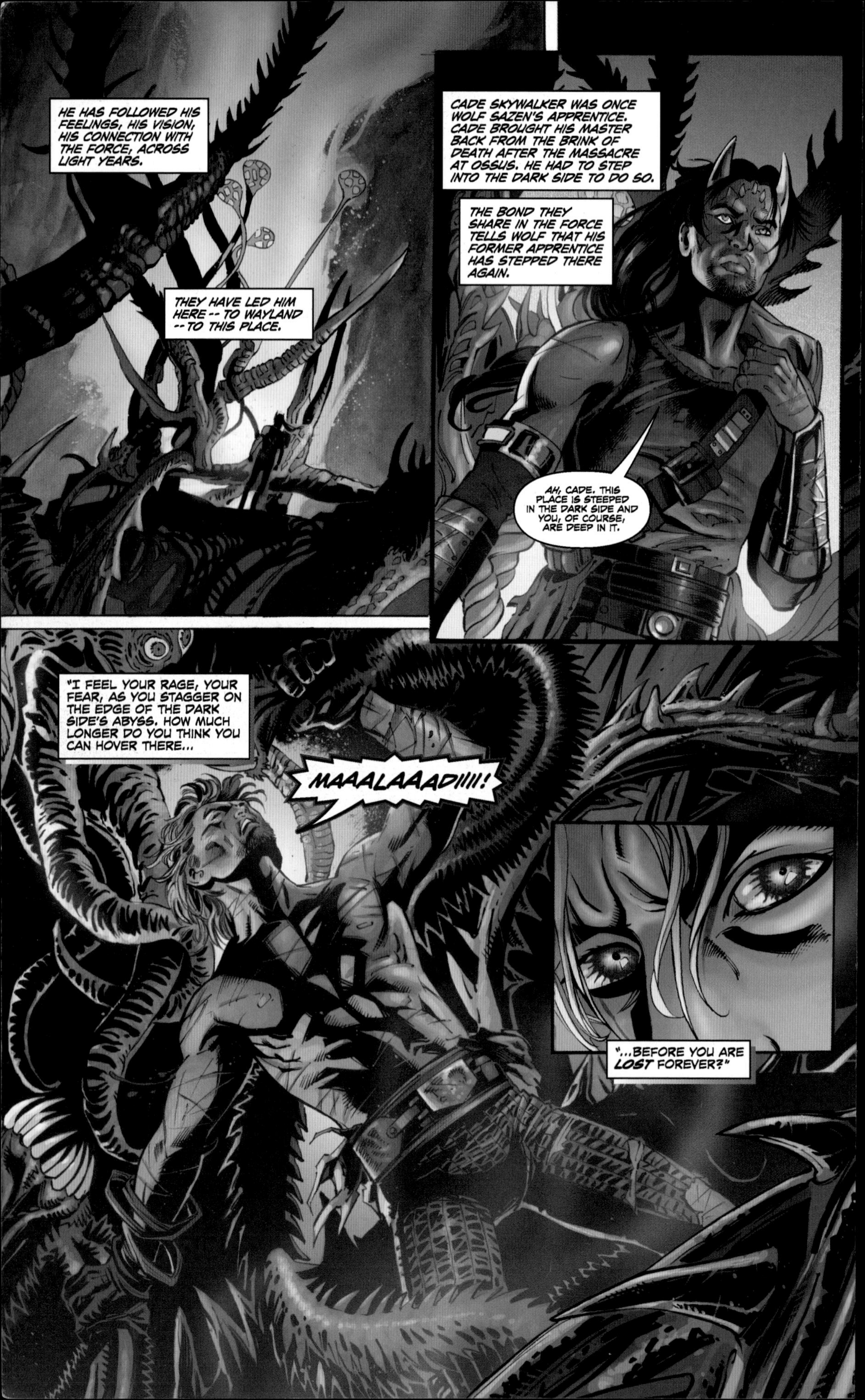
HE HAS FOLLOWED HIS FEELINGS, HIS VISION, HIS CONNECTION WITH THE FORCE, ACROSS LIGHT YEARS.
THEY HAVE LED HIM HERE -- TO WAYLAND -- TO THIS PLACE.
CADE SKYWALKER WAS ONCE WOLF SAZEN'S APPRENTICE. CADE BROUGHT HIS MASTER BACK FROM THE BRINK OF DEATH AFTER THE MASSACRE AT OSSUS. HE HAD TO STEP INTO THE DARK SIDE TO DO SO.
THE BOND THEY SHARE IN THE FORCE TELLS WOLF THAT HIS FORMER APPRENTICE HAS STEPPED THERE AGAIN.
AH, CADE. THIS PLACE IS STEEPED IN THE DARK SIDE AND YOU, OF COURSE, ARE DEEP IN IT.
"I FEEL YOUR RAGE, YOUR FEAR, AS YOU STAGGER ON THE EDGE OF THE DARK SIDE'S ABYSS. HOW MUCH LONGER DO YOU THINK YOU CAN HOVER THERE...
MAAALAAADIIII!
"...BEFORE YOU ARE LOST FOREVER?"

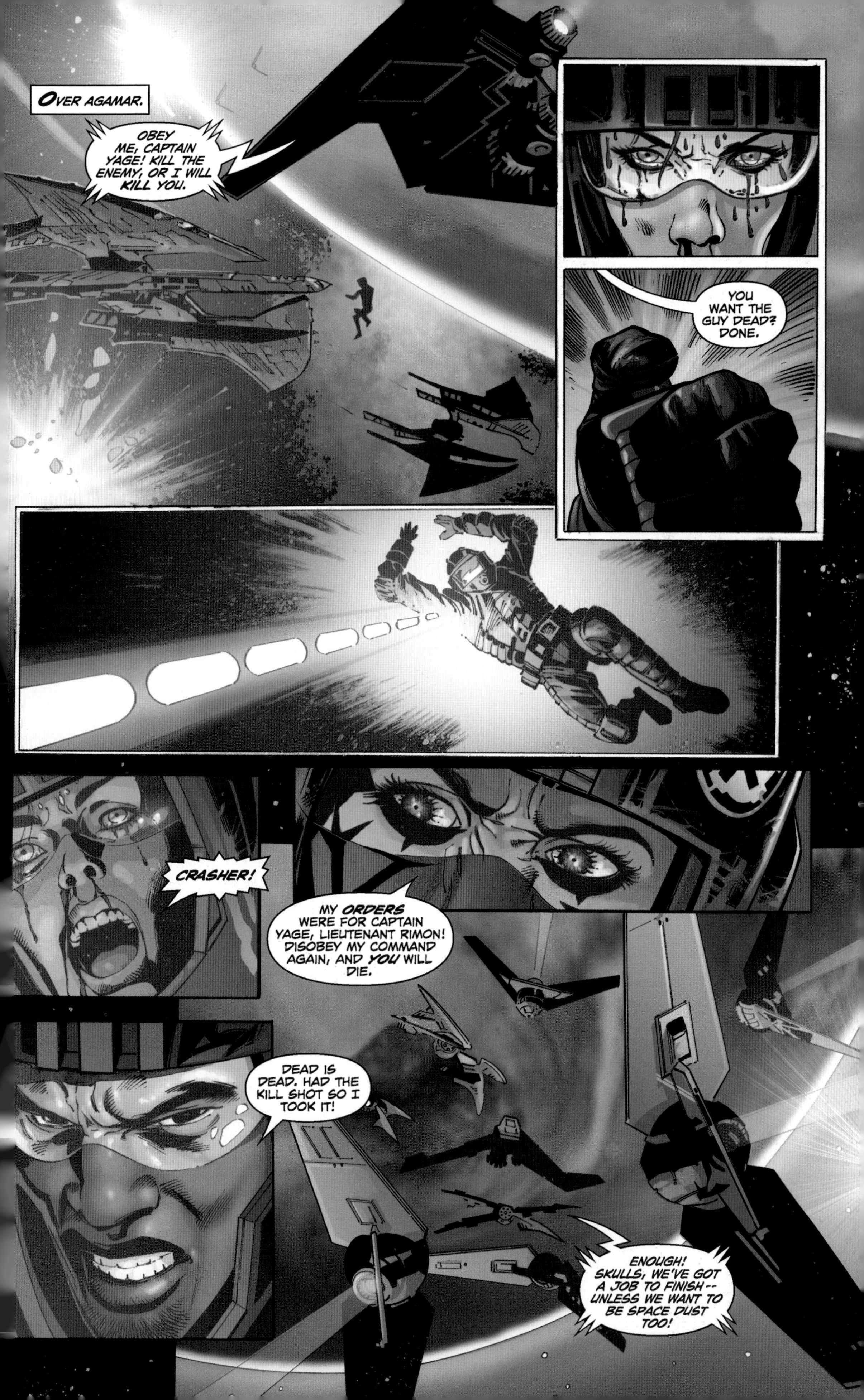
OVER AGAMAR.
OBEY ME, CAPTAIN YAGE! KILL THE ENEMY, OR I WILL KILL YOU.
YOU WANT THE GUY DEAD? DONE.
CRASHER!
MY ORDERS WERE FOR CAPTAIN YAGE, LIEUTENANT RIMON! DISOBEY MY COMMAND AGAIN, AND YOU WILL DIE.
DEAD IS DEAD. HAD THE KILL SHOT SO I TOOK IT!
ENOUGH! SKULLS, WE'VE GOT A JOB TO FINISH-- UNLESS WE WANT TO BE SPACE DUST TOO!

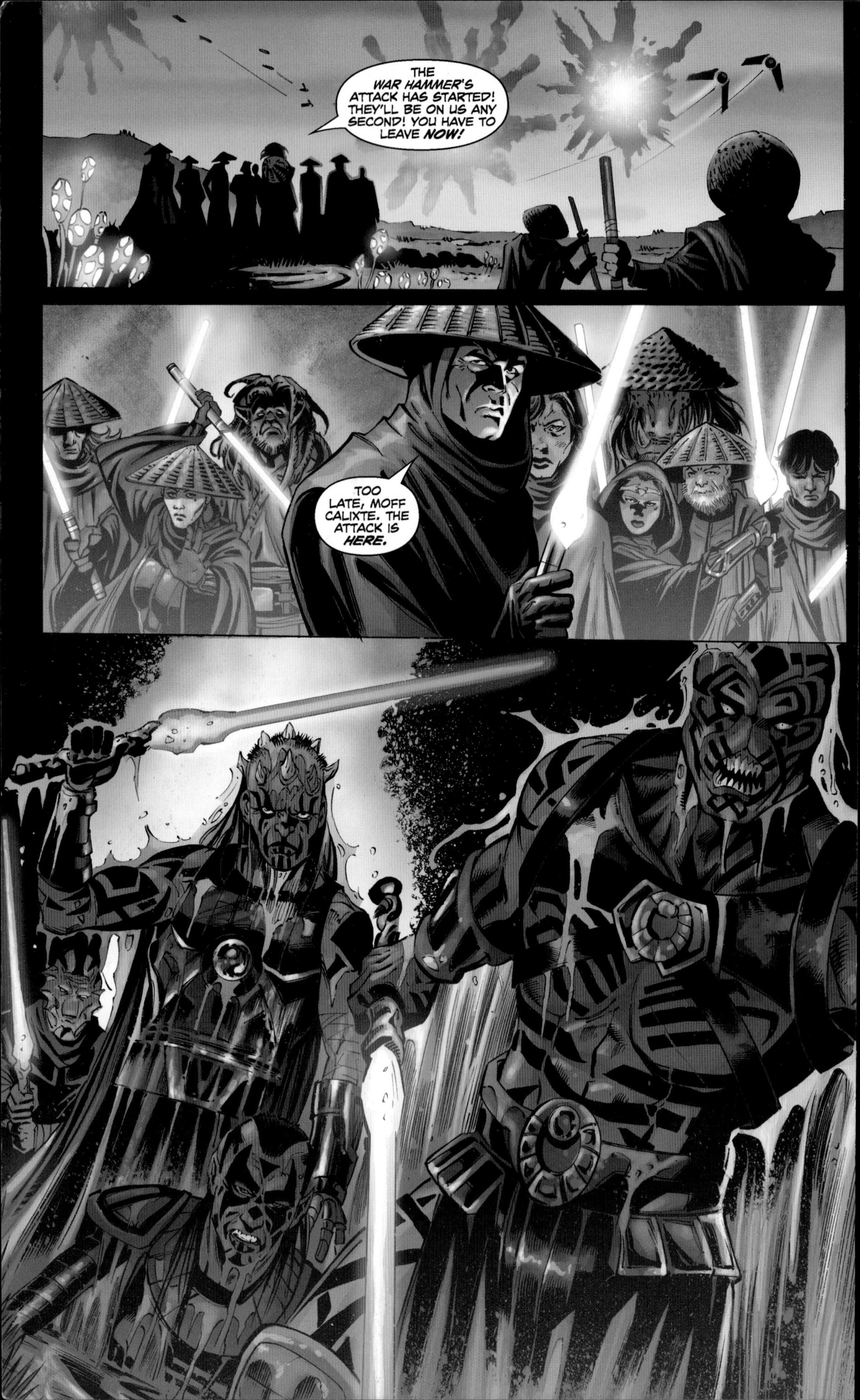
THE *WAR HAMMER'S* ATTACK HAS STARTED! THEY'LL BE ON US ANY SECOND! YOU HAVE TO LEAVE ***NOW!***
TOO LATE, MOFF CALIXTE. THE ATTACK IS ***HERE.***

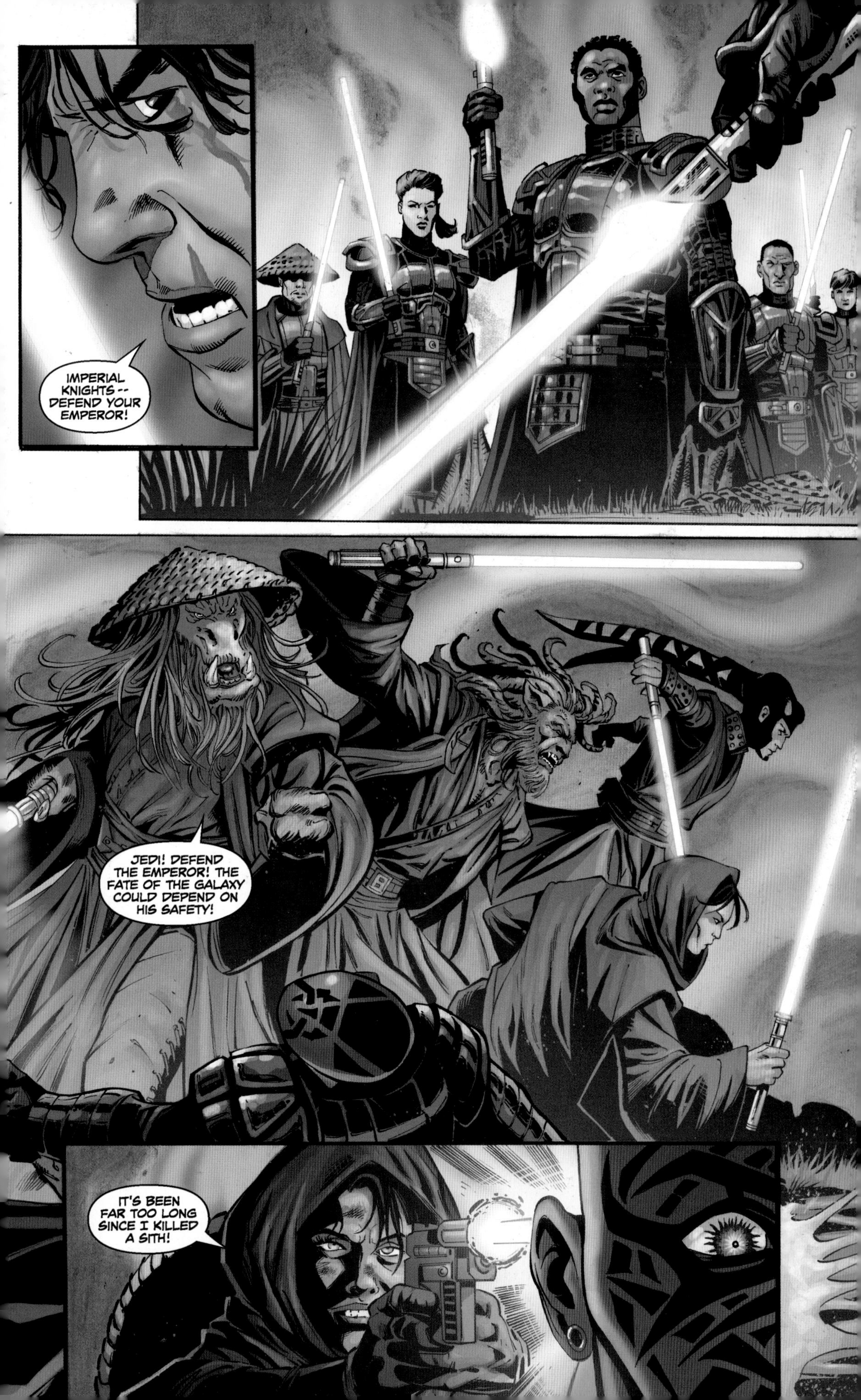
IMPERIAL KNIGHTS -- DEFEND YOUR EMPEROR!
JEDI! DEFEND THE EMPEROR! THE FATE OF THE GALAXY COULD DEPEND ON HIS SAFETY!
IT'S BEEN FAR TOO LONG SINCE I KILLED A SITH!

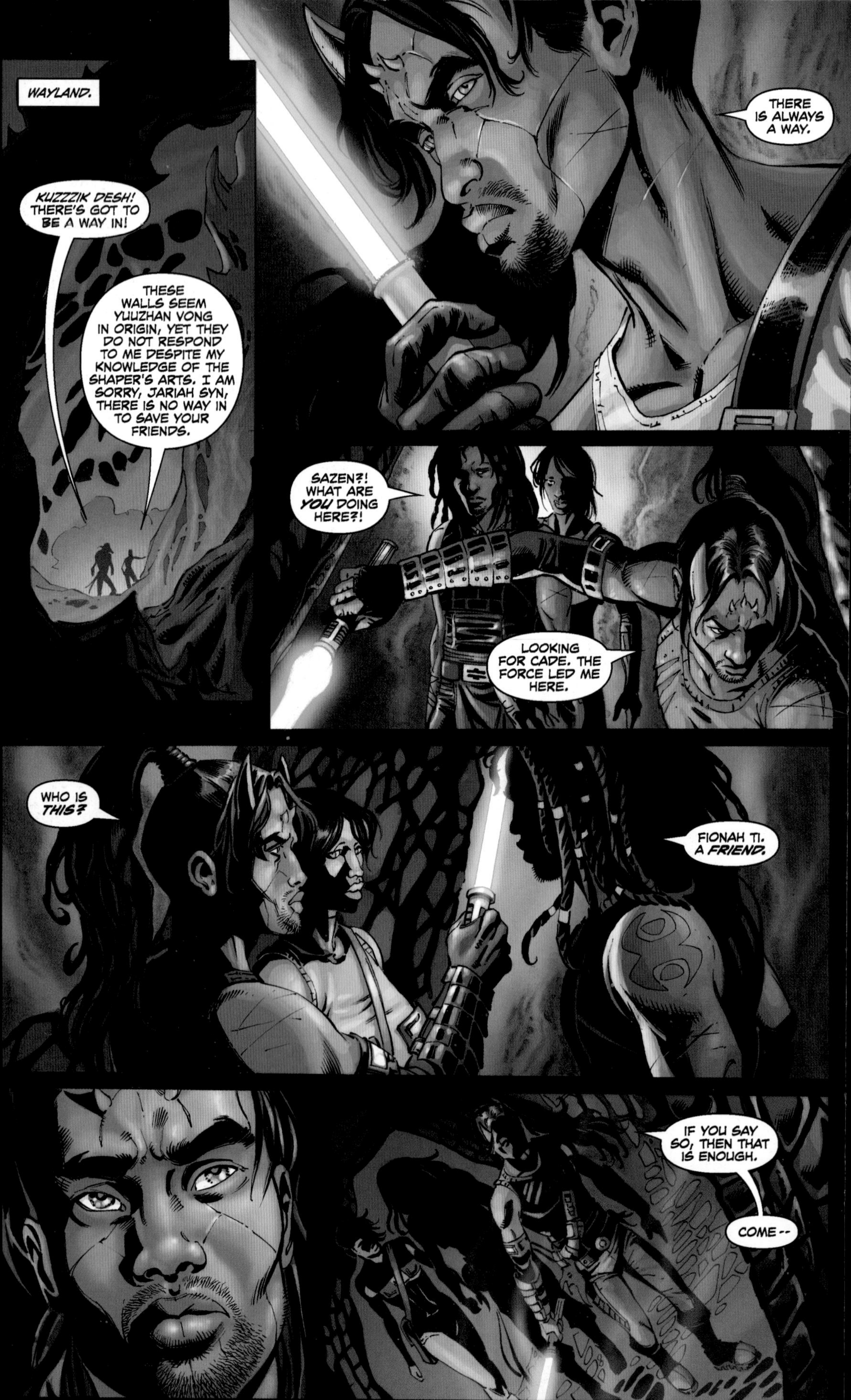

WAYLAND.
KUZZZIK DESH! THERE'S GOT TO BE A WAY IN!
THESE WALLS SEEM YUUZHAN VONG IN ORIGIN, YET THEY DO NOT RESPOND TO ME DESPITE MY KNOWLEDGE OF THE SHAPER'S ARTS. I AM SORRY, JARIAH SYN, THERE IS NO WAY IN TO SAVE YOUR FRIENDS.
THERE IS ALWAYS A WAY.
SAZEN?! WHAT ARE YOU DOING HERE?!
LOOKING FOR CADE. THE FORCE LED ME HERE.
WHO IS THIS?
FIONAH TI. A FRIEND.
IF YOU SAY SO, THEN THAT IS ENOUGH.
COME --

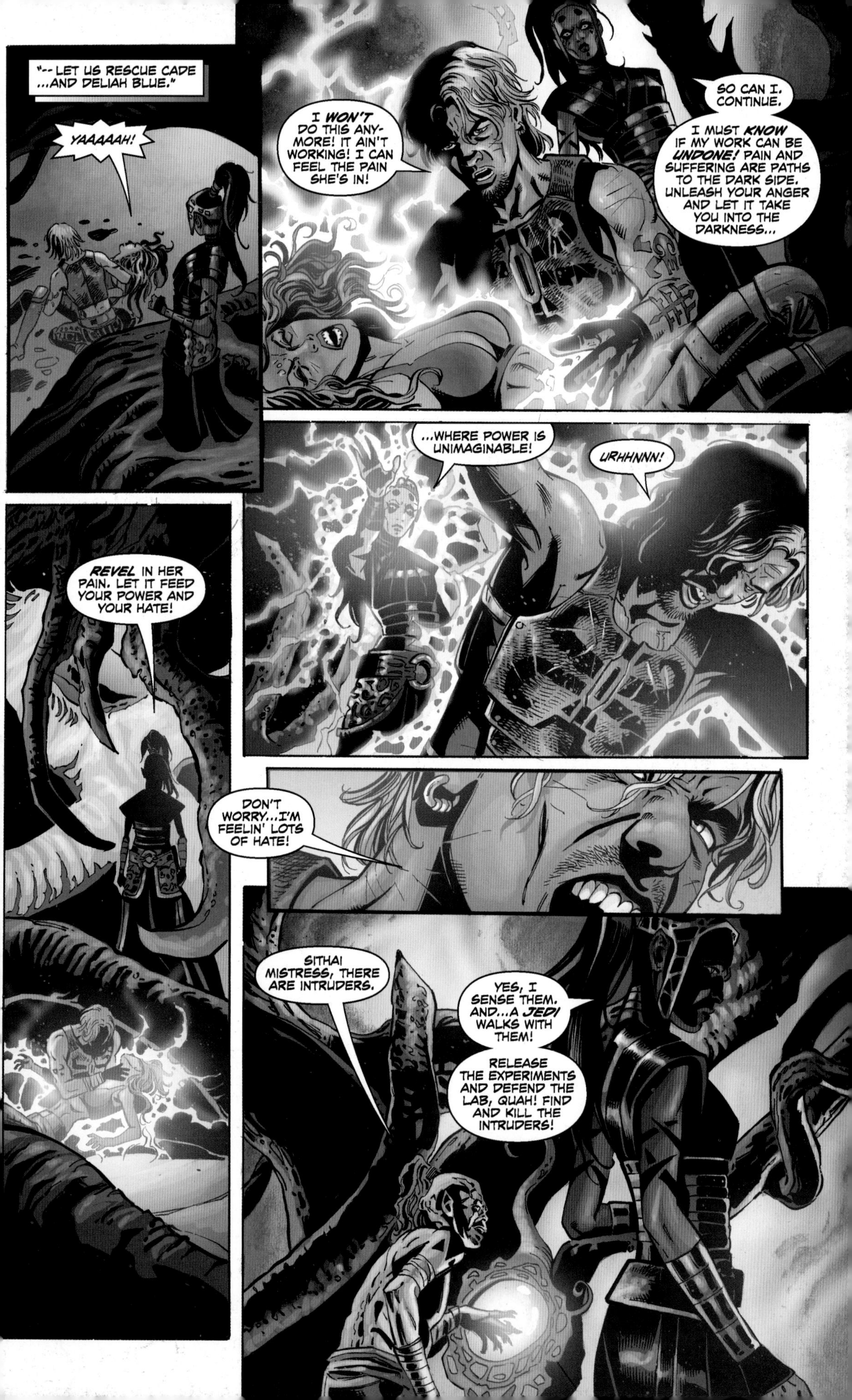
"-- LET US RESCUE CADE ...AND DELIAH BLUE."
YAAAAAH!
I WON'T DO THIS ANYMORE! IT AIN'T WORKING! I CAN FEEL THE PAIN SHE'S IN!
SO CAN I. CONTINUE.
I MUST KNOW IF MY WORK CAN BE UNDONE! PAIN AND SUFFERING ARE PATHS TO THE DARK SIDE. UNLEASH YOUR ANGER AND LET IT TAKE YOU INTO THE DARKNESS...
...WHERE POWER IS UNIMAGINABLE!
URHHNNN!
REVEL IN HER PAIN. LET IT FEED YOUR POWER AND YOUR HATE!
DON'T WORRY...I'M FEELIN' LOTS OF HATE!
SITHAI MISTRESS, THERE ARE INTRUDERS.
YES, I SENSE THEM. AND...A JEDI WALKS WITH THEM!
RELEASE THE EXPERIMENTS AND DEFEND THE LAB, QUAH! FIND AND KILL THE INTRUDERS!

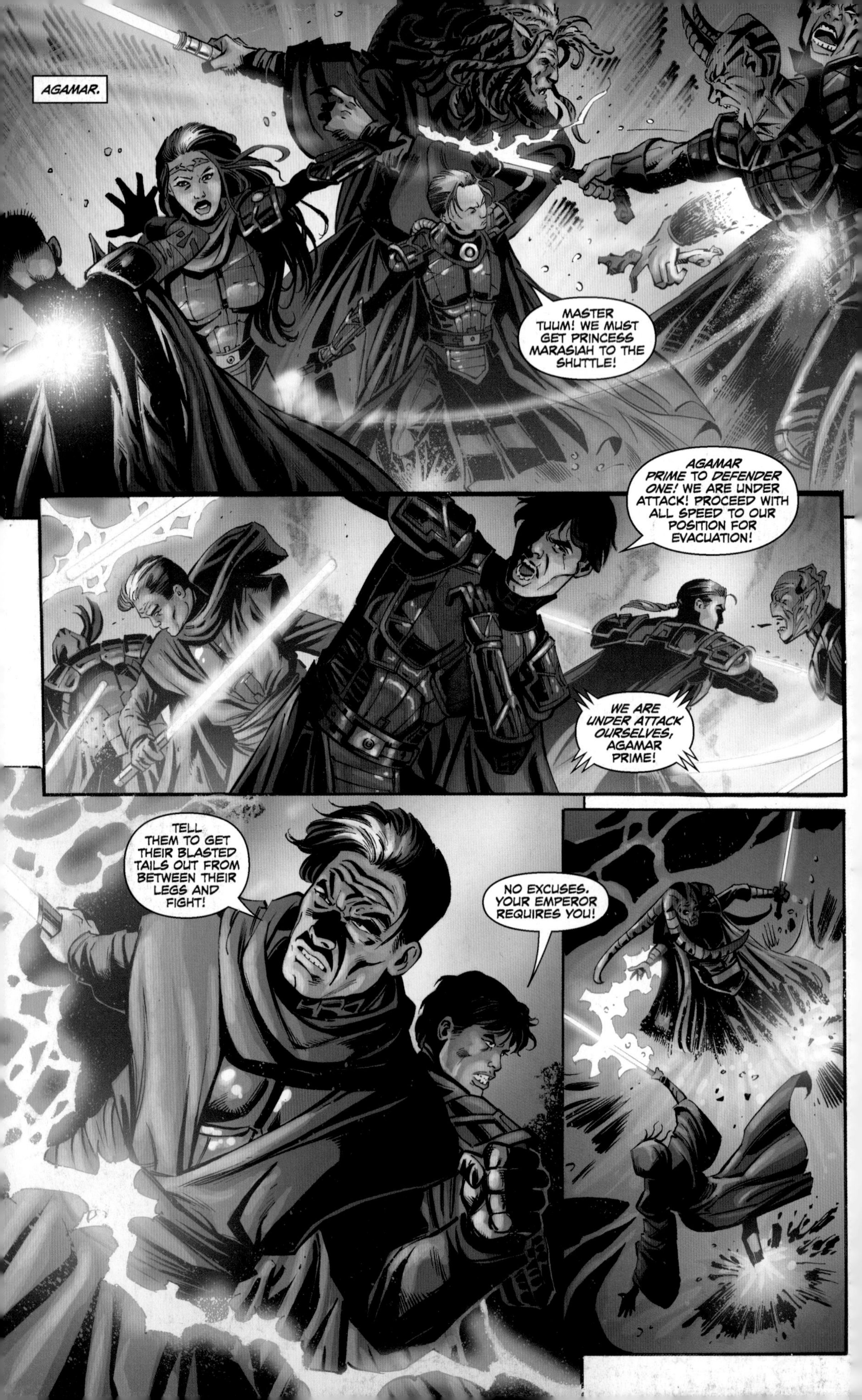
AGAMAR.
MASTER TUUM! WE MUST GET PRINCESS MARASIAH TO THE SHUTTLE!
AGAMAR PRIME TO DEFENDER ONE! WE ARE UNDER ATTACK! PROCEED WITH ALL SPEED TO OUR POSITION FOR EVACUATION!
WE ARE UNDER ATTACK OURSELVES, AGAMAR PRIME!
TELL THEM TO GET THEIR BLASTED TAILS OUT FROM BETWEEN THEIR LEGS AND FIGHT!
NO EXCUSES. YOUR EMPEROR REQUIRES YOU!

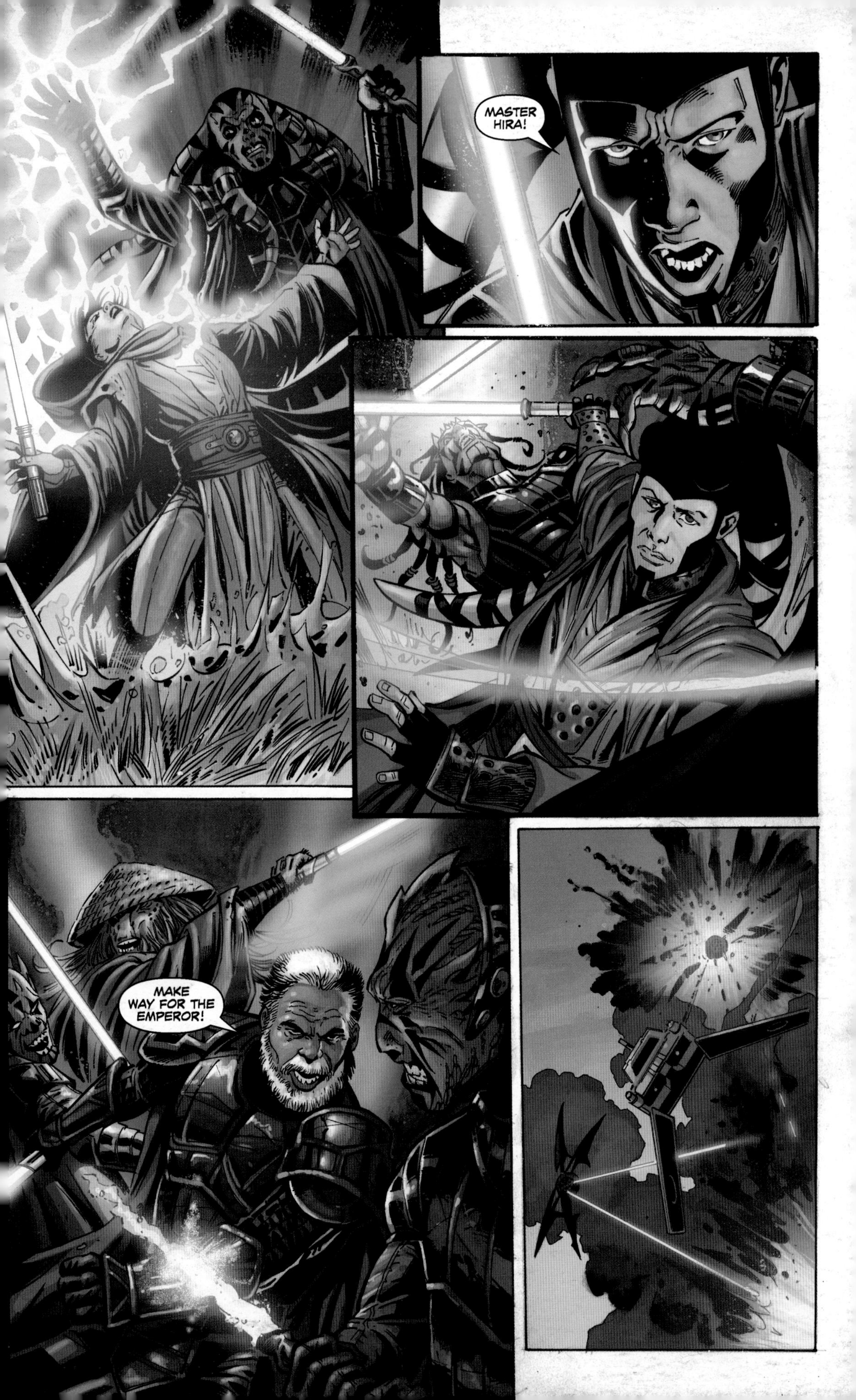
MASTER HIRA!
MAKE WAY FOR THE EMPEROR!

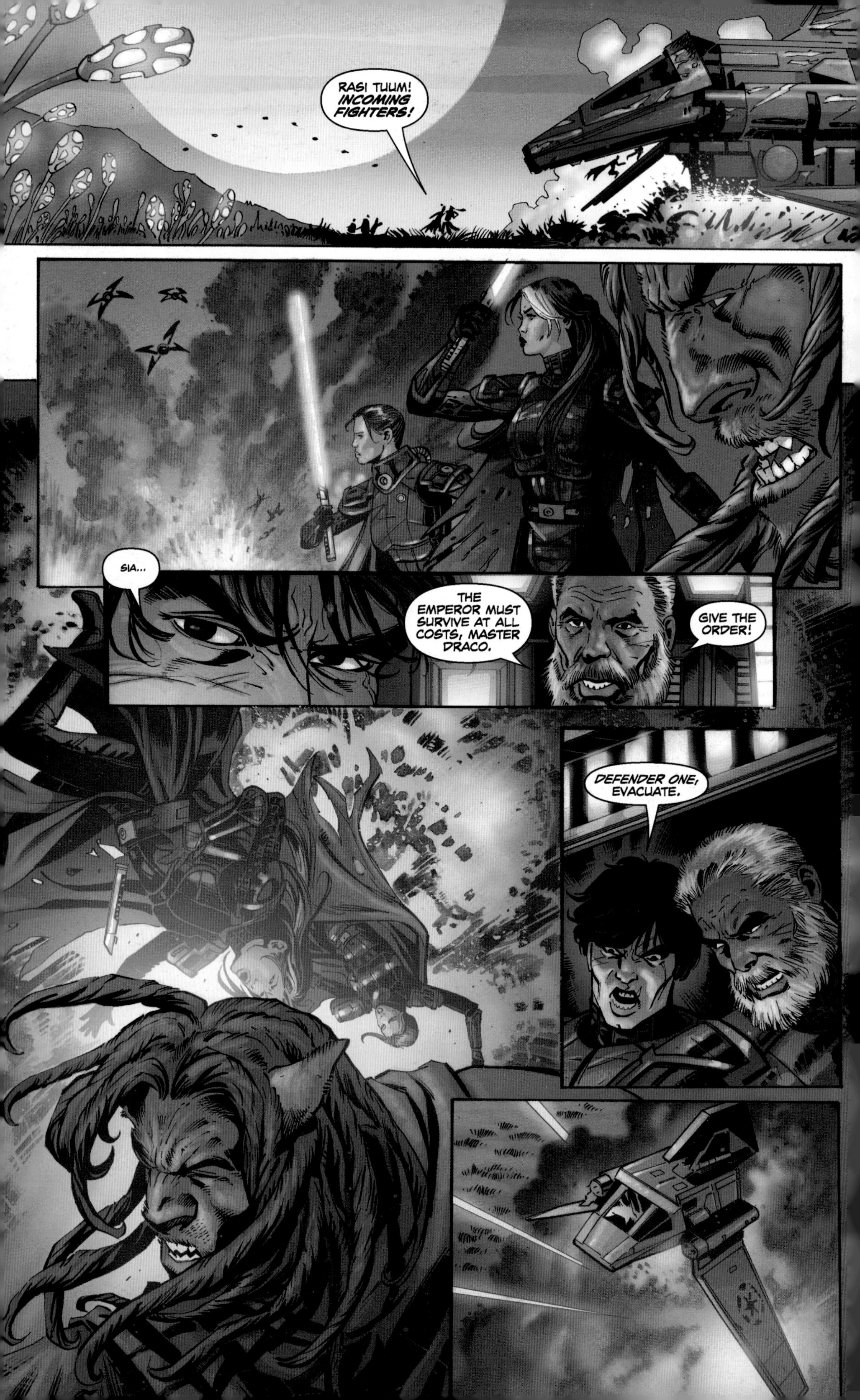
RASI TUUM! INCOMING FIGHTERS!
SIA...
THE EMPEROR MUST SURVIVE AT ALL COSTS, MASTER DRACO.
GIVE THE ORDER!
DEFENDER ONE, EVACUATE.

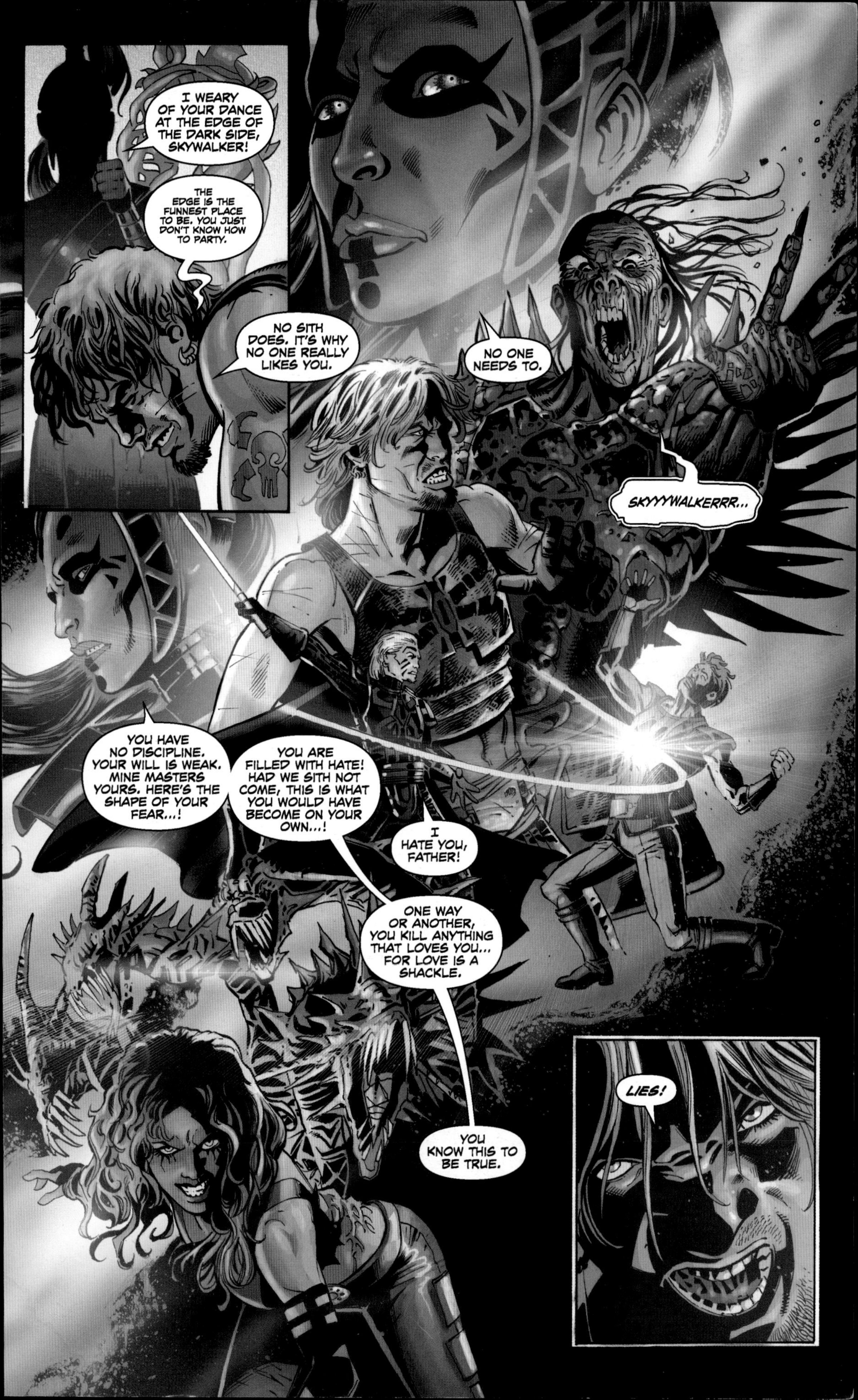
I WEARY OF YOUR DANCE AT THE EDGE OF THE DARK SIDE, SKYWALKER!
THE EDGE IS THE FUNNEST PLACE TO BE. YOU JUST DON'T KNOW HOW TO PARTY.
NO SITH DOES. IT'S WHY NO ONE REALLY LIKES YOU.
NO ONE NEEDS TO.
SKYYYWALKERRR...
YOU HAVE NO DISCIPLINE. YOUR WILL IS WEAK. MINE MASTERS YOURS. HERE'S THE SHAPE OF YOUR FEAR...!
YOU ARE FILLED WITH HATE! HAD WE SITH NOT COME, THIS IS WHAT YOU WOULD HAVE BECOME ON YOUR OWN...!
I HATE YOU, FATHER!
ONE WAY OR ANOTHER, YOU KILL ANYTHING THAT LOVES YOU... FOR LOVE IS A SHACKLE.
YOU KNOW THIS TO BE TRUE.
LIES!

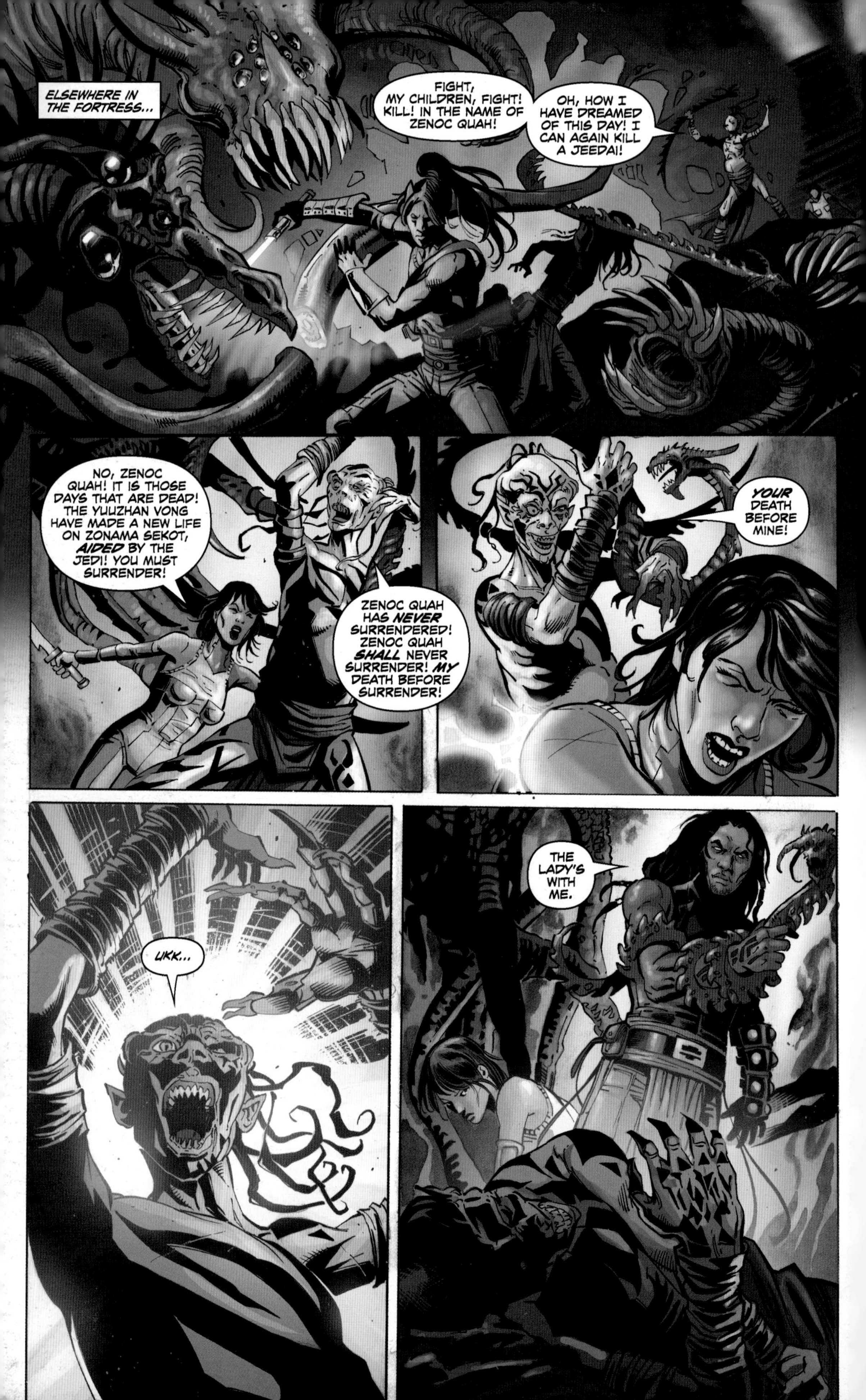
ELSEWHERE IN THE FORTRESS...
FIGHT, MY CHILDREN, FIGHT! KILL! IN THE NAME OF ZENOC QUAH!
OH, HOW I HAVE DREAMED OF THIS DAY! I CAN AGAIN KILL A JEEDAI!
NO, ZENOC QUAH! IT IS THOSE DAYS THAT ARE DEAD! THE YUUZHAN VONG HAVE MADE A NEW LIFE ON ZONAMA SEKOT, AIDED BY THE JEDI! YOU MUST SURRENDER!
ZENOC QUAH HAS NEVER SURRENDERED! ZENOC QUAH SHALL NEVER SURRENDER! MY DEATH BEFORE SURRENDER!
YOUR DEATH BEFORE MINE!
UKK...
THE LADY'S WITH ME.

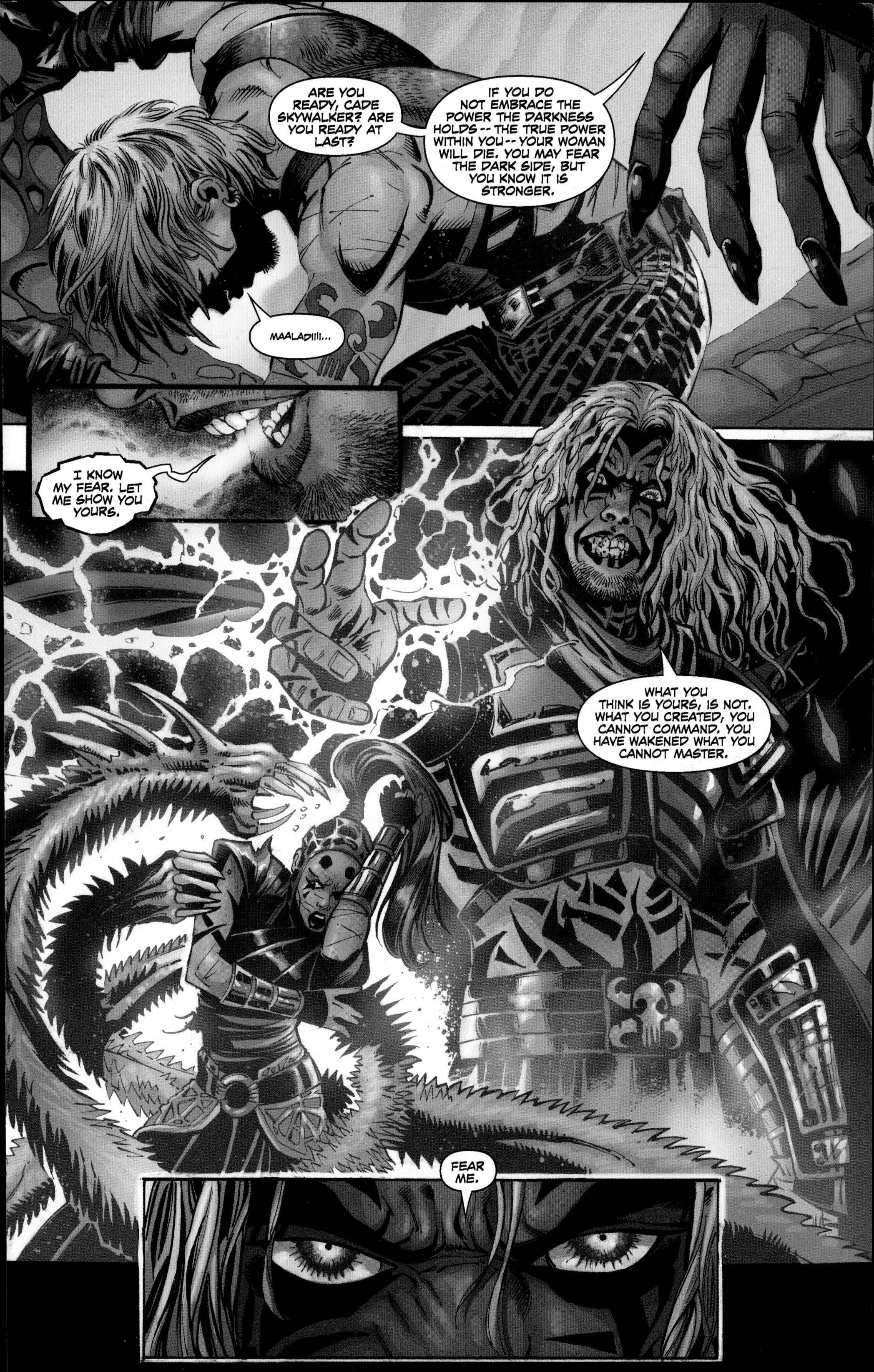
ARE YOU READY, CADE SKYWALKER? ARE YOU READY AT LAST?
IF YOU DO NOT EMBRACE THE POWER THE DARKNESS HOLDS -- THE TRUE POWER WITHIN YOU -- YOUR WOMAN WILL DIE. YOU MAY FEAR THE DARK SIDE, BUT YOU KNOW IT IS STRONGER.
MAALADIIII...
I KNOW MY FEAR. LET ME SHOW YOU YOURS.
WHAT YOU THINK IS YOURS, IS NOT. WHAT YOU CREATED, YOU CANNOT COMMAND. YOU HAVE WAKENED WHAT YOU CANNOT MASTER.
FEAR ME.

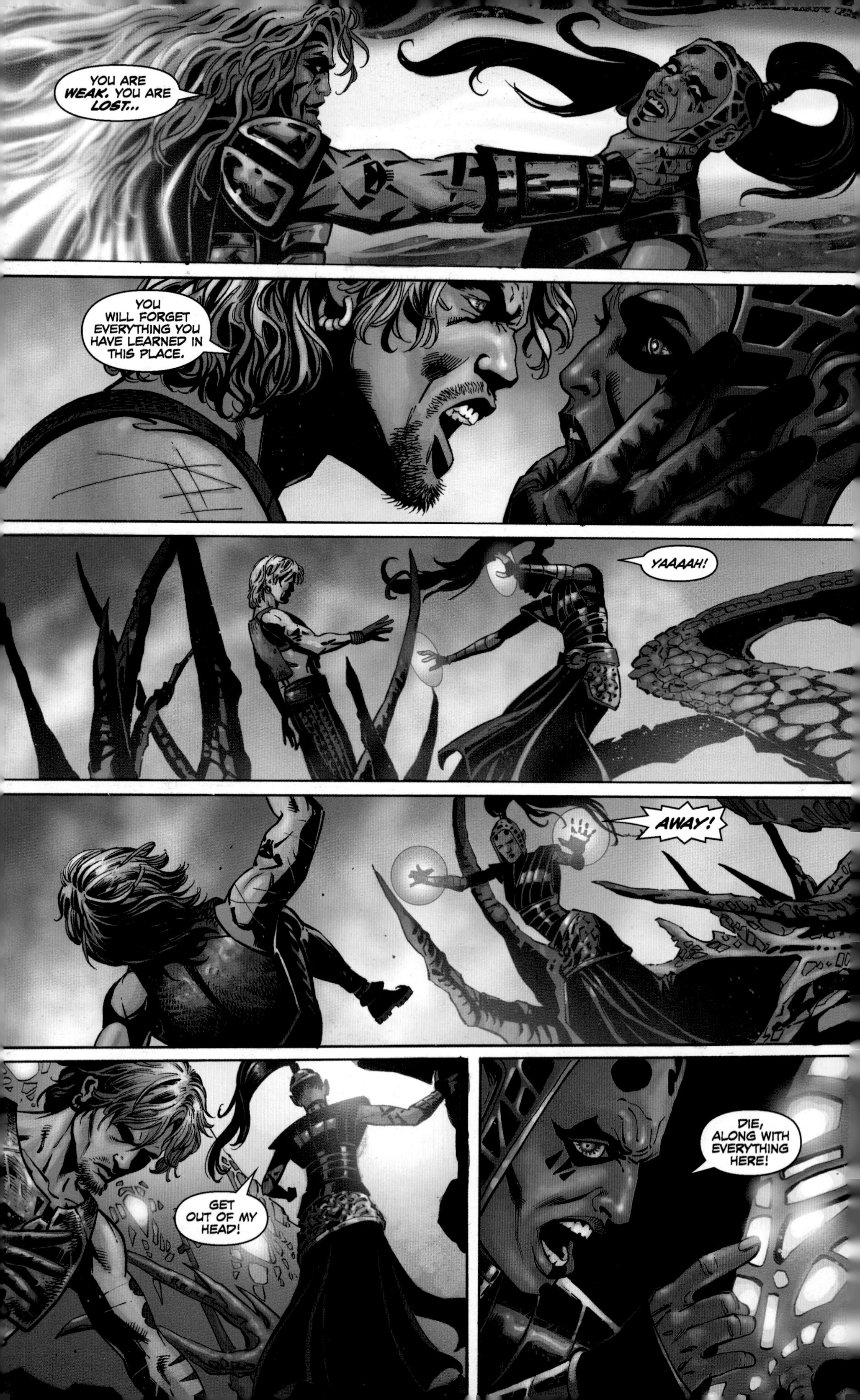
YOU ARE *WEAK.* YOU ARE *LOST...*
YOU WILL FORGET EVERYTHING YOU HAVE LEARNED IN THIS PLACE.
YAAAAH!
AWAY!
GET OUT OF MY HEAD!
DIE, ALONG WITH EVERYTHING HERE!

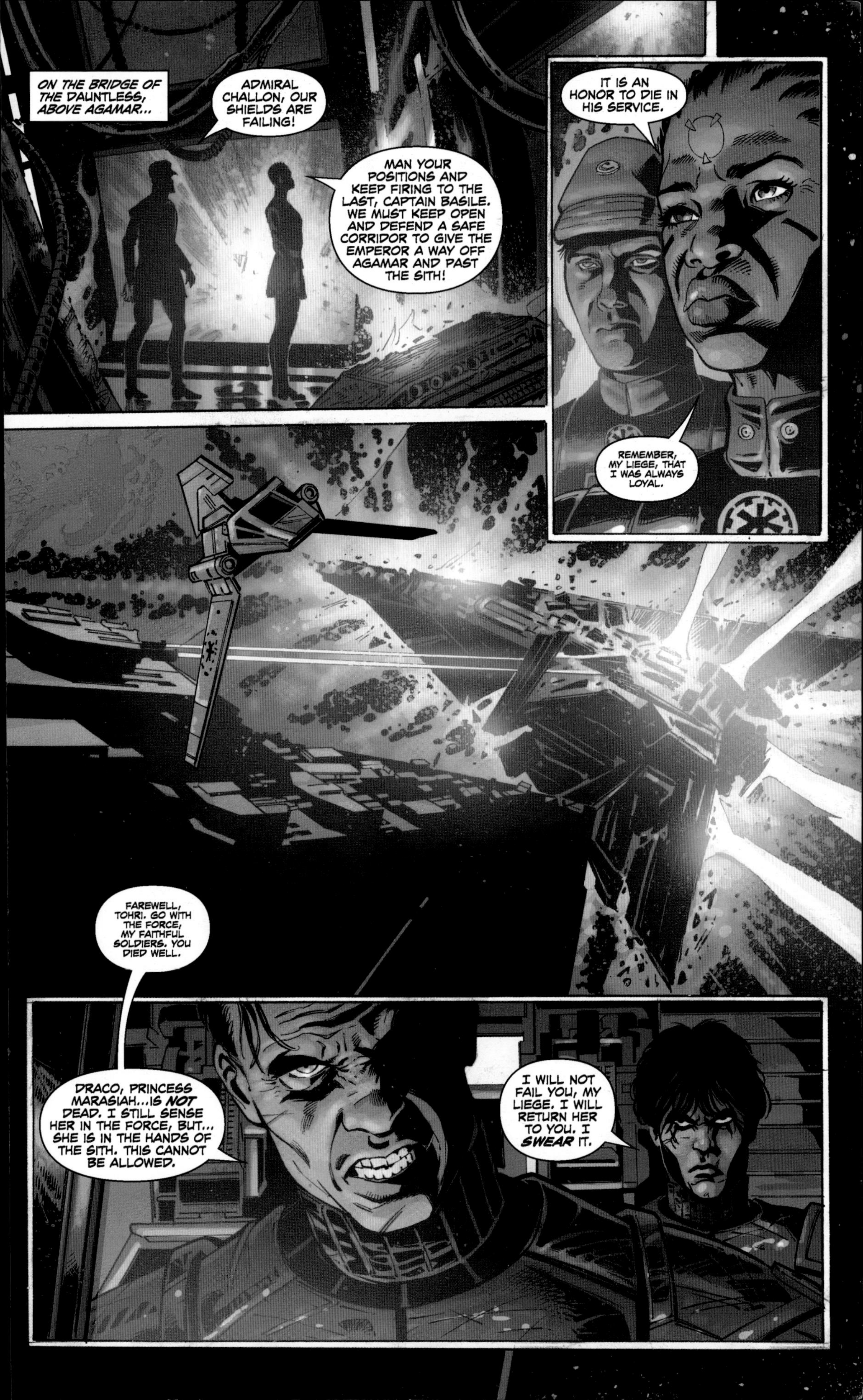
ON THE BRIDGE OF THE DAUNTLESS, ABOVE AGAMAR...
ADMIRAL CHALLON, OUR SHIELDS ARE FAILING!
MAN YOUR POSITIONS AND KEEP FIRING TO THE LAST, CAPTAIN BASILE. WE MUST KEEP OPEN AND DEFEND A SAFE CORRIDOR TO GIVE THE EMPEROR A WAY OFF AGAMAR AND PAST THE SITH!
IT IS AN HONOR TO DIE IN HIS SERVICE.
REMEMBER, MY LIEGE, THAT I WAS ALWAYS LOYAL.
FAREWELL, TOHRI. GO WITH THE FORCE, MY FAITHFUL SOLDIERS. YOU DIED WELL.
DRACO, PRINCESS MARASIAH...IS **NOT** DEAD. I STILL SENSE HER IN THE FORCE, BUT... SHE IS IN THE HANDS OF THE SITH. THIS CANNOT BE ALLOWED.
I WILL NOT FAIL YOU, MY LIEGE. I WILL RETURN HER TO YOU. I **SWEAR** IT.

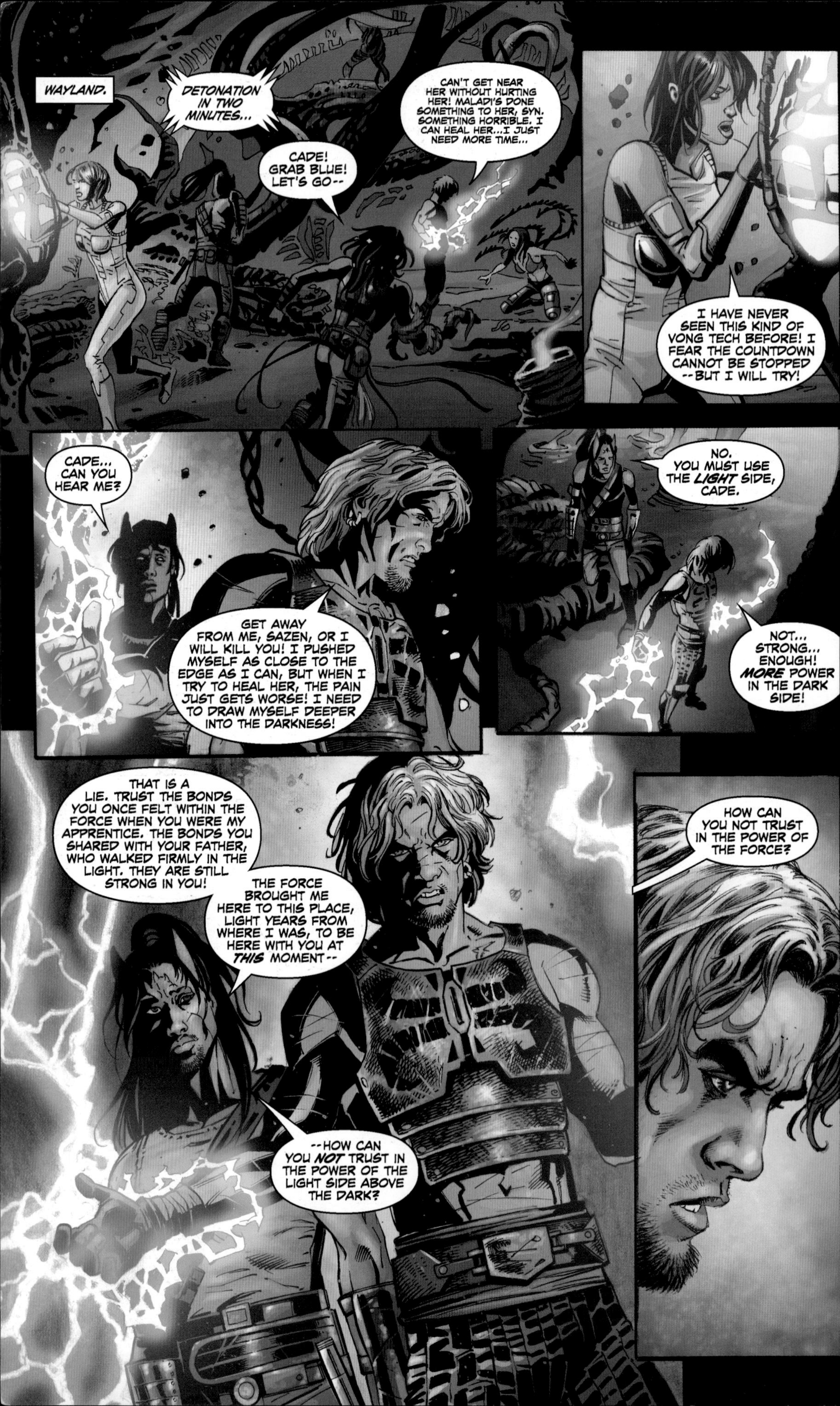

WAYLAND.
DETONATION IN TWO MINUTES...
CADE! GRAB BLUE! LET'S GO--
CAN'T GET NEAR HER WITHOUT HURTING HER! MALADI'S DONE SOMETHING TO HER, SYN. SOMETHING HORRIBLE. I CAN HEAL HER...I JUST NEED MORE TIME...
I HAVE NEVER SEEN THIS KIND OF VONG TECH BEFORE! I FEAR THE COUNTDOWN CANNOT BE STOPPED --BUT I WILL TRY!
CADE... CAN YOU HEAR ME?
GET AWAY FROM ME, SAZEN, OR I WILL KILL YOU! I PUSHED MYSELF AS CLOSE TO THE EDGE AS I CAN, BUT WHEN I TRY TO HEAL HER, THE PAIN JUST GETS WORSE! I NEED TO DRAW MYSELF DEEPER INTO THE DARKNESS!
NO. YOU MUST USE THE LIGHT SIDE, CADE.
NOT... STRONG... ENOUGH! MORE POWER IN THE DARK SIDE!
THAT IS A LIE. TRUST THE BONDS YOU ONCE FELT WITHIN THE FORCE WHEN YOU WERE MY APPRENTICE. THE BONDS YOU SHARED WITH YOUR FATHER, WHO WALKED FIRMLY IN THE LIGHT. THEY ARE STILL STRONG IN YOU!
THE FORCE BROUGHT ME HERE TO THIS PLACE, LIGHT YEARS FROM WHERE I WAS, TO BE HERE WITH YOU AT THIS MOMENT--
--HOW CAN YOU NOT TRUST IN THE POWER OF THE LIGHT SIDE ABOVE THE DARK?
HOW CAN YOU NOT TRUST IN THE POWER OF THE FORCE?

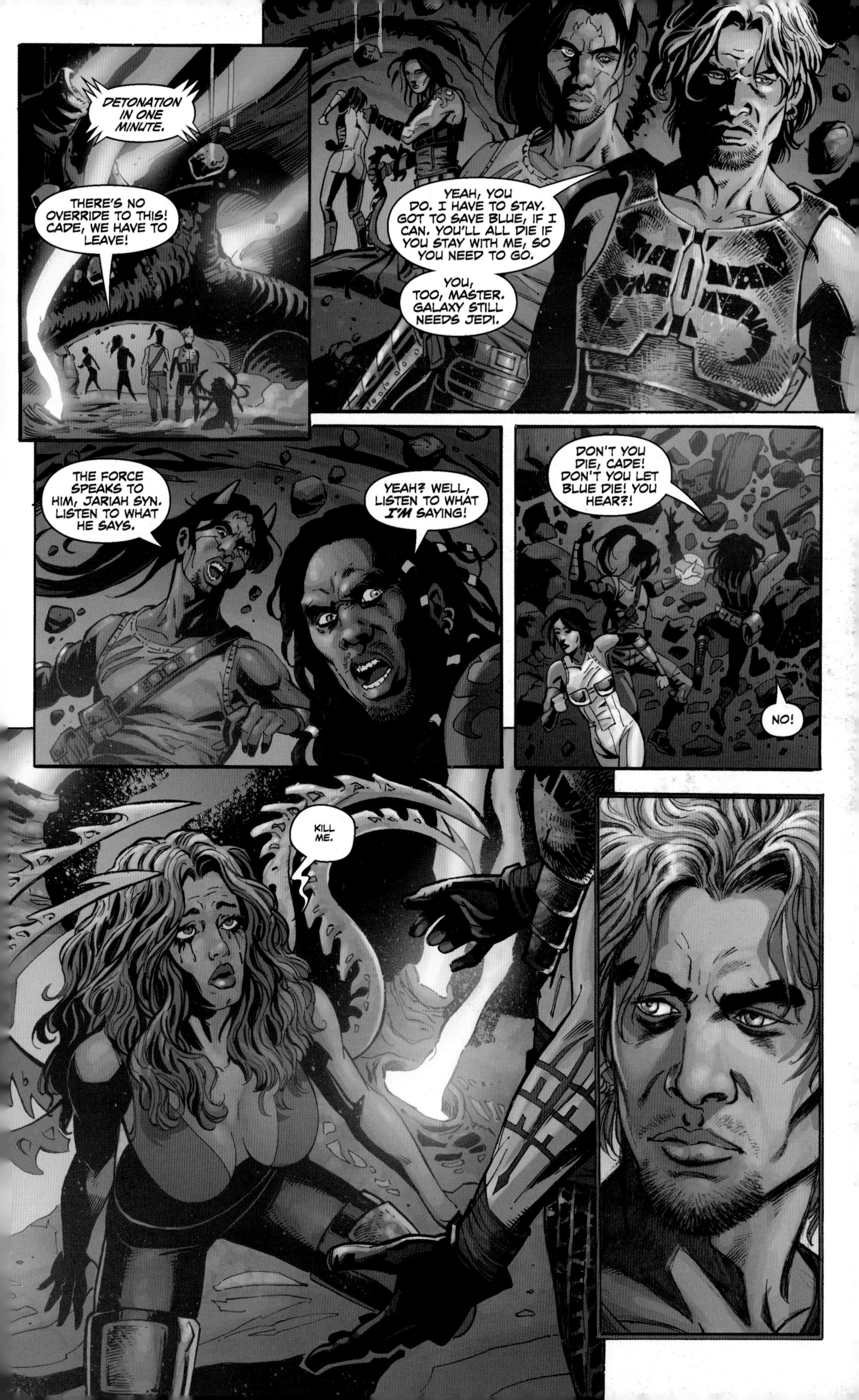
DETONATION IN ONE MINUTE.
THERE'S NO OVERRIDE TO THIS! CADE, WE HAVE TO LEAVE!
YEAH, YOU DO. I HAVE TO STAY. GOT TO SAVE BLUE, IF I CAN. YOU'LL ALL DIE IF YOU STAY WITH ME, SO YOU NEED TO GO.
YOU, TOO, MASTER. GALAXY STILL NEEDS JEDI.
THE FORCE SPEAKS TO HIM, JARIAH SYN. LISTEN TO WHAT HE SAYS.
YEAH? WELL, LISTEN TO WHAT I'M SAYING!
DON'T YOU DIE, CADE! DON'T YOU LET BLUE DIE! YOU HEAR?!
NO!
KILL ME.

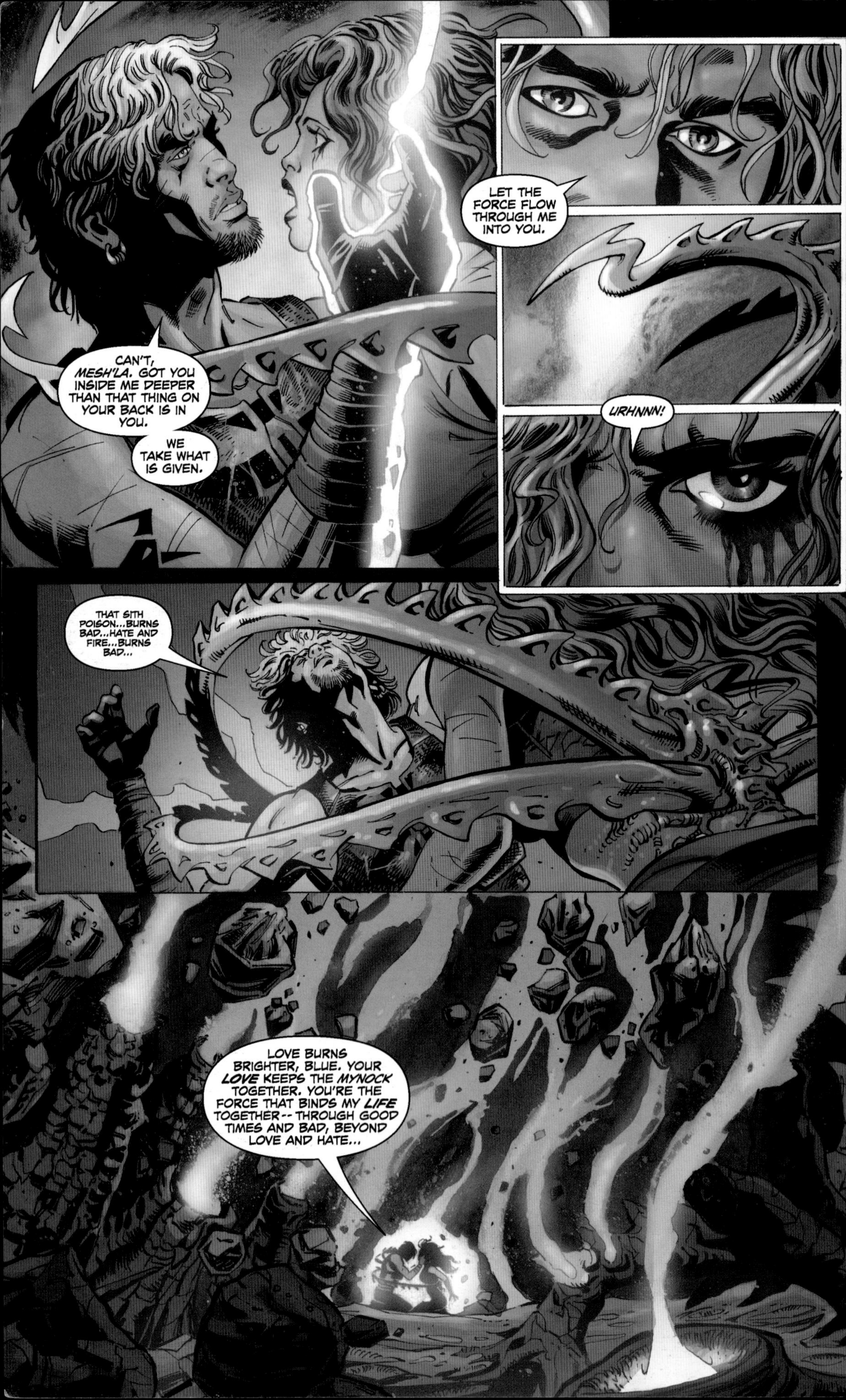
CAN'T, *MESH'LA*. GOT YOU INSIDE ME DEEPER THAN THAT THING ON YOUR BACK IS IN YOU.
WE TAKE WHAT IS GIVEN.
LET THE FORCE FLOW THROUGH ME INTO YOU.
URHNNN!
THAT SITH POISON...BURNS BAD...HATE AND FIRE...BURNS BAD...
LOVE BURNS BRIGHTER, BLUE. YOUR *LOVE* KEEPS THE *MYNOCK* TOGETHER. YOU'RE THE FORCE THAT BINDS MY *LIFE* TOGETHER-- THROUGH GOOD TIMES AND BAD, BEYOND LOVE AND HATE...

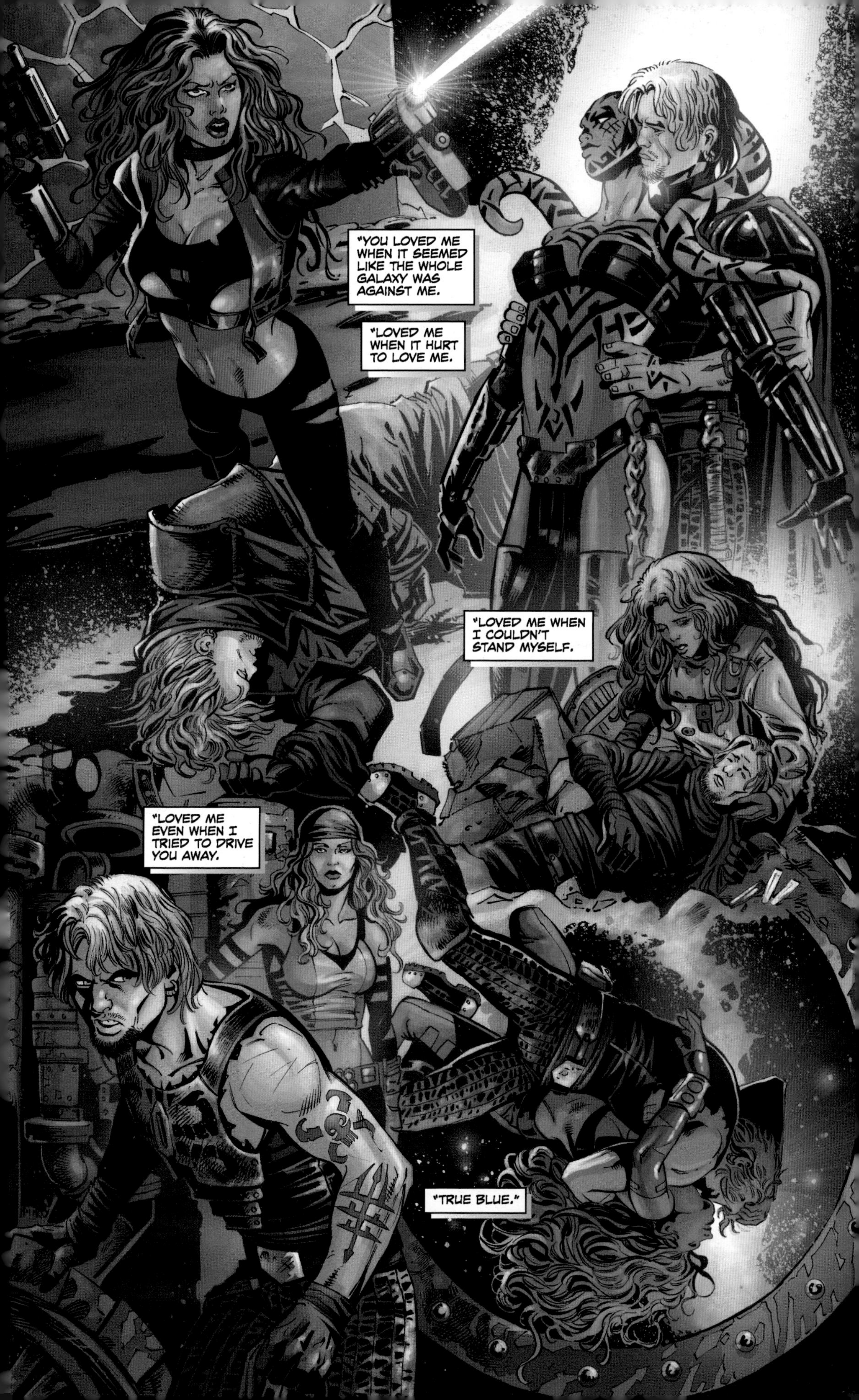
"YOU LOVED ME WHEN IT SEEMED LIKE THE WHOLE GALAXY WAS AGAINST ME.
"LOVED ME WHEN IT HURT TO LOVE ME.
"LOVED ME WHEN I COULDN'T STAND MYSELF.
"LOVED ME EVEN WHEN I TRIED TO DRIVE YOU AWAY.
"TRUE BLUE."

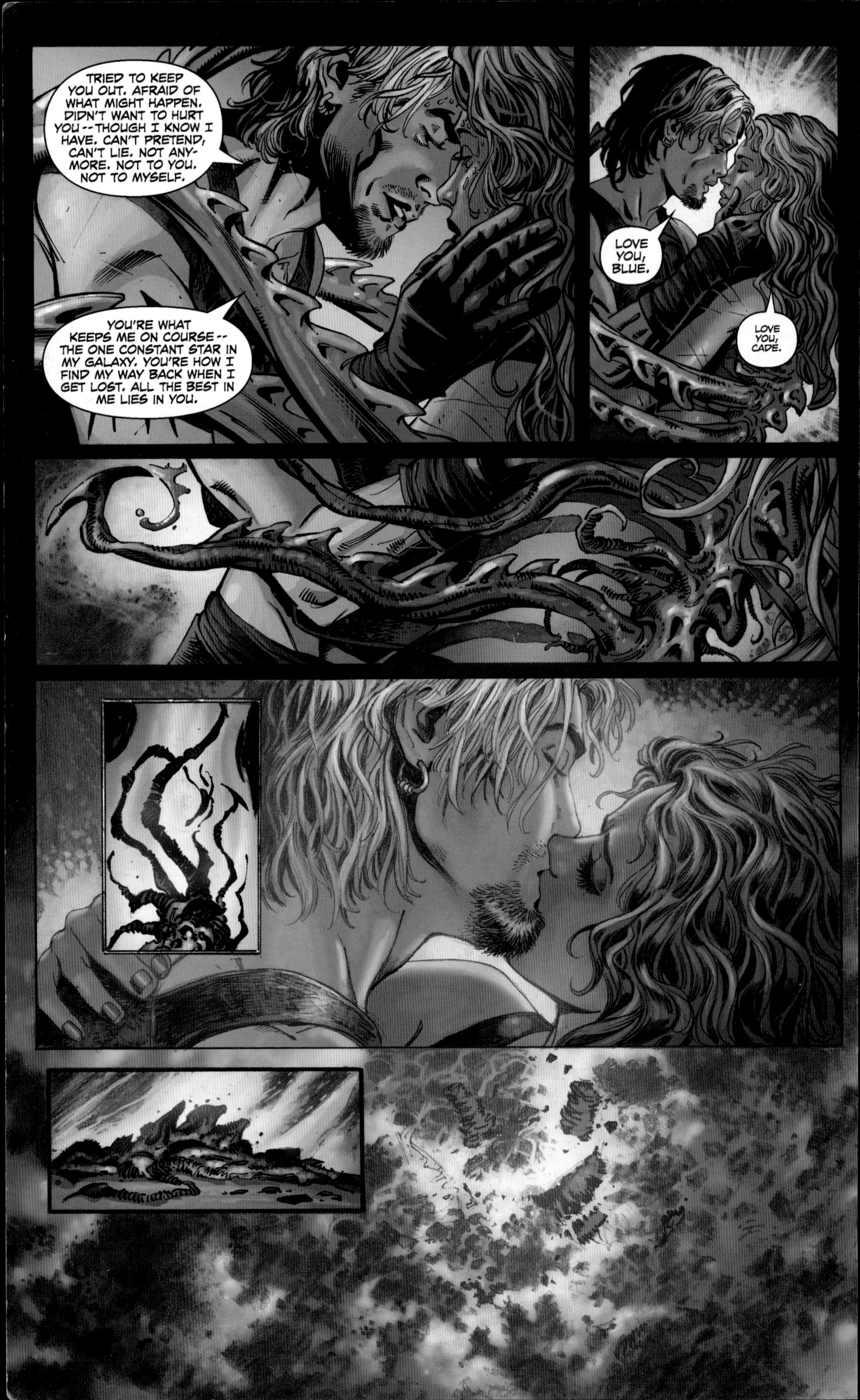
TRIED TO KEEP YOU OUT. AFRAID OF WHAT MIGHT HAPPEN. DIDN'T WANT TO HURT YOU--THOUGH I KNOW I HAVE. CAN'T PRETEND, CAN'T LIE. NOT ANYMORE. NOT TO YOU. NOT TO MYSELF.
YOU'RE WHAT KEEPS ME ON COURSE--THE ONE CONSTANT STAR IN MY GALAXY. YOU'RE HOW I FIND MY WAY BACK WHEN I GET LOST. ALL THE BEST IN ME LIES IN YOU.
LOVE YOU, BLUE.
LOVE YOU, CADE.

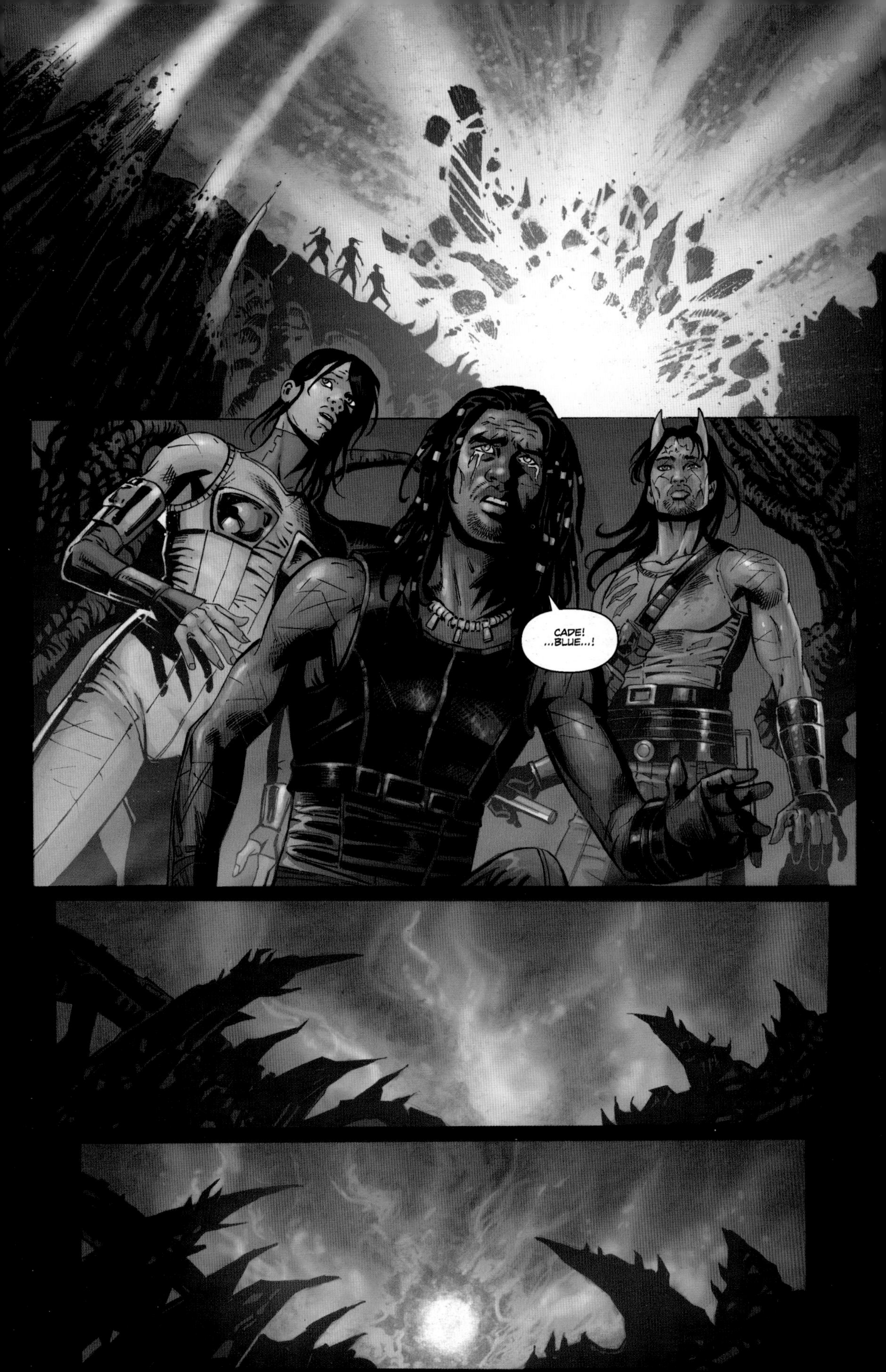
CADE!
...BLUE...!

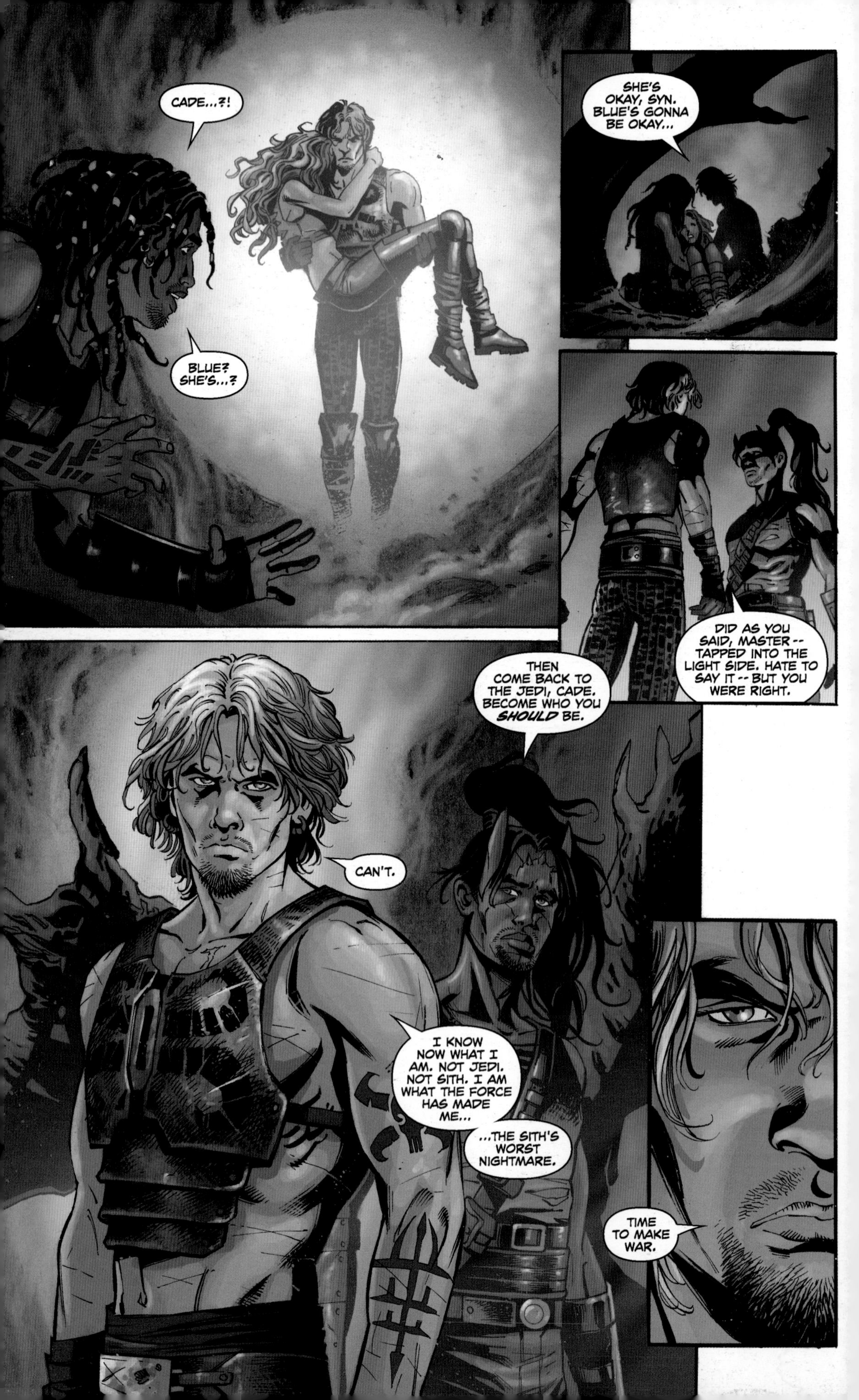
CADE...?!
BLUE? SHE'S...?
SHE'S OKAY, SYN. BLUE'S GONNA BE OKAY...
DID AS YOU SAID, MASTER -- TAPPED INTO THE LIGHT SIDE. HATE TO SAY IT -- BUT YOU WERE RIGHT.
THEN COME BACK TO THE JEDI, CADE. BECOME WHO YOU SHOULD BE.
CAN'T.
I KNOW NOW WHAT I AM. NOT JEDI. NOT SITH. I AM WHAT THE FORCE HAS MADE ME...
...THE SITH'S WORST NIGHTMARE.
TIME TO MAKE WAR.

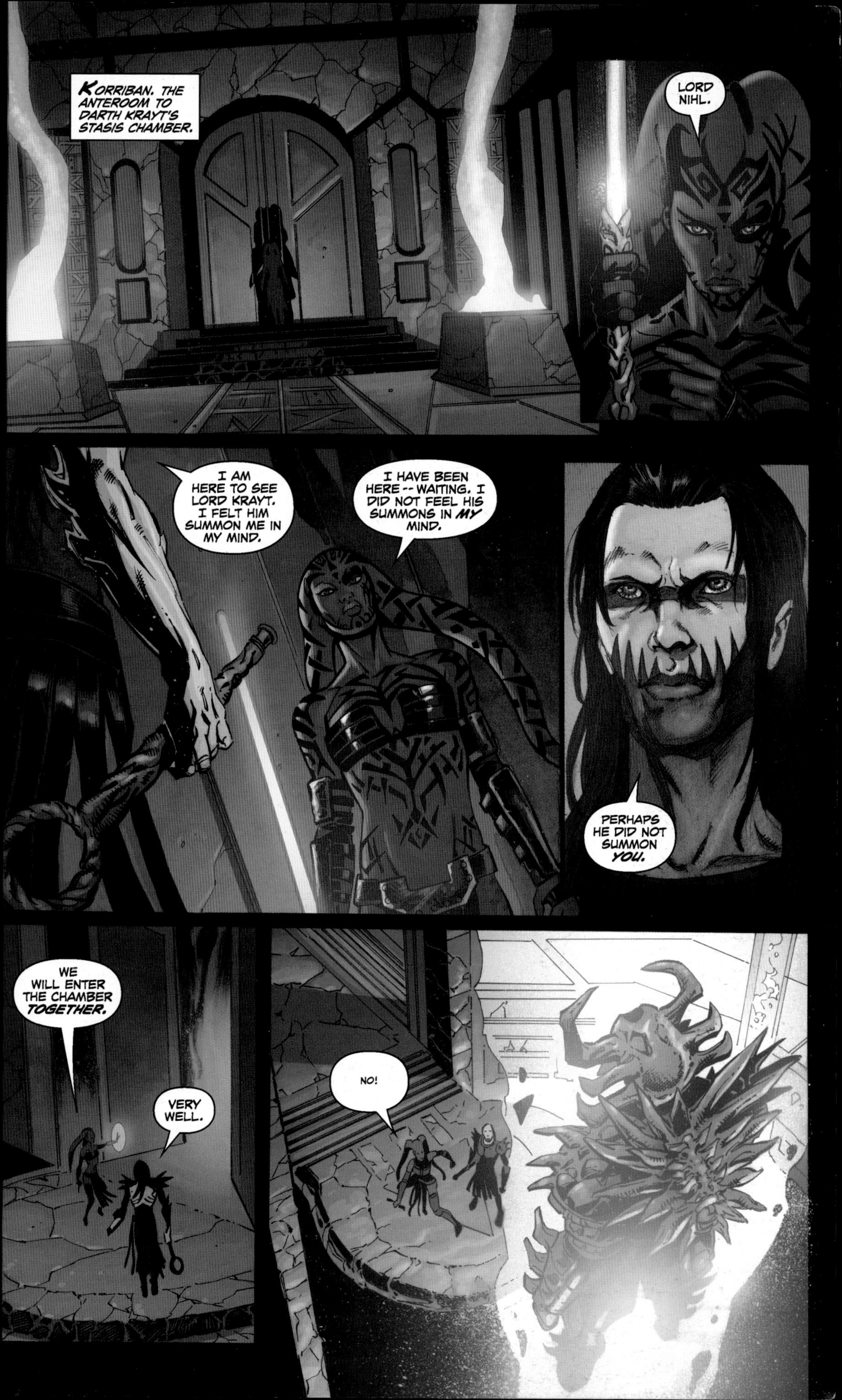
KORRIBAN. THE ANTEROOM TO DARTH KRAYT'S STASIS CHAMBER.
LORD NIHL.
I AM HERE TO SEE LORD KRAYT. I FELT HIM SUMMON ME IN MY MIND.
I HAVE BEEN HERE -- WAITING. I DID NOT FEEL HIS SUMMONS IN *MY* MIND.
PERHAPS HE DID NOT SUMMON *YOU.*
WE WILL ENTER THE CHAMBER *TOGETHER.*
VERY WELL.
NO!

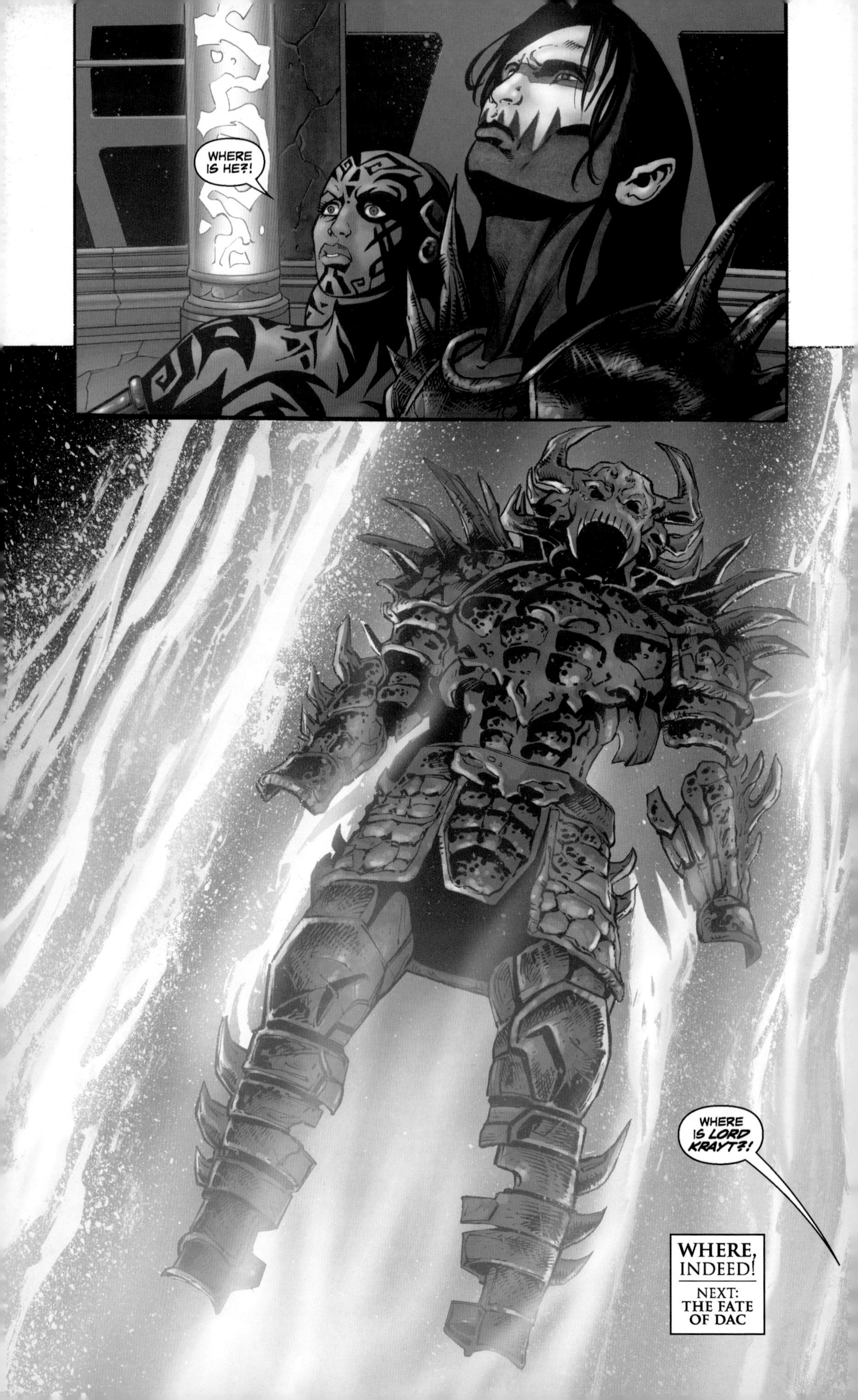
WHERE IS HE?!
WHERE IS LORD KRAYT?!
WHERE, INDEED!
NEXT: THE FATE OF DAC

HUTTESE
GLOSSARY

cheeka: woman
chizk: junk
kriffing: expletive
kwee-kunee: queen
loz noy jitat: a curse
mesh'la: beautiful
nek: war dog
pateesa: friend; term of affection
skocha kung: burnout scum
sleemo: slimeball
stoopa: stupid
sweets patogga: sweetie pie

Chuba doompa, dopa-maskey kung!: You low-down,
two-faced scum!
Kuzzzik desh!: a pirate curse

STAR WARS GRAPHIC NOVEL TIMELINE (IN YEARS)

Omnibus: Tales of the Jedi—5,000–3,986 BSW4
Knights of the Old Republic—3,964–3,963 BSW4
Jedi vs. Sith—1,000 BSW4
Omnibus: Rise of the Sith—33 BSW4
Episode I: The Phantom Menace—32 BSW4
Omnibus: Emissaries and Assassins—32 BSW4
Twilight—31 BSW4
Bounty Hunters—31 BSW4
The Hunt for Aurra Sing—30 BSW4
Darkness—30 BSW4
The Stark Hyperspace War—30 BSW4
Rite of Passage—28 BSW4
Jango Fett—27 BSW4
Zam Wesell—27 BSW4
Honor and Duty—24 BSW4
Episode II: Attack of the Clones—22 BSW4
Clone Wars—22–19 BSW4
Clone Wars Adventures—22–19 BSW4
General Grievous—22–19 BSW4
Episode III: Revenge of the Sith—19 BSW4
Dark Times—19 BSW4
Omnibus: Droids—5.5 BSW4
Boba Fett: Enemy of the Empire—3 BSW4
Underworld—1 BSW4
Episode IV: A New Hope—SW4
Classic Star Wars—0–3 ASW4
A Long Time Ago . . . —0–4 ASW4
Empire—0 ASW4
Rebellion—0 ASW4
Boba Fett: Man with a Mission—0 ASW4
Omnibus: Early Victories—0–3 ASW4
Jabba the Hutt: The Art of the Deal—1 ASW4
Episode V: The Empire Strikes Back—3 ASW4
Shadows of the Empire—3.5 ASW4
Episode VI: Return of the Jedi—4 ASW4
Mara Jade: By the Emperor's Hand—4 ASW4
Omnibus: X-Wing Rogue Squadron—4–5 ASW4
Heir to the Empire—9 ASW4
Dark Force Rising—9 ASW4
The Last Command—9 ASW4
Dark Empire—10 ASW4
Boba Fett: Death, Lies, and Treachery—10 ASW4
Crimson Empire—11 ASW4
Jedi Academy: Leviathan—12 ASW4
Union—19 ASW4
Chewbacca—25 ASW4
Legacy—130–137 ASW4

Old Republic Era
25,000 – 1000 years before
Star Wars: A New Hope

Rise of the Empire Era
1000 – 0 years before
Star Wars: A New Hope

Rebellion Era
0 – 5 years after
Star Wars: A New Hope

New Republic Era
5 – 25 years after
Star Wars: A New Hope

New Jedi Order Era
25+ years after
Star Wars: A New Hope

Legacy Era
130+ years after
Star Wars: A New Hope

Infinities
Does not apply to timeline

Sergio Aragonés Stomps Star Wars
Star Wars Tales
Star Wars Infinities
Tag and Bink
Star Wars Visionaries

BSW4 = before *Episode IV: A New Hope*. ASW4 = after *Episode IV: A New Hope*.

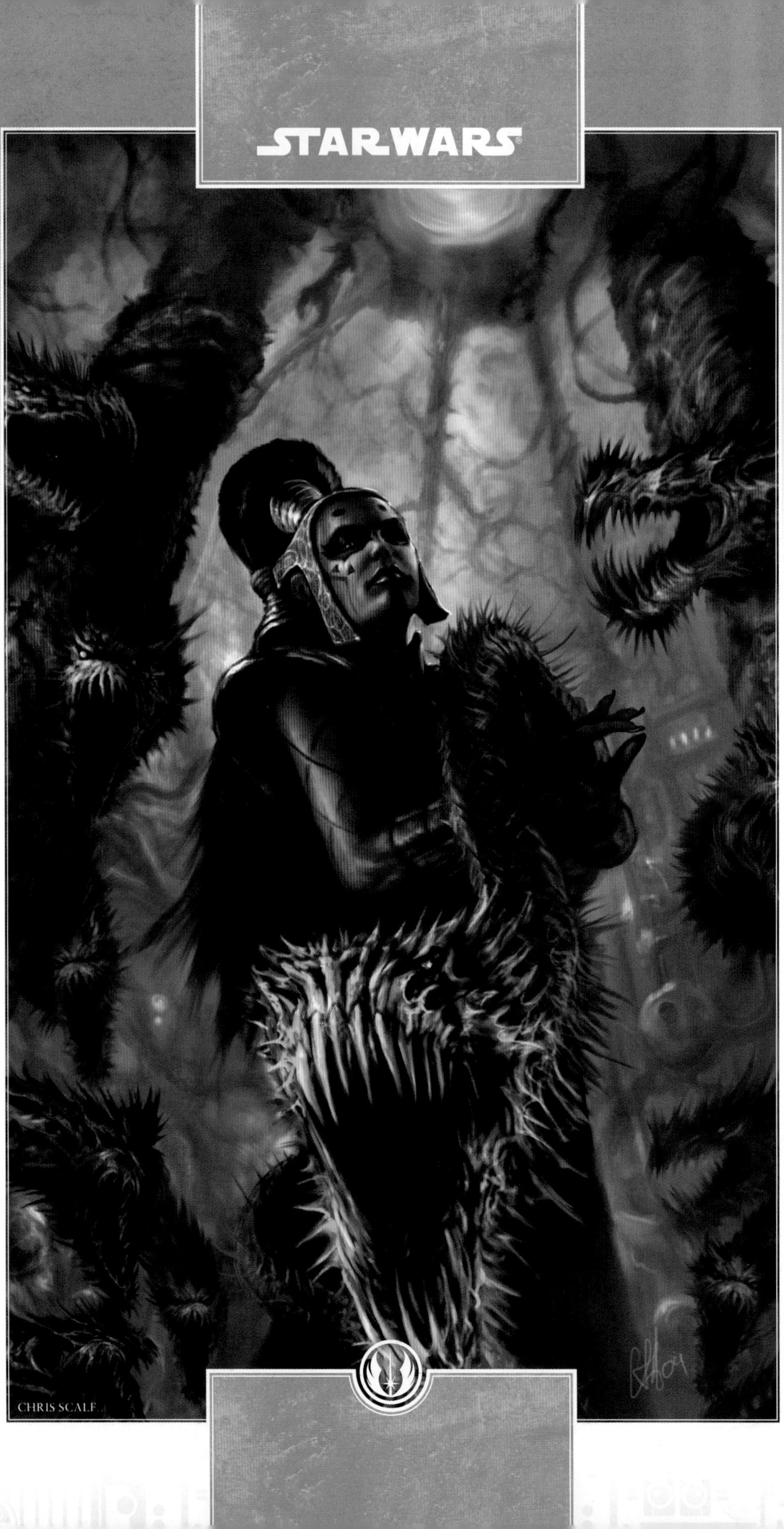
STAR WARS
CHRIS SCALF

STAR WARS

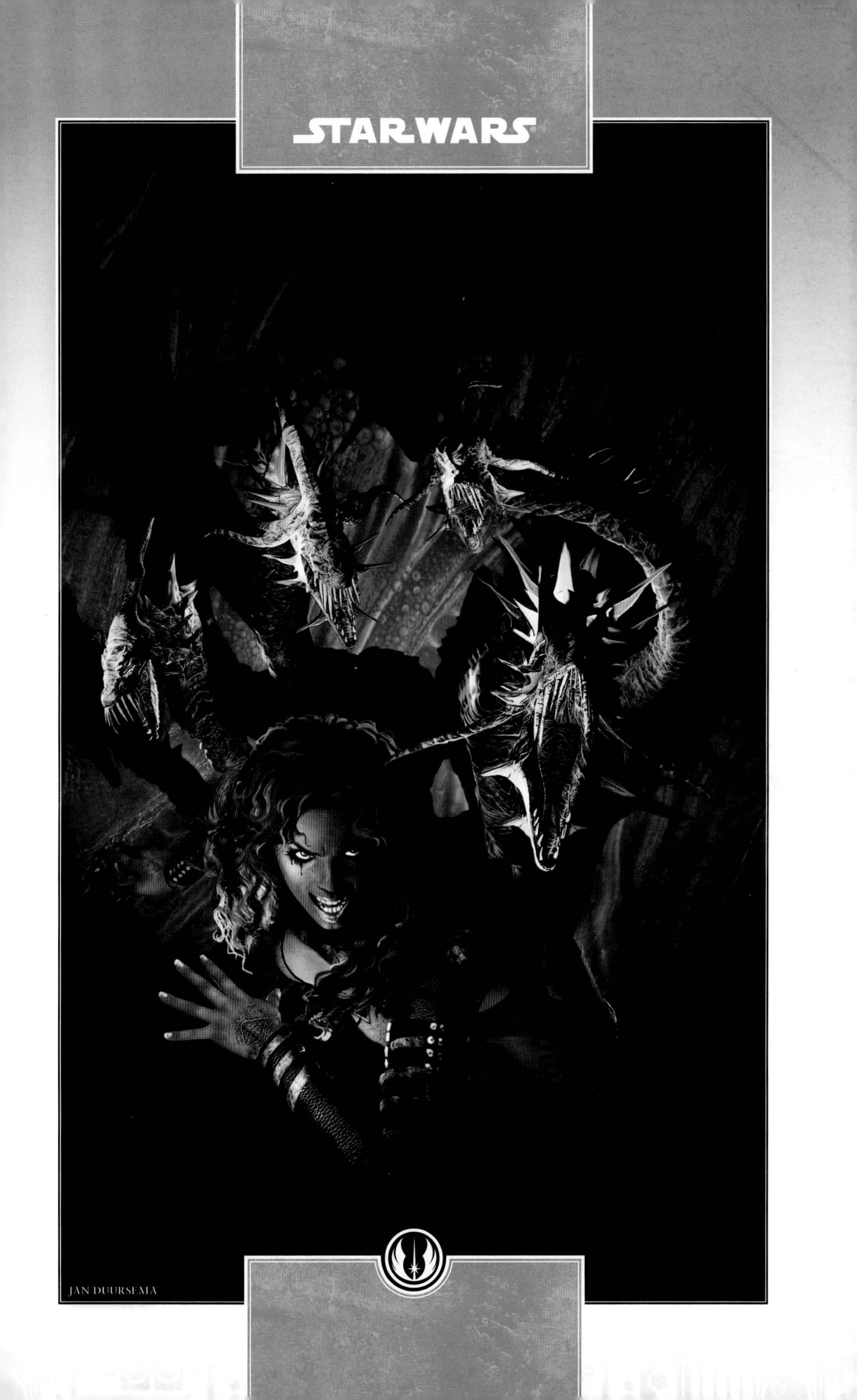
JAN DUURSEMA

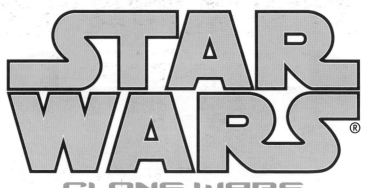

STAR WARS®
CLONE WARS ADVENTURES

Don't miss any of the action-packed adventures of your favorite STAR WARS® characters, available at comics shops and bookstores in a galaxy near you!

STAR WARS
CLONE WARS ADVENTURES
Vol 1
THREE NEW STORIES! ALL-JEDI ACTION!

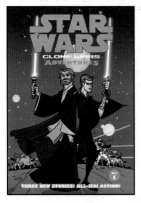

Volume 1
ISBN-10: 1-59307-243-0
ISBN-13: 978-1-59307-243-8

STAR WARS
CLONE WARS ADVENTURES
THREE TALES OF HYPERKINETIC JEDI ACTION!

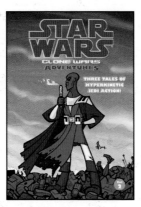

Volume 2
ISBN-10: 1-59307-271-6
ISBN-13: 978-1-59307-271-1

STAR WARS
CLONE WARS ADVENTURES
FOUR TALES OF SINISTER SEPARATIST SCHEMING AND ROCKING REPUBLIC COMBAT!

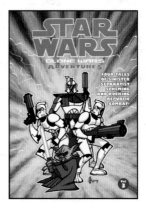

Volume 3
ISBN-10: 1-59307-307-0
ISBN-13: 978-1-59307-307-7

STAR WARS
CLONE WARS ADVENTURES
FOUR RIVETING ADVENTURES IN ONE FANTASTIC VOLUME!

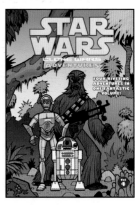

Volume 4
ISBN-10: 1-59307-402-6
ISBN-13: 978-1-59307-402-9

STAR WARS
CLONE WARS ADVENTURES
FOUR AMAZING TALES OF HEROISM AND GALAXY-SHAKING ACTION!

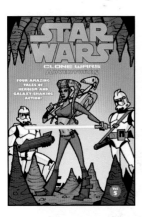

Volume 5
ISBN-10: 1-59307-483-2
ISBN-13: 978-1-59307-483-8

STAR WARS
CLONE WARS ADVENTURES
FOUR TALES OF PLANETS IN PERIL AND JEDI IN JEOPARDY!

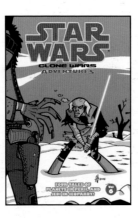

Volume 6
ISBN-10: 1-59307-567-7
ISBN-13: 978-1-59307-567-5

STAR WARS
CLONE WARS ADVENTURES

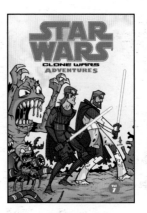

Volume 7
ISBN-10: 1-59307-678-9
ISBN-13: 978-1-59307-678-8

STAR WARS
CLONE WARS ADVENTURES

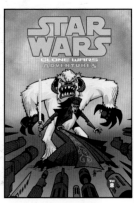

Volume 8
ISBN-10: 1-59307-680-0
ISBN-13: 978-1-59307-680-1
Coming in June!

$6.95 each!

To find a comics shop in your area, call 1-888-266-4226

For more information or to order direct: • On the web: darkhorse.com • Phone: 1-800-862-0052 Mon.-Fri. 9 A.M. to 5 P.M. Pacific Time.
• E-mail: mailorder@darkhorse.com *Prices and availability subject to change without notice.

STAR WARS®
KNIGHTS OF THE OLD REPUBLIC

DARK HORSE BOOKS

TO FIND A COMICS SHOP IN YOUR AREA, CALL 1-888-266-4226.

For more information or to order direct: *On the web: darkhorse.com *E-mail: mailorder@darkhorse.com
*Phone: 1-800-862-0052 Mon.-Fri. 9 A.M. to 5 P.M. Pacific Time.

*prices and availability subject to change without notice. STAR WARS © 2010 Lucasfilm Ltd. & TM (BL 8023)

STAR WARS OMNIBUS COLLECTIONS

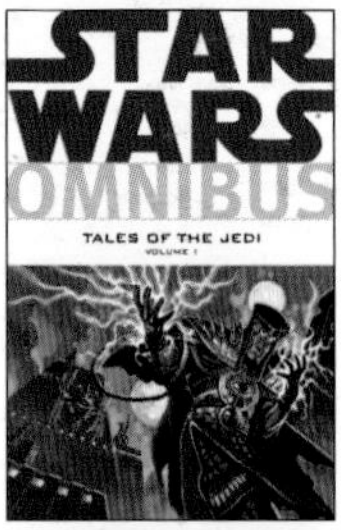
STAR WARS
OMNIBUS
TALES OF THE JEDI

STAR WARS: TALES OF THE JEDI

Including the *Tales of the Jedi* stories "The Golden Age of the Sith," "The Freedon Nadd Uprising," and "Knights of the Old Republic," these huge omnibus editions are the ultimate introduction to the ancient history of the *Star Wars* universe!

Volume 1 ISBN 978-1-59307-830-0 | $24.99 Volume 2 ISBN 978-1-59307-911-6 | $24.99

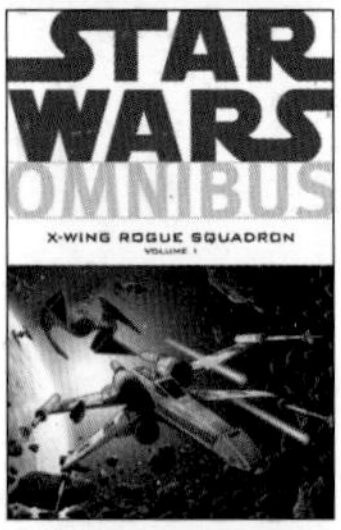
STAR WARS
OMNIBUS
X-WING ROGUE SQUADRON

STAR WARS: X-WING ROGUE SQUADRON

The greatest starfighters of the Rebel Alliance become the defenders of a new Republic in this massive collection of stories featuring Wedge Antilles, hero of the Battle of Endor, and his team of ace pilots known throughout the galaxy as Rogue Squadron.

Volume 1 ISBN 978-1-59307-572-9 | $24.99 Volume 2 ISBN 978-1-59307-619-1 | $24.99

Volume 3 ISBN 978-1-59307-776-1 | $24.99

STAR WARS: BOBA FETT

Boba Fett, the most feared, most respected, and most loved bounty hunter in the galaxy, now has all of his comics stories collected into one massive volume!

ISBN 978-1-59582-418-9 | $24.99

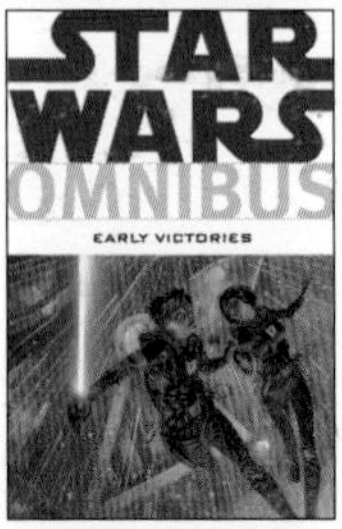
STAR WARS
OMNIBUS
EARLY VICTORIES

STAR WARS: EARLY VICTORIES

Following the destruction of the first Death Star, Luke Skywalker is the new, unexpected hero of the Rebellion. But the galaxy hasn't been saved yet–Luke and Princess Leia find there are many more battles to be fought against the Empire and Darth Vader!

ISBN 978-1-59582-172-0 | $24.99

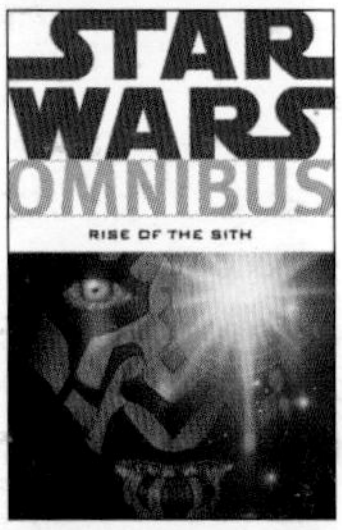
STAR WARS
OMNIBUS
RISE OF THE SITH

STAR WARS: RISE OF THE SITH

Before the name of Skywalker–or Vader–achieved fame across the galaxy, the Jedi Knights had long preserved peace and justice . . . as well as preventing the return of the Sith. These thrilling tales illustrate the events leading up to *The Phantom Menace*.

ISBN 978-1-59582-228-4 | $24.99

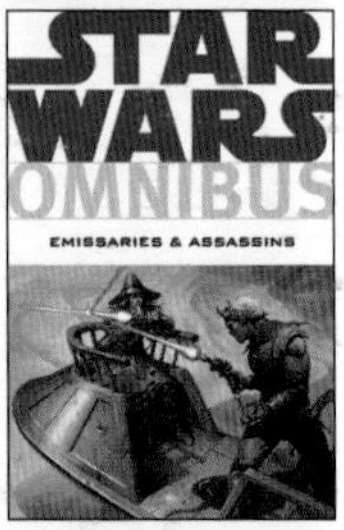
STAR WARS
OMNIBUS
EMISSARIES & ASSASSINS

STAR WARS: EMISSARIES AND ASSASSINS

Discover more stories featuring Anakin Skywalker, Amidala, Obi-Wan, and Qui-Gon set during the time of Episode I: *The Phantom Menace* in this mega collection!

ISBN 978-1-59582-229-1 | $24.99

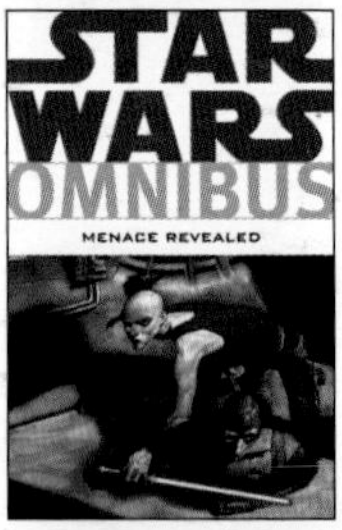
STAR WARS
OMNIBUS
MENACE REVEALED

STAR WARS: MENACE REVEALED

This is our largest omnibus of never-before-collected and out-of-print *Star Wars* stories. Included here are one-shot adventures, short story arcs, specialty issues, and early Dark Horse Extra comic strips! All of these tales take place after Episode I: *The Phantom Menace*, and lead up to Episode II: *Attack of the Clones*.

ISBN 978-1-59582-273-4 | $24.99

STAR WARS: SHADOWS OF THE EMPIRE

Featuring all your favorite characters from the *Star Wars* trilogy—Luke Skywalker, Princess Leia, and Han Solo—this volume includes stories written by acclaimed novelists Timothy Zahn and Steve Perry!

ISBN 978-1-59582-434-9 | $24.99

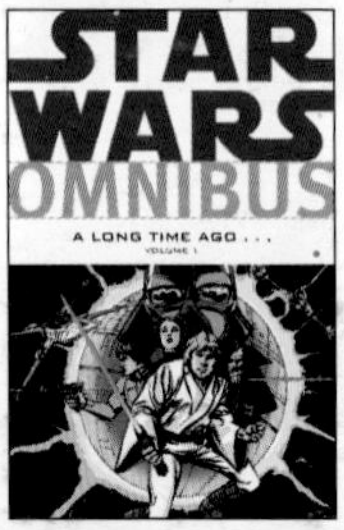
STAR WARS
OMNIBUS
A LONG TIME AGO . . .

STAR WARS: A LONG TIME AGO. . . .

Star Wars: A Long Time Ago. . . . omnibus volumes feature classic *Star Wars* stories not seen in over twenty years! Originally printed by Marvel Comics, these stories have been recolored and are sure to please *Star Wars* fans both new and old.

Volume 1: ISBN 978-1-59582-486-8 | $24.99 Volume 2: ISBN 978-1-59582-554-4 | $24.99

DARK HORSE BOOKS

AVAILABLE AT YOUR LOCAL COMICS SHOP OR BOOKSTORE!

To find a comics shop in your area, call 1-888-266-4226

For more information or to order direct: • On the web: darkhorse.com

• E-mail: mailorder@darkhorse.com • Phone: 1-800-862-0052 Mon.–Fri. 9 AM to 5 PM Pacific Time